Never Too Late
To Remember

for Temple Emanu-El

Rochelle G Saidel

1/30/97

New Perspectives
Jewish Life and Thought

Never Too Late To Remember

The Politics Behind New York City's Holocaust Museum

ROCHELLE G. SAIDEL

HM

HOLMES & MEIER

New York/London

Published in the United States of America 1996 by
Holmes & Meier Publishers, Inc.
160 Broadway
New York, NY 10038

This book has been printed on acid-free paper.

Library of Congress Cataloging-in-Publication Data

Saidel, Rochelle G.
    Never too late to remember : the politics behind New York City's
Holocaust Museum / Rochelle G. Saidel.
        p.   cm.
    Includes bibliographical references and index.
    ISBN 0-8419-1367-6 (cloth : alk. paper)
    1. Holocaust, Jewish (1939–1945)—Museums—New York (State)—New
York. 2. Jews—United States—Politics and government. 3. New York
(N.Y.)—Politics and government—1951–   4. New York (State)—
Politics and government—1951–   I. Title.
D804.175.N49S25   1996
940.53'18'0747471—dc20   96-12944
                                                                CIP

Manufactured in the United States of America

*In memory of my great-grandfather David Ovchinskis
of Koptchevo, Lithuania,
murdered by the Nazis in Lazdei, on November 3, 1941,
and his children and grandchildren who perished there and
at the Ninth Fort, Kovno.*

Contents

Photographs appear after page 114.

Preface

The year of my birth, 1942, has been singled out by historians as statistically the worst year in the entire history of the Jewish people. I was born on January 30, on the ninth anniversary of the very day that Adolf Hitler took power in 1933. To commemorate this anniversary, Hitler proclaimed in Berlin on the day I was born that "the result of this war will be the total annihilation of the Jews."

Although I grew up with a strong commitment to Judaism, I was born in safe and secure upstate New York and it took some years for the Holocaust to affect me personally. My general interest in the Holocaust solidified in 1977, when I attended one of the first Nazi war criminal hearings in the United States in Albany, New York, and spoke with survivors who were witnesses. This led to my writing many articles and a book on this specific aspect of the Holocaust. Additionally, as part of my responsibility on the staff of Senator Manfred Ohrenstein from 1981 until 1989, I organized a permanent exhibit in the New York State Museum in Albany that detailed the odyssey of Holocaust refugees who were interned in Oswego, New York.

When I decided to write about the effort to create a major Holocaust memorial museum in New York City, I did so with deep personal interest in the subject. As part of my work for Senator Ohrenstein, as his liaison to the Jewish community and consultant on the Holocaust, I followed the New York City project closely, almost from its initiation by Mayor Edward I. Koch in 1981. At that early date, and even in 1988–89 when I began research on the topic at The Graduate Center of City University of New York, it seemed destined for ultimate success. However, the intricacies of the political coalition behind the museum, the changes in the coalition over time, and other circumstances created problems and delays in the implementation process. This book comes to an end when the project finally seems to be reaching a successful conclusion. After thirteen years of history, and a prehistory that goes back to 1946, ground was broken for A Living Memorial to the Holocaust–Museum of Jewish Heritage on October 16, 1994. Forty-seven years earlier, on October 19, 1947, a similar ceremony in Riverside Park was supposed to result in a Holocaust memorial for the City of New York. It is ironic that New York City, with its huge Jewish population, was the first Jewish community to attempt to create a major memorial in the United States and still did not have one fifty years after World War II ended. By the spring of 1996, however, the current memorial museum project was rising in Battery Park City, and in the not too distant future the victims of the Holocaust will be suitably remembered in New York City.

Acknowledgments

Without the help and encouragement of many people, it would not have been possible to complete this book. I conducted many interviews to gather information, and I thank the people in New York, Washington, Jerusalem, and Los Angeles who took the time to share with me their expertise on memorializing the Holocaust or their involvement with the creation of Holocaust memorials. They include Dr. David Altshuler, Dr. Michael Berenbaum, Dr. David Blumenfeld, Hyman Bookbinder, Stuart Eizenstat, David Emil, Meyer S. Frucher, Benjamin Gebiner, Dr. Yoav Gelber, Ellen Goldstein, Rabbi Irving Greenberg, Dr. Israel Gutman, Edward I. Koch, Yitzchak Mais, Rabbi Meyer May, Benjamin and Vladka Meed, Ernest Michel, Dr. Michael Nutkiewicz, Richard Ravitch, Herbert Rickman, Menachem Rosensaft, Irit Salmon, Julius Schatz, Rebecca Shanor, Mark Siegel, Simcha Stein, Hon. Herbert Tenzer, Shaike Weinberg, and Professor Elie Wiesel.

I am also grateful to the following experts on the Holocaust, memorialization, and the American Jewish community who shared with me their unpublished works: Aviva Cantor, Dr. Harold Fisch, Dr. Franklin Littell, Yitzchak Mais, Dr. Sybil Milton, Dr. Barry Schwartz, and Dr. James E. Young.

Archival research was carried out at the archives of the Jewish Labor Bund, the YIVO Institute for Jewish Research, the American Jewish Committee library, the New York State Library, the President Jimmy Carter Library, the Warsaw Ghetto Resistance Organization (WAGRO), the offices of the Jewish Community Relations Council, the New York City Municipal Archives, and A Living Memorial to the Holocaust-Museum of Jewish Heritage. I appreciate the kind cooperation of the staff members in all of these institutions. Shari Segel of the Holocaust Museum and Leo Greenbaum of YIVO were helpful in locating photographs for the book. In addition, I thank Marian Craig, Daniel McGlone, Dr. William L. Shulman, Jim Sleeper, and Mark Weitzman for providing written background materials.

New York State Senator Manfred Ohrenstein gave me the opportunity to see firsthand the activities of the New York Holocaust Memorial Commission while I was a member of his staff, and I thank him and my former colleagues who have been supportive of my interest in working on this project.

This book began as research for my doctorate in political science at City University Graduate Center in New York, and I acknowledge Professors Asher Arian and Marshall Berman, both of whom supervised my dissertation with wisdom, keen insights, infinite patience, and kindness. They and Professors John Mollenkopf, Joseph Murphy, and Frances Fox Piven all encouraged me to write this book. I also appreciate the generosity of the National Foundation for Jewish Culture, which presented me with their 1994 Sidney and Hadassah Musher Publication Prize, and the Meinhart Spielman bequest to the City College Jewish Studies Department, which provided financial support while I was researching and writing the dissertation.

I am especially grateful to Miriam Holmes, director of Holmes & Meier Publishers, and to Dr. Berel Lang, both of whom understood the importance of publishing the story of the politics of memorializing the Holocaust in New York City and had confidence in my ability to write about it. Sheila Friedling, the in-house editor at Holmes & Meier, did a superb job of helping me to make this a better, more readable book, as did executive editor Katharine Turok and copy editor Miriam Hurewitz. Dr. Sarah Blacher Cohen and Aviva Cantor suggested that Holmes & Meier was the appropriate publisher for this book, and I thank them for their good advice. Aviva, along with Louis Sepersky, kept me abreast of last-minute changes in New York while I was far away geographically and on a deadline to finish the book. I am indebted to them for their persistence, thoroughness, time, and especially their friendship. With great generosity, they have always faithfully served as my informal "clipping service" when I am away from the city. I am also grateful to other friends who have shared books, newspaper clippings, ideas, hospitality, and a sympathetic ear during the duration of this effort, including Charles R. Allen, Jr., Janis Colton, Doris Eisen, Elizabeth Howitt, Hannah Koevary, Arieh Lebowitz, Rogerio Marx, Hella Moritz,

Dr. Ahuva Passow, Dr. Gertrude Schneider, Leida Snow, Marcia Talmage, Murray Zuckoff, my sister Mindy Mangot, and my daughter, Esther Wolk-Cohen. Dr. Eva Alterman Blay and Suzanna Sassoun provided physical as well as intellectual support, by carrying early versions of the manuscript from São Paulo to New York. I especially thank my son, Daniel Wolk, for patiently improving my computer skills.

Last, but certainly not least, I thank my husband, Dr. Guilherme Ary Plonski, for seeing me through this endeavor with loving and generous encouragement, forbearance, and intelligent suggestions; and my parents, Florence and Joseph Saidel, for instilling in me a sense of responsibility to remember the Holocaust and its ongoing ramifications.

Introduction: Where Is New York City's Holocaust Memorial Museum?

There's no monument in New York. . . .
In the dark silent night
They throng without lament,
Wreathe New York's expanse
Of steel and concrete;
Carry water, sand, cement
To build a monument
For themselves—
The s i x m i l l i o n . . ."

—*Wolf Pasmanik,* World Union Press, *ca. 1964*

Memorializing the significant events that have marked the twentieth century has become a common part of the landscape in the United States, with museums and monuments to commemorate such diverse milestones as American participation in wars, women receiving the right to vote, and astronauts traveling in outer space. Within this effort to commemorate modern history, the Holocaust has an unusually large number of memorials of all types. These range from small monuments in hundreds of locations to huge multimillion dollar museums in Washington, D.C., and Los Angeles. Such big cities as Miami, Detroit, Philadelphia, and San Francisco have substantial and disparate memorials, and Boston has just constructed a major memorial on the Freedom Trail. The communal remembering of an event is a selective act, involving complex choices about how and what to preserve, record, and symbolize. Every time a memorial is constructed to commemorate the Holocaust or any other historical event, the process of memorialization is inevitably political—embedded in practical as well as ideological and aesthetic issues. The choice between a monument and a museum as the vehicle for memorialization, along with decisions about which historical facts are emphasized, diminished, or eliminated, are deliberately political acts.

In New York City, the process of Holocaust memorialization is political because it has been subject to pressures, opinions, conflicts, power struggles, and compromises within the organized Jewish community and within the local government, as well as to the interplay of these same forces in the community and the government. The struggle to decide on an appropriate way to memorialize the Holocaust has been affected both by internal political debates about the memorial's substance and form and by the pressures imposed by external political conditions. As a result, New York City, the most Jewish of cities outside of Israel and a city filled with monuments and museums, did not yet have a major memorial to the victims and heroes of the Holocaust in 1996. More than half a century after the end of World War II and a quarter of a century into a period of great interest in the Holocaust, there was still no major memorial standing in New York City. Instead, this city with the largest Jewish and Holocaust survivor populations in the United States had seen a series of failed attempts that began in 1946. Now that the latest project appears finally to be reaching a successful conclusion, what happened during the fifty years between the first initiative in the 1940s and the creation of a memorial museum in the 1990s is in danger of being ignored or forgotten. However, the prehistory of the New York City Holocaust museum project needs to be recounted and recorded because it enables us to understand how this memorial evolved. Perhaps more important, it contributes to a better understanding of the politics of memorialization, the politics of the organized American Jewish community, and the politics of New York City.

This most recent attempt at commemoration began in 1981,

when Mayor Edward I. Koch appointed a Holocaust Memorial Task Force (later a commission) to begin working to create such an institution. In the fall of 1994, more than thirteen years after this project's initiation, there was finally a ceremonial ground breaking. This book examines the politics behind Holocaust memorialization in New York City from the original aborted attempt in 1946 to the memorial museum under construction today. By placing this latest effort to create a major memorial in New York in its political, historical, and cultural context, the book explores the process of memorialization and the role in New York City of the proposed museum in remembering the Holocaust now and in the future.

The current project is much different from its predecessors because it is the product of a coalition that includes New York State and the state's governor, New York City and the city's mayor, politically influential cochairmen, many other elected officials, and a professionally coordinated commission. Earlier failed attempts to create a Holocaust memorial in the city were initiated by individuals and small, disorganized interest groups. Although Mayor Koch's predecessors publicly said that they supported the idea of a Holocaust memorial, none of them made the idea his own and aggressively led the effort. It always remained a private endeavor (although a small parcel of city land for a site was offered more than once).

The first attempt to create a Holocaust memorial in New York City occurred in 1946–47. In Riverside Park at West Eighty-third Street there is an engraved stone, placed there in October 1947 and intended as a cornerstone, which reads: "This is the site for the American memorial to the heroes of the Warsaw Ghetto battle April–May 1943 and to the 6 million Jews of Europe martyred in the cause of human liberty." On April 26, 1993, more than forty-five years after the October 1947 dedication, an "American" memorial museum, the United States Holocaust Memorial Museum, opened its doors in Washington, D.C. While there are a number of small monuments and sculptures in the city of New York, a major memorial (in its most recent incarnation designated for a site in Battery Park City) was still not completed fifty years after the end of World War II.

In retrospect, it is more remarkable that an effort at memorialization was initiated in New York City in the political atmosphere of 1946–47 than that it failed. When the first Holocaust memorial was being planned in Riverside Park, the city's Jewish community was only loosely organized, its foremost purpose was the creation of a homeland in Palestine, and it was still in shock and denial over the losses of the Holocaust. Anti-Semitism was still a real threat in the United States, and accusations of Communist connections were also real and growing threats.

By the time of the second major attempt to create a Holocaust memorial in New York City in the 1960s, the Jewish community was much more organized than in 1947. A committee was again formed, and this time the effort had the backing of Jewish organizations rather than individuals. Several sites and designs were considered by the memorial committee and by the city. Mayors were supportive, but there was still not enough political advantage from such a memorial for the city administration to strongly back it. Other priorities in the organized Jewish community, such as money for Israel and immigration from the Soviet Union, were also factors contributing to the failure. The community itself gave up the project and focused on helping Israel, especially after the 1967 Six Day War and the 1973 Yom Kippur War.

By the end of the 1970s, the situation had changed, and memorialization of the Holocaust had gained increasing acceptance in the organized Jewish community. After this culminated in President Jimmy Carter's 1978 announcement of a national memorial, there was political advantage from strongly backing a Holocaust memorial in New York City. This advantage did not go unnoticed in Mayor Koch's office. Like most high-level government officials, the mayor employed "political entrepreneurs"— aides with the savvy and connections to build coalitions, seize opportunities, move projects along, and gain political advantages. Mayor Koch's political entrepreneur and liaison to the Jewish community, Herbert Rickman, saw a ripe opportunity. He encouraged the mayor to intervene and co-opt the issue of Holocaust memorialization to gain political favor with the city's Jewish community.

In 1978 a presidential political entrepreneur had proposed to President Carter that such a project might help him strengthen his position in the organized Jewish community on a national level. This intervention by the federal government for a national Holocaust memorial project in turn gave the then dormant New York project legitimacy and made it more important for New

York City's organized Jewish community. In 1981 the mayor of New York City created a task force, and then a memorial commission, for the purpose of building a memorial and at the same time strengthening his position vis-à-vis the established organized Jewish community. The mayor's specific "interest group" included some of the same players who had been trying to create a Holocaust memorial for many years; but he added people who would give him control and influence, especially in the person of his powerful chairman, Barton's Candy heir and real estate developer George Klein.

There are both internal and external reasons why the newest New York City project was at an impasse for so long. Internal reasons flow from the unwieldy and changing structure of the coalition of political forces responsible for implementation, as well as the length of time the project has dragged on. These include changes in political alliances over time (including new elected and appointed officials); having at the helm (for much of the time) both the mayor and the governor, sometimes with different agendas; other priorities (especially fund-raising crises) in the organized Jewish community, which influence commission members and potential donors; disagreement among the cochairmen and members of the commission; the politics of site selection; and the personalization of the project by one of the cochairmen. Notwithstanding these internal problems, a positive influence should have been the fact that since the 1970s the idea of memorialization had grown in the organized American Jewish community. This was because non-Orthodox segments of the community were seeking a new secular link with Judaism in the United States, the community generally had underlying fears of history repeating itself, and a number of new historic events brought these fears closer to home.

From 1946 through the 1960s, the major external reason for failure to create the early Holocaust memorial projects in New York City was the lack of interest on the part of government officials. The issue was not considered "hot": that is, there was little political capital to be gained from supporting it. But the increasing importance of Holocaust memorialization for the organized American Jewish community, beginning gradually in 1961 and heightened later in the decade and in the 1970s, acted as a catalyst for government interest and intervention. Ironically, this very intervention later was responsible for holding up the New York memorial project even longer.

The commission that Mayor Koch had originated for a city Holocaust project changed to a joint New York City–New York State commission for a city-state project in 1986. That year, Governor Mario Cuomo retroactively became "founding cochairman" along with Mayor Koch, and a new political alliance between the city and the state was initiated. At that time, the site of the museum was changed from the Federal Custom House to Battery Park City, then a new development controlled by the state on landfill on the west side of the tip of lower Manhattan. The new city-state alliance ultimately had a negative impact on the project, resulting from the state government's trying to influence its final outcome and the governor's policies producing bureaucratic problems and delayed implementation. Friction between the city and the state over the project, along with the election and appointment of new state and city government officials, also disrupted the continuity of the project's implementation. The Cuomo administration's intervention to block a real estate deal in Battery Park City and to drastically increase rent for the museum resulted in delays and unexpected new decisions by the commission. The state and the commission finally reached a compromise agreement to go ahead with the project on a smaller scale in August 1994, perhaps coincidentally during the governor's campaign for reelection that November.

In addition, an external delay in the decision path was caused by "Black Monday" on Wall Street, October 19, 1987, and subsequent economic crises in the city. The economic climate both dropped property values in Battery Park City and financially wiped out many potential donors, necessitating new decisions on how best to fund the museum.

The New York City Holocaust museum project should have been destined for smooth sailing. Unlike earlier attempts in New York, the latest project was placed on the agenda by the mayor and then eagerly embraced by a well-established and organized Jewish leadership (including developers and other supporters of Mayor Koch). The project also had as a precedent President Carter's creation of the President's Commission on the Holocaust three years earlier, which gave the city project added prestige. Moreover, by 1981, memorialization of the Holocaust had become a hot item for the major Jewish American organizations.

During the 1980s, memorializing the Holocaust had become a "growth industry." Until the early 1970s it was not even on the agendas of the organized Jewish community; nor was it a priority when it was finally placed there. After 1978, when Holocaust memorialization was placed on the agenda of the United States government, the idea became more important for the organized Jewish community and thus ripe for adoption by Mayor Koch.

By that time a number of unrelated factors had converged to make memorialization of the Holocaust an appropriate issue for elected officials and candidates to place on their political agendas. For example, the 1967 Six Day War and the 1973 Yom Kippur War had brought images of another Holocaust to the fore. Menachem Begin, who masterfully used the Holocaust for his own political purposes, became the prime minister of Israel in June 1977. At about the same time, leaders of survivor organizations began to realize that their biological clocks were ticking fast, and they began to encourage other survivors to share their stories. Meanwhile, the much-publicized television program *Holocaust* was the first major network airing on the (fictionalized) subject of the Holocaust in 1978. In addition, children of survivors reached adulthood and began asking questions about their parents' past; secular American Jews who were disillusioned with Israel were seeking a substitute secular tie to Judaism; and the United States Justice Department in 1977 set up its Special Litigation Unit to investigate and bring to trial Nazi war criminals living in the United States. When President Carter's people were searching for a domestic issue that would mend fences with Jewish voters in 1978, the issue of the Holocaust was "a natural." It was an idea whose time had come.

Mayor Koch began to intervene when Herb Rickman, his special assistant and liaison to the Jewish community, approached developer George Klein in the spring of 1981, an election year, and suggested the creation of a mayor's task force. Klein took the chairmanship and, in July 1981, twenty-eight Jewish communal leaders, survivors, Holocaust scholars, and other prominent and wealthy Jews were named as members. In 1982 this task force recommended a permanent commission, and in 1983 the New York City Holocaust Memorial Commission was appointed by Mayor Koch.

In 1986 Governor Cuomo became, retroactively, a founding cochairman along with Mayor Koch. Cuomo was allowed to appoint additional commission members and a cochairman, and the name was changed to the New York Holocaust Memorial Commission (deleting the word "City"). Because the governor offered to house the museum in Battery Park City—which he controlled through the Battery Park City Authority, a state entity—the power structure of government intervention changed dramatically.

Mayor Koch, like President Carter, did not create his Holocaust commission in response to pressure from Jewish interest groups. Instead, these two elected officials co-opted the issue of the memorialization of the Holocaust in order to gain favor with the organized Jewish community and thereby obtain Jewish votes and financial backing for their upcoming election campaigns. Carter, and then Koch, created a specific Holocaust memorialization interest group that could potentially bring in votes and money. When Governor Cuomo's political entrepreneur, Meyer S. (Sandy) Frucher, decided that Cuomo, too, could and should have a piece of this pie, the city-state partnership became a reality.

Mayor Koch's co-opting the project should have made it more likely to succeed than earlier efforts to create a major Holocaust memorial in New York City, because he had a vested interest in its success and gave it active governmental backing. However, a series of setbacks delayed completion of the memorial during Koch's term as mayor. The most significant setbacks were caused by the intervention of Governor Cuomo or several of his high-level officials. When Koch left office at the end of December 1989, there was not even a hole in the ground for his proposed Holocaust memorial and museum. His absence after so prominently linking himself with the project, along with Mario Cuomo's shifting interest when he was considering a run for president during the 1992 elections, were factors that impeded implementation.

After Herb Rickman, Koch's liaison to the established Jewish community, suggested the creation of a mayor's task force on the Holocaust in 1981, Koch and Rickman chose George Klein as its chairman. He was not only a multimillionaire developer and major Koch campaign contributor but also a vice president of the New York Jewish Community Relations Council. At this time, Koch, as founding chairman of the task force, was at the apex, with sole power of appointment. Klein, as the chairman of the task force, ran the show, working closely with Rickman. Klein was then in a position to encourage his friends, other wealthy developers, to be generous both to the effort to create a Holocaust memorial and to Koch's mayoral campaign.

The politics of site selection is of special interest. The location was originally the U.S. Custom House, and then more than one site was considered at Battery Park City. Just when the city administration had secured the Custom House as a site, Sandy Frucher, on behalf of Governor Cuomo, dangled the promise of an apparently better site in Battery Park City if Cuomo could be the project's cochairman. Koch's acquiescence and the Holocaust commission's ensuing decision to change to this site led to further complications and stagnation.

The government intervention by Mayor Koch, and then by Governor Cuomo, in efforts to create a Holocaust memorial museum in New York City, have affected the content and philosophy of the project. Their intervention as well as the location of the project in the United States, and specifically, in New York City, give the museum's concept a particular slant. Along with specific governmental demands, there is also a kind of self-censorship by the Jewish leadership of the Holocaust commission to emphasize the positive aspects of the role of the United States—although this is much more evident in the Washington museum. In addition, the governor's office insisted on removing any doubts about the possibility that the museum would be a Jewish *religious* institution. This culminated in the state's citing the First Amendment—that is, separation of church and state—in the 1991 and 1993 memoranda of agreement and the 1994 lease between Battery Park City Authority and the Holocaust commission. The two memoranda prescribe that "the Building shall be operated at all times during the term of the New Museum Lease in accordance with the then current requirements of the First Amendment to the Constitution of the United States." The 1994 lease, which supersedes the earlier memoranda, makes the same statement in slightly different language.

The specific conception and evolution of this Holocaust museum could occur only in New York City, where the museum's viewpoint, or way of remembering, is influenced by the large, organized Jewish population. This concentration of nearly 2 million Jews, many of them prominent in government, real estate development, finance, the arts, public relations, higher education, and the other worlds that make New York "move and

10248

shake," gives the city an ambience that is uniquely Jewish in the United States.

The location of the proposed museum in New York City thus influences its planned content, giving it a decidedly Jewish viewpoint or slant. When Mayor Koch opened the door by providing an opportunity to create a Holocaust memorial, the leaders he chose to carry out the task expected to be able to significantly control the content of the memorial museum and make it uniquely Jewish. Because New York is such an ethnically Jewish city, they thought politicians and elected officials would approve of a particularistic Jewish memorialization of the Holocaust. They further believed that, in the New York City of the 1980s, the Holocaust was a potent symbol that would enable the powerful Jewish community to make political demands for a uniquely Jewish approach to memoralization. Koch, who needed to please Jewish sources of campaign money and influence (and also seemed to agree with the parochial concept), approved of the narrow Jewish approach to the memorial.

Later, once the proposed museum became a joint city-state project, the political coalition supporting it changed, and both the mayor and the governor were given powers of approval. Because the governor's office was inclined to make the museum's message less parochial, the commission made some changes in its plans for the museum's presentation. After Governor Cuomo had intervened by offering Battery Park City as a site, he learned too late about the narrow, or Jewish, scope of the planned museum and exhibits. Fearing criticism from advocates of separation of church and state, and requests for parcels of land or air rights from other religious groups, his office tried to change the message of the museum. For example, they insisted that the name of the museum be changed, so that "The Museum of Jewish Heritage–A Living Memorial to the Holocaust" became "A Living Memorial to the Holocaust–Museum of Jewish Heritage." Governor Cuomo's office was concerned about the Jewish "image" conveyed by the museum's original name. The governor's association with the museum would be helpful with his Jewish voters in both the city and state, but could be detrimental if he opted to run for president. He decided to walk the tightrope of pleasing both his local and potential national electorates by keeping the hyphenated name but reversing its components to minimize the Jewish aspect.

When a final arrangement between the Battery Park City Authority and the Holocaust commission was announced at the ceremonial signing of a new lease on August 18, 1994, Governor Cuomo had long since decided against running for president. Instead, he was once again standing for reelection as governor of New York State in November. Once again he needed to present a good image to his Jewish constituents in the state—especially in New York City—and he no longer had to worry about his national political image. Perhaps this influenced his public message regarding the imminent ground breaking for the museum. In the press release announcing that construction would soon begin, the governor acknowledged the museum's projected plans for remembering pre-Holocaust Jewish life in Europe, the Holocaust, and Jewish immigration to the United States, stating: "This museum will tell New Yorkers and visitors from around the world the story of the Jewish people before, during, and after the Holocaust, and document the long and proud history of the Jews who helped build America. This is a story that all of us—not just Jews—need to learn. Just as we must never forget the lessons of hatred gone mad taught by the Holocaust, we must never forget the lessons of Jewish survival and achievement over the centuries." At one time in the history of the project, the state had reneged on its promise of rent-free government land, perhaps coincidentally after the governor's office discovered that the museum was particularistically Jewish. Later, in 1994, the governor seems to have reevaluated this position. Meanwhile, the museum creators had been trying to adapt their plans to make the museum acceptable to the state government, agreeing to separation-of-church-and-state mandates.

Governor Cuomo received 75 percent of the Jewish vote in New York State in 1994, but he lost the election to Republican state senator George Pataki, 49 percent to 45 percent. Governor Pataki is likely to continue to support completion of the Holocaust memorial museum because his most important political ally during the campaign, Senator Alfonse D'Amato, is close to George Klein and a longtime backer of the project. Since the project was already well under way and the legal issues between the state and the commission had been settled before his election, it would have been difficult for Pataki to renege on Cuomo's action. Furthermore, approval and strong support for the project can help Pataki build closer ties to Jewish constituents. However,

Governor Cuomo, like Mayor Koch, was personally identified with the project as a founding cochairman. When the mayoralty of New York City passed from Ed Koch to David Dinkins, and then to Rudolph Giuliani, the Holocaust commission had to learn to negotiate with new partners, resulting in an inevitable interruption of momentum. And now the commission had to begin dealing with a new cast of characters in the Capitol in Albany.

Like other politicians before him, most notably President Carter, Mayor Koch captured the powerful symbol of the Holocaust soon after its emergence as a hot issue and used it to gain approval from Jewish constituents. Governor Cuomo then got on the bandwagon and pretended to be there from the beginning. Yet even at this stage, despite the powerful political symbolism of the Holocaust, the project failed to go forward smoothly. A series of delays and restructured plans resulted in a vicious circle: no visible progress because of insufficient funds, and unsuccessful fund-raising because of the lack of concrete progress. The successful implementation of the Washington Holocaust museum may also have been detrimental to fund-raising efforts for the New York project. During the construction of the Washington museum, and especially after its successful completion, potential donors questioned whether the American Jewish community needed another major memorial museum. The opening of the Simon Wiesenthal Center's Beit HaShoah–Museum of Tolerance in Los Angeles in February 1993 added to the controversy.

Finally, thirteen years after Mayor Koch initiated his task force, an agreement was reached in the summer of 1994 to begin to build a Holocaust memorial museum in New York City. The project is much smaller and less expensive than the Washington and Los Angeles museums, and much more modest than the one originally planned by the commission. There had already been two successors in City Hall to museum initiator Mayor Koch. His immediate successor, Democratic mayor David Dinkins, did nothing significant to move the project along. In 1994 Republican mayor Rudolph Giuliani was in office, and he joined Governor Cuomo to announce the new deal and take credit for it. Then, in November, soon after ground was broken, Cuomo was voted out of office.

The idea of memorializing the Holocaust has come a long way in the United States during the past three decades. With few exceptions, thirty years ago the Holocaust was spoken of in whispers or ignored. There were virtually no university courses on the topic, or books, movies, television programs, or Holocaust centers and museum exhibits. This book helps to explain why it has since become a national civic issue as well as a multimillion-dollar industry in the United States, with a national memorial museum on the Mall in Washington, D.C., other memorials and museums throughout the country, a national association of Holocaust organizations, a national network of children of survivors, national gatherings of survivors, national academic conferences, courses in numerous universities, and public-school curricula in some states and cities, not to mention hundreds of fiction and nonfiction books, as well as movies, art exhibits, plays, and television programs. The most publicized (and popular) manifestation of this interest was the box-office success of Steven Spielberg's movie *Schindler's List* and its choice as winner of the Academy Award for the best American film of 1993.

Despite this recent history of heightened interest, creating a major Holocaust memorial in New York City, the center of the organized Jewish community in the United States, has been a slow, shaky, and arduous process. Now that this fifty-year process is coming to an end, tracing the efforts to create a memorial from their very beginnings provides insights into the new memorial museum's evolution and its potential impact on the city's complex ethnic politics. The message of this museum will be instrumental in shaping the memory of the Holocaust for the hundreds of thousands of Jewish and non-Jewish New Yorkers and tourists who will visit the museum annually.

1

The American Jewish Community's Emergence as an Interest Group

Jewish life without committees would be like lox without bagels. —Albert Vorspan, My Rabbi Doesn't Make House Calls, *1969*

In order to understand how government intervention and changing circumstances contributed to the impasse of the most recent attempt to create a Holocaust memorial museum in New York City, it is first necessary to examine the historical setting in which this intervention occurred. The first effort to create a major Holocaust memorial in the city occurred in 1946, but the first municipal intervention in the issue of Holocaust memorialization did not take place there until 1981, following the lead of the Carter administration in 1978. These interventions by President Carter and Mayor Koch did not happen in a vacuum. Nor did Governor Cuomo's climbing aboard the bandwagon in 1986, which altered the structure of forces behind the New York City memorial project. Their interventions in Holocaust memorialization were directly related to two developments. The first one, the rise of the organized Jewish community as an interest group in the United States since the end of World War II, is the subject of this chapter. The second, the emergence of Holocaust memorialization as an issue for this interest group, will be addressed in Chapter 2.

It is important to understand the New York project within

the context of the established, national, organized American Jewish community. If this broader interest group had not been in place and influential, the Carter administration would have had no reason to intervene on the issue of Holocaust memorialization—and thus give Mayor Koch increased impetus for initiating a New York City project. Placing the project's history in a national framework is also necessary because from 1946 until 1978, various plans for Holocaust memorials in New York City were intended as a national memorial. Furthermore, because almost every major national American Jewish organization has its headquarters in New York City, local government intervention in a project of interest to the organized Jewish community in the city also has national implications. As will be seen in Chapter 7, at one time President Carter's commission on the Holocaust even considered placing the national memorial in New York City rather than in Washington, D.C. Mayor Koch at first encouraged this possibility, and when it was ruled out by the president's commission, he more vigorously pursued the creation of a museum in New York City under the auspices of a local commission.

Between the time President Carter and then Mayor Koch announced intentions to create major government-backed Holocaust memorials and the time of the Holocaust itself, the Jewish community in the United States underwent a transformation. Following World War II, the organized American Jewish community's effort to organize as an interest group included the same two key items that had been on its agenda during the war: the rescue of Jews from countries where they were endangered and the creation of a Jewish homeland in Israel—with the latter now more important. However, after the war this effort to become an influential interest group was intensified. One reason for its escalation after World War II may have been the organized Jewish community's guilt about not having done enough to influence the American government to rescue Jews during the war. Even after reports on the death camps had been received during the war, organized efforts continued to focus on building a Jewish homeland rather than rescue. Although this book begins with the first attempt to create a Holocaust memorial in New York City after the war, in 1946, what the organized Jewish community did or did not do during World War II is not irrelevant. Its activities during the war are summarized here because of their ramifications for postwar Jewish organizational life.[1]

During the war and until Israel became a reality in 1948, the issues of the creation of a Jewish homeland in Palestine and the rescue of the victims of Nazi Europe (refugees and later survivors) were intertwined. The organized American Jewish community's strongest argument for the creation of a Jewish state was that it could provide a haven for Europe's Jewish refugees and survivors (and shield the United States from bearing that burden). After the creation of the State of Israel, the organized Jewish community continued to link the need for a Jewish homeland with rescue. The argument was made that a secure Jewish homeland—Israel—was necessary to prevent another Holocaust and to rescue Jews from oppression across the globe (and again, protect the United States from bearing that burden). This was an especially powerful argument when the Soviet Union was considered the number-one menace by both the American Jewish community and the U.S. government.

The first attempt of the Jewish community to unify as an interest group in the United States did not take place until January 23–24, 1943, in the midst of World War II. The meeting was called by Henry Monsky, then the president of B'nai B'rith, the American Jewish fraternal organization that had been founded about one hundred years earlier. Monsky invited delegates from thirty-four national Jewish organizations "to seek agreement on the role the American Jewish community would play in representing Jewish demands after the war." In retrospect this is incredible. The genocide of the Jews of Europe had already been reported; but instead of clamoring for the U.S. government to rescue the Jews immediately, the leaders of the organized American Jewish community were planning for afterward. Nevertheless, this was the first endeavor to create an umbrella organization that would serve as a central channel to communicate the consensus of organized American Jewish opinion to the American government. The thirty-two organizations that sent representatives to this meeting formed the American Jewish Conference, which held its first session on August 29, 1943. The conference, which represented 1.5 million Jews directly and another million indirectly, overwhelmingly endorsed the 1942 Biltmore Platform, which had called for a reaffirmation of the Balfour pledge to establish a Jewish homeland in Palestine.[2] Although this meeting took place during the depth of World War II and of the Holocaust, its major focus was the creation of a Jewish national homeland. Throughout the war the major emphasis remained on Zionism and its mission—a homeland necessary for the rescue of European Jewry—while actual rescue efforts remained secondary.

The American Jewish Committee resigned from the American Jewish Conference almost immediately, and the American Council for Judaism was anti-Zionist. The latter "viewed any friendly gesture toward Israel by an American Jew as evidence of divided political loyalties."[3] The American Council for Judaism had been founded in the early 1940s by Arthur Hays Sulzberger, owner of the *New York Times,* and other "patrician" Jews who feared being accused of divided loyalties.[4]

When the Zionist effort was organized as the American Jewish Conference in 1943, it was headed by Rabbi Stephen S. Wise, who had led the American Zionist movement from the beginning. After the more aggressive Rabbi Abba Hillel Silver took over in 1944, he formed the American Zionist Emergency Council to lobby on the issue. For the 1944 presidential elections, both the Democrats and the Republicans included strong pro-Zionist planks in their platforms.

The American Zionist Emergency Council began to do what an interest group does, that is, lobbying elected officials and candidates on its issue of a Jewish homeland. It spread the Zionist message by means of a monthly political bulletin, *Palestine,* sent to more than 16,000 educational, political, and religious leaders. It also "orchestrated an extensive campaign of personal contacts" with editors, church and educational leaders, political candidates, congressmen and senators, and "at critical junctures flooded the White House, the State Department, and congressional offices with literally thousands upon thousands of letters and telegrams."[5] The emphasis continued to be Zionist, rather than a plea to rescue Hitler's victims.

After the war, the leaders of the organized Jewish community chastised themselves for not working harder to influence the American government to save the European Jews. As a result, their bid to organize as a powerful interest group was stepped up dramatically, and the picture began to change. Most people who are knowledgeable about the American Jewish community support the idea that efforts to organize after the war were related to the realization that not enough had been done during the war. According to rabbi and historian Arthur Hertzberg, for example, the American Jewish community learned during the war that they did not have enough power to rescue the Jews of Europe. "During the Holocaust," he observed, "Jews had not been powerful enough among all the factions and fractions of America to make the President and Congress feel their Jewish pain. In the 1940s, this knowledge was not yet spelled out in public. Jews continued to speak the language of goodwill, and of 'Americans all,' but Jews would spend the next two decades making sure that power in America was not the monopoly of the uncaring."[6]

Historian Melvin Urofsky has noted that, immediately after the war, awareness of the Holocaust changed the American Jewish community's formerly passive interest in working for creation of a Jewish homeland in Palestine to an active commitment. "And in the face of vested interests opposed to the Zionist dream, American Jewry mounted one of the most intense and successful lobbying efforts in American politics," he explains. "More than at any other time in its history, American Jewry stood united behind the Zionists [in 1945–48]. On the eve of Jewish statehood, 955,000 men and women formally belonged to one of dozens of Zionist organizations. In addition, millions of other American Jews endorsed the Zionist position through their membership in groups affiliated with the American Jewish Conference or through any of the more than fifty national agencies engaged in practical work in Palestine or political support of Zionism in the United States."[7] Thus Jewish statehood still remained the raison d'être for the Jewish community's escalated lobbying from the end of World War II until 1947–48.

Another reason for the increased political activity of the organized Jewish community immediately following World War II, not unrelated to their guilt, was the fact that this community had become by default the largest and most powerful Jewish community in the world. As political scientist Daniel Elazar noted: "American Jewry had become the foremost Jewish community in the world, larger by far than any other functioning Jewish community; indeed, it was ten times larger than its nearest functioning counterpart. It owned the bulk of the wealth that world Jewry could mobilize to undertake the tremendous tasks of relief and reconstruction confronting it as a result of the Holocaust, tasks which increasingly came to be concentrated in the development of the new state of Israel. . . . At the same time,

American Jewry confronted a new situation at home: barriers against full participation in American society rapidly fell away."[8]

Elazar was explaining both the internal and external circumstances that gave the American Jewish community the impetus to organize as a powerful interest group. On the one hand, the American Jewish community gained the responsibility, incurred through guilt and default, of taking on a world leadership role to fight for a Jewish homeland, security at home, and the rescue of Jews in the aftermath of the war. On the other hand, after the war ended and the full impact of the genocide of the Jews of Europe was revealed in the United States, the atmosphere changed: overt anti-Semitism diminished and the government became more receptive to the demands of the organized American Jewish community.

Leonard Fein, the founder of *Moment* magazine, explained the general involvement of Jews in politics as follows: "Politics, for Jews, is the displacement of Jewish motives onto public objects. What are those motives? To be a Jew means to belong to a people, not merely to adhere to a doctrine. It means, more specifically, to belong to a people that has perforce developed special sensitivities, through the course of its wanderings, to the acts of rulers and governments. It means, therefore, that the Jew *as Jew* has learned to pay attention to the political, to engage with it in order to ensure that princes and parliaments do not, wittingly or casually, do harm to one's people."[9] Although Fein's explanation does not deal specifically with the aftermath of World War II, it captures the reasons behind the intensified effort by the organized Jewish community in the United States to create a strong interest group at that time.

In 1946 a new Zionist Political Action Committee was created. There is evidence that by 1947 the organized Jewish community had met with some success in making its presence known as an interest group seeking to influence the federal government. Harry Truman, at least, took it into account during his campaign for president: "In November 1947 two political advisers, James H. Rowe, Jr., and Clark M. Clifford, presented Truman with a state-by-state plan for a campaign strategy. Rowe acknowledged that Jews hold the key to New York, and the key to the Jewish voters is what the Administration does about Palestine. But New York was probably the only state in which Jews would vote as a bloc."[10] The issue continued to be a Jewish homeland in Palestine; and the large concentration of Jews in New York City, then the city with the largest Jewish population in the world, was a target for those politicians seeking the support of Jewish voters.

In November 1947 the United States and the United Nations accepted the partition plan that ultimately created Israel. According to Urofsky, "The success of the Zionist effort in 1947 represented nearly five years of work, organization, publicity, education, and the careful cultivation of key people in different fields . . . securing the help of influential men and women in the press, the church, the arts, and above all, the government."[11] During the 1948 presidential election, candidates Truman, Thomas Dewey, and Henry Wallace all issued pro-Zionist statements. (Truman won 75 percent of the Jewish vote, with Wallace receiving 15 percent.)

Even the first attempt to create a major Holocaust memorial in New York in 1946 had a Zionist orientation. The ceremony to unveil the cornerstone for this original, and never completed, New York Holocaust memorial in Riverside Park was held on October 19, 1947, right before the United Nations vote to create Israel on November 29. Because of the timing of the memorial ceremony, it seemed likely to me that it was at least partially connected to Zionist efforts to convince the public of a link between a Jewish homeland and the Holocaust. My assumption was verified when I discovered in an archive the unpublished memoirs of the man who had led this effort. "My decision to hold the dedication ceremony in September or October [1947]," he had written, "was chiefly influenced by the acute situation in Palestine where a bitter fight raged between the Jews and the English which caused the United Nations to put the Palestine question on the agenda before the Assembly in October, 1947."[12]

In 1954, six years after the birth of Israel, an official pro-Israel Jewish lobby was created. The Zionist factions' Emergency Committee, which fell apart after the 1948 War of Independence, had been reorganized in 1949 as the American Zionist Council (composed of the fourteen leading Zionist organizations). In March 1954 the council established the American Zionist Committee for Public Affairs, an organization created specifically to lobby Washington on issues concerning Israel; since 1959 it has been called the American Israel Public Affairs Committee (AIPAC). For the first time, pro-Israel lobbying was coordinated by a single office.

Throughout the 1950s the American Jewish community continued to become more organized around the central issue of Israel. The umbrella organization called the Conference of Presidents of Major American Jewish Organizations (Presidents' Conference) was formally established in 1959. Starting in 1955, leaders of twenty organizations began meeting on a regular basis to lay the foundation for the creation of the conference.[13]

The organized Jewish community in the United States today is being defined here as that part of the Jewish population of about 6,840,000 that is in some way connected with a constituent organization of the Presidents' Conference.[14] The Jewish community is not monolithic. Many American Jews are unaffiliated and/ or dissent from views represented by the Presidents' Conference or some of its constituents. Often these constituent organizations disagree with each other. Although only about 40 percent of the Jews in the United States are affiliated with a Jewish organization today, the Presidents' Conference claims to speak for the Jewish community, mainly on issues of foreign policy. The conference can legitimately speak only for this organized 40 percent. However, since there is no spokesperson for the *un*organized others, the effectiveness of the organized Jewish community as an interest group must be traced through the Presidents' Conference.

Daniel Elazar observed that the Presidents' Conference was established because "increased American Jewish involvement in the concerns of the Jewish people as a whole [had] sharpened the need for a communal voice that speaks as one, at least in the field of foreign relations."[15] Analyzing the conference as "a structural device that has been developed to coordinate a weak multiple-element oligarchy, in those areas in which the constituent groups are willing to coordinate," he defined the organized Jewish community as an oligarchy, "a substantially closed group of individuals [who] enjoy a virtual monopoly of power by reserving control over all significant decision making"; in a number of aspects, he noted, oligarchy is "far more prevalent in the American Jewish world than autocracy."[16]

A recent brochure of the Conference of Presidents of Major American Jewish Organizations defines the group's aims as follows: "The purpose of the Presidents' Conference is to strengthen the U.S.–Israel alliance and to protect and enhance the security and dignity of Jews abroad. Toward this end, the Conference of

Presidents speaks and acts on the basis of consensus on issues of national and international Jewish concern, as the most all-embracing coalition of the world's largest Jewish community. . . . It also serves as the representative body to which officials of the Executive and Legislative branches of the American government, Israeli leaders, foreign statesmen and Jewish communities in other lands turn in dealing with issues of mutual concern." After 1968, AIPAC, the official pro-Israel lobby, was permitted to inform Congress that the Presidents' Conference (then with 22 member organizations) had endorsed, in principle, AIPAC's views. By 1974 the Conference of Presidents had 32 member organizations, and by 1978, 37 members.[17] In 1996 there were 54 constituent organizations and five official observers.[18] Memorialization of the Holocaust is the province of the National Jewish Community Relations Advisory Council (NJCRAC), a member organization of the Presidents' Conference.

Political scientist Daniel Elazar wrote in 1989 that the President's Conference had begun to be eclipsed by AIPAC in the 1970s, and that "today a new balance is in the making."[19] This statement is perplexing for two reasons. First, obviously, if AIPAC, the official pro-Israel lobby, is informing Congress that the Presidents' Conference has endorsed its views, the two organizations are working together and not competing. AIPAC is, in fact, an important member of the Presidents' Conference. Second, the two groups are and have been closely linked for the purpose of maximizing impact as an interest group: AIPAC is the mechanism whereby the major Jewish organizations can lobby by proxy, without registering as lobbyists or agents of a foreign government and thereby losing their tax-exempt status. Unofficially, member organizations of the Presidents' Conference ask their members to lobby their representatives and the administration. Officially, however, only AIPAC lobbies.

AIPAC has a reputation as one of the most effective lobbying organizations in Washington, dealing strictly with issues relating to Israel. As Melvin Urofsky wrote of AIPAC, "I.L. Kenen, and his successor, Morris J. Amitai, have made the America-Israel Public Affairs Committee a respected voice in Washington. When necessary, AIPAC can also call upon the national Jewish organizations for letter, telephone, and telegram campaigns to impress Congress or the White House with just how important Israel is to their constituents."[20] AIPAC lost some ground in 1993, when some of its leadership were forced to resign after what could be briefly described as their boasting too much about powerful connections. Afterward, attorney Neal Sher, who had headed the Office of Special Investigations (OSI), the Justice Department's unit to seek out and prosecute Nazi war criminals living in the United States, was named the new director of AIPAC. Among his most important qualifications for his new post were the connections he had made on Capitol Hill during his years in the OSI.

One of the twenty original organizations that met to form the Presidents' Conference is the National Jewish Community Relations Advisory Council (NJCRAC). An umbrella in its own right, NJCRAC was founded in 1944 as a voluntary association of Jewish community relations agencies. (It originally had no *J* in its initials, because the word *Jewish* was then not part of its name. This reflected the organized Jewish community's fear, in 1944, of displaying a high profile.) NJCRAC was founded by the Council of Jewish Federations, which is itself the umbrella for local federations of Jewish philanthropy throughout the United States.[21] NJCRAC portrays itself in its program plan as "a unique partnership of 117 local and 13 national agencies throughout the United States. NJCRAC member agencies represent the broadest range of political and social thought in the organized Jewish community, yet they are linked by a dual commitment to safeguarding the rights of Jews and assuring the vitality of the United States' pluralist democracy. The NJCRAC partnership brings together both national and local perspectives in the formulation of consensus positions and approaches on national issues."[22] Its *Joint Program Plan*, first issued annually in 1953, is designed to serve as an advisory guide to assist member agencies in their own program planning; each agency may accept, reject, modify, or extend any of the recommendations, according to individual concerns and needs. NJCRAC is the member organization of the President's Conference under whose jurisdiction issues such as memorializing the Holocaust fall; and this topic first appeared in NJCRAC's *Joint Program Plan* for 1972–73 (see Chapter 2).

By 1960, when John F. Kennedy was elected president, both the Presidents' Conference and AIPAC were in place and working in tandem on their agenda for promoting the best interest of Israel as perceived by the organized American Jewish community. Kennedy's election was a milestone in the organized Jewish

community's effort to become a mainstream interest group, because the election of a Catholic president (whom it had strongly
backed) broadened the opportunities for political power by non-
Protestants in the United States. As journalist and scholar
Charles Silberman saw it, Kennedy's election was "an event that
symbolized the transformation of the United States from an essentially Protestant to a religiously pluralistic society." After
Kennedy's election, he points out, there was a steady decrease
in all types of prejudice, including anti-Semitism. According to
Silberman, "the reduction in hostility toward Jews has been accompanied, in fact, by a growth in positive attitudes. In 1940, for
example, 63 percent of Americans said that Jews as a group had
'objectionable traits'; by 1981, when a Gallup poll asked Americans to rate Jews on a ten-point scale, 81 percent had favorable
and only 8 percent had unfavorable opinions."[23]

Furthermore, because the Jewish community had so strongly
backed Kennedy, it was in a favorable position with his administration. (He received 82 percent of the Jewish vote, carrying New
York by 384,000 votes, with Jewish precincts giving him a plural-
ity of more than 800,000.) The Jews had played a major role in
electing the first Catholic president. As Urofsky explains, "The
understanding that marked relations between the Kennedy
administration and American Jews reinforced the sense of belonging that characterized Jewish life in the early 1960s. . . . Kennedy reportedly told David Ben-Gurion in New York in 1961,
'You know, I was elected by the Jews of New York, and I would
like to do something for the Jewish people.'"[24]

President Kennedy did not live to see the 1967 Six Day War,
when he clearly could have paid this "debt." The war brought an
enormous resurgence of support for Israel from the organized
American Jewish community. In addition to lobbying Washington for help, a 1967 emergency fund-raising campaign by the
United Jewish Appeal raised $240 million, and $190 million
worth of Israel bonds were purchased. As will be discussed in
the next chapter, the Six Day War was one of the earliest catalysts
for the emergence of the organized American Jewish community's interest in memorializing the Holocaust.

By the late 1970s, the individual major Jewish organizations,
the Presidents' Conference, and AIPAC were cohesive and working more aggressively and knowledgeably in the political arena.
In addition, Jewish PACs (political action committees) were rais-

ing money for targeted candidates who were pro-Israel. Kennedy's election, the 1967 Six Day War and 1973 Yom Kippur War, and the ethnic movements of the 1960s had all increased the ability of the organized Jewish community to function as an effective interest group. Menachem Begin, who took over as prime minister of Israel in June 1977, was a master at using the Holocaust for Zionist and his own Likud party political purposes, which helped make the organized American Jewish community receptive to the idea of memorializing the Holocaust. This new receptiveness in the Jewish community opened a policy door for elected officials and candidates in the United States to make political use of the idea of Holocaust memorialization. In order to use the issue effectively, President Jimmy Carter and then Mayor Koch created their own specialized interest groups to support such memorialization.

President Carter desperately needed an issue to appeal to the organized Jewish community in 1978, when he created his President's Commission on the Holocaust. When he ran against Gerald Ford in 1976, the Jewish community organizations—which cannot legally keep their tax-exempt status and support a candidate, but nevertheless informally make their views known to their constituents—were wary of this unknown Southern Baptist. Gerald Ford, however, won only 28 percent of the Jewish vote. Nevertheless, the American Jewish community came to believe between 1977 and 1980 that their 1976 fears about President Carter had not been unfounded. His policies and statements about Israel, the Palestinians, and providing military equipment for Israel and other countries in the Middle East turned the Jewish community away from him. It was an effort by the Carter administration to assuage these fears within the Jewish community—a community that was then ready to acknowledge the importance of memorializing the Holocaust—that led to the creation of the President's Commission on the Holocaust in 1978.

Carter's attempt to capture the vote of the Jewish community in the 1980 presidential elections did not succeed. Only 45 percent of the Jewish electorate voted for him, the "lowest Jewish vote for a Democratic candidate since Franklin D. Roosevelt brought Jews firmly into the Democratic fold." Fifteen percent of Jews voted for John Anderson in 1980, and a high 39 percent for Ronald Reagan.[25] Despite his initiation of a national effort to memorialize the Holocaust, Carter had a hard time keeping Jewish voters voting Democratic in 1980. More than one in four Jewish voters who had voted for Carter in 1976 voted for Reagan in 1980, and the Jewish majority that traditionally voted with the Democratic Party was reduced to a margin of four to three.[26]

At this stage in the history of the organized American Jewish community, memorialization of the Holocaust became an issue for the federal and then the New York City government. Although President Carter's creation of a national President's Commission on the Holocaust and subsequent U.S. Holocaust Memorial Commission did not win him the Jewish vote (or the presidency) in 1980, he should be recorded in American and Jewish history as the president who placed this issue on the agenda of the U.S. government. The idea of constructing a memorial museum remained on the agenda and moved forward during the presidencies of Ronald Reagan and George Bush, coming to fruition during President Bill Clinton's term in 1993. President Carter's governmental intervention in an area that had previously been the private domain of the American Jewish community was the first step in the federal, New York State, and New York City governments' ability to influence how the American Jewish community would memorialize the Holocaust.

2

Memory of the Holocaust as an Issue in the American Jewish Community

Dear love, Auschwitz made me more of a Jew than ever Moses did. —Dannie Abse, "White Balloon," 1990

Tracing the growing significance of Holocaust memorialization for the increasingly organized American Jewish community makes it easy to comprehend why Mayor Edward I. Koch became interested in creating a major Holocaust memorial museum in New York City. Memorialization of the Holocaust became the project of the mayor—and then of a complicated city-state-private coalition headed by the mayor and the governor of New York State—only after the issue had become important for the community. When President Jimmy Carter intervened on the issue in 1978, it was already becoming a "hot" topic in the organized Jewish community, and the president's placing it on the national governmental agenda made it even more important.

Before the subject of Holocaust memorialization was placed on the federal, and then the New York City and New York State agendas, it had to have become significant for the organized American Jewish community. Otherwise, President Carter's political entrepreneurs, and then those of Mayor Koch and Governor Mario Cuomo, would not have chosen a Holocaust memorial as the critical item in their agenda to attract Jewish votes and money. Therefore, before explaining how memorializing the Holocaust evolved into a city-state-private project in New York City, it is necessary to trace when and how this topic emerged and became important for the organized American Jewish community.

Interest in the Holocaust and its memorialization did not appear instantly or follow a straight path. Various historical, psychological, political, and cultural factors interacted to bring about the organized Jewish community's gradual and growing interest in studying and memorializing the Holocaust. Some key events are possible to pinpoint, but, as I will demonstrate, not all historians of the Holocaust and the American Jewish community agree on which historical event was most significant. The community's interest in the Holocaust did not suddenly emerge where it had not been before. Latent awareness was pushed to the forefront by specific events and also by the passing of time.

Starting with the trial of Adolf Eichmann in Jerusalem in 1961, and gaining in intensity during Israel's Six Day War in 1967, the organized American Jewish community began to face the Holocaust and its implications for their present and future. There was a proliferation of books, college courses, movies, and commemorations, beginning slowly in the 1960s. (One of the few earlier exceptions was *The Diary of Anne Frank*, published in English in 1952, made into a movie in 1959, and dramatized on Broadway in the interim.) The popularization of the Holocaust culminated in the NBC miniseries *Holocaust* in April 1978 (the month before President Carter announced his President's Commission on the Holocaust).

Once Carter had made memorialization of the Holocaust an official program of the U.S. government, the action generated a reaction. The organized Jewish community jumped on the bandwagon, applauded the project, and made the Holocaust a more prominent issue on their agenda. Holocaust survivor and Nobel laureate Elie Wiesel told me that in making memorialization of the Holocaust part of government policy, President Carter changed the social psychology of the country. The subject became aggrandized in the Jewish community, and survivors who were previously considered second-class by the community suddenly gained new status[1]. During the 1980s, after President Carter's intervention, the number of books, movies, television programs, symposiums, courses, and institutions for study of the Holocaust continued to grow more rapidly.[2]

After the organized Jewish community's general interest in the Holocaust emerged in the 1960s, but before President Carter intervened in 1978, the community had not been catalyzed into creating a major national memorial or museum. Small groups of individuals had attempted to do so at different times in New York City since 1946, but for the most part the major Jewish organizations were not enthusiastic about these projects. (I have found no record of any attempt to create a major Holocaust memorial in the United States before the first effort in New York City in 1946–47.)

Beginning in the 1960s and continuing through the early 70s, the idea of memorializing the Holocaust gradually took hold in the bureaucracy of the Jewish community. By the mid-1970s the concept of memorialization (but *not* a national memorial) was firmly on the community's agenda. It was an idea for which the time had come in the national organized Jewish community. According to political scientist John Kingdon, an expert on public policy, agendas are set when three streams come together: problem recognition, policy formulation and refinement, and politics.[3] In the case of Holocaust memorialization, these three forces coalesced at the critical time of two major wars during which Israel faced possible annihilation. The situation created a policy window, or an opportunity for action, for Holocaust memorialization. "Problem recognition" refers to the American Jewish community's acknowledgment that Israel was not an idealistic utopia: its very existence had been endangered by two wars, and afterward its policies of occupation were difficult for some parts of the community to defend. Many secular American Jews began, consciously or unconsciously, to search for a less controversial symbol of Jewish identity. This recognition led to policy formulation and refinement and, subsequently, to the creation of a new policy for retaining the organized American Jewish community's allegiance to Israel. The new policy introduced the memorialization of the Holocaust as a supplement to loyalty to Israel.

This, in turn, led to the political component of agenda setting: the organized American Jewish community's support of Israel's use of the Holocaust to explain or make excuses for the country's behavior. Regarding Israel's use of the Holocaust as a rationalization (for its West Bank policies, requests for economic aid, or arguments against Arab countries receiving military aid), the organized American Jewish community, through the Presidents' Conference and AIPAC, supported Israel's position. This position, especially after Menachem Begin became prime minister in 1977, was that, as a result of the Holocaust, Israel deserved special treatment as well as approval for all of its actions. As Boaz Evron, a leftist Israeli writer, remarked: "The exploitation of the memory for these purposes has been developed into a fine art. Almost any Israeli official appearance abroad involves an invocation of the Holocaust, in order to inculcate in the listeners the proper feelings of guilt."[4] Conor Cruise O'Brien, an Irish journalist, made the same point from his perspective as a non-Israeli and non-Jew. "Among Gentiles interested in Israel, there is impatience with Israeli Holocaust consciousness—and especially with what is seen as the exploitation of the Holocaust by Israeli leaders, since 1977, especially by Menachem Begin."[5]

The organized American Jewish community's general interest in the Holocaust and specific interest in creating memorials grew slowly, and in spurts, after the 1961 Eichmann trial and the 1967 Six Day War. Some communities, such as Philadelphia, created small Holocaust memorials or monuments in the 1960s; and in New York City, Jewish groups made a number of attempts to create a large-scale memorial in the 1960s and '70s. (The earlier 1946 effort in New York City was an exception.) After 1973 the *Joint Program Plan* of the National Jewish Community Relations Advisory Council (NJCRAC) encouraged the creation of small local memorials, reflecting the leadership's acknowledgment of Holocaust memorialization as an important issue for the organized American Jewish community. However, there was no national Jewish program or organizational platform for a major national memorial until after President Carter placed this specific item on the federal agenda. As Chapter 7 documents, in the case of the federal Holocaust memorial the organized Jewish community was reactive rather than active. In the late 1970s, after the issue of memorializing the Holocaust had been institutionalized in the organized Jewish community (through NJCRAC), more localities began to build small memorials. It must be emphasized, however, that the Jewish community did not request that the federal government create a national memorial.

Although the community's interest in memorializing the Holocaust was gradual, most experts agree that the 1967 Six Day War was *the* event that turned the tide. The connection between the Hitlerian Holocaust and the possibility of another in Israel was so frightening and blatant that it could not be ignored. Creation of a Jewish homeland, ran the Zionist argument in 1945–47, had as its purpose the redemption of survivors of the Holocaust. Then, in 1967, this very redemption was threatened with the possibility of another genocide. Even the creation of a Jewish homeland in Israel seemed not to be saving the Jewish people from the possibility of annihilation. And if the Jews could be destroyed in Israel, perhaps they could also be destroyed in the United States. This was the reason the Six Day War so powerfully raised Holocaust consciousness in the American Jewish community.

The connection between the Holocaust and the Six Day War in the minds of American Jews is accepted by most scholars. For example, historian Jacob Neusner wrote in 1979 that the Six Day War marked the beginning of interest in the Holocaust. "What turned an historical event into a powerful symbol of contemporary social action and imagination," he observed, "was a searing shared experience. For millions of Jews, the dreadful weeks before the 1967 war gave a new vitality to the historical record of the years from 1933 to 1945—the war and its result."[6]

Rabbi Irving (Yitz) Greenberg, Director of CLAL, The National Jewish Center for Learning and Leadership, and one of the first advocates of teaching about the Holocaust, also cited the Six Day War (and, to a lesser degree, the Eichmann trial) as the catalyst for interest in the Holocaust by the organized American Jewish community. He told me that in the 1950s the subject of the Holocaust was all but totally neglected by the community. "People were 'ashamed' of the 'sheep to the slaughter' idea," he observed. Rabbi Greenberg described the Eichmann trial as a "turning point" because "it moved the Holocaust from the sense of shame to the sense of pity, compassion, and feeling. And it gave it significant publicity, although the ground was still not saturated, and the publicity was soaked up and didn't show up on the surface."[7] (Greenberg's analogy compares the situation to planting seeds in dry soil, which needs to absorb water deep in the ground before irrigated topsoil can produce vegetation.)

In 1962, Rabbi Greenberg was a professor at Yeshiva University, one of New York's most prestigious institutions of Jewish scholarship. He told me that he wanted to teach a course on the Holocaust there, but the faculty and administration showed little interest. He finally was able to "sell" the idea to the dean after he renamed the course "Totalitarianism and Ideology in the Twentieth Century." His research in 1962 found only one course on the Holocaust in existence, at Brandeis University. Greenberg believes that the Six Day War was the breakthrough. "There was a tremendous urgency that the Holocaust is coming again," he told me. "I think 1967 opened the emotional floodgates."

Holocaust historian Saul Friedlander also targets the Six Day War as stimulating interest in the Holocaust in the United States. He pointed out that Elie Wiesel and Raul Hilberg had difficulties finding publishers in the early 1960s. "Why the change? The Six Day War. There was a need for definition by the community. They were losing their Zionist dream, and this led to the centrality of the Jewish experience of the Holocaust. It wasn't meant to be that way, but two things came together and made it happen."[8]

Melvin Urofsky, a historian of Zionism, and Charles Silberman, a journalist/scholar who has studied the dynamics of the American Jewish community, also identified the Six Day War with the organized American Jewish community's emerging interest in the Holocaust. Urofsky contrasted "the emotional outburst which erupted following the victory" with "the gloom and despair which characterized American Jewry during May 1967." According to Urofsky, "the imagery of the Holocaust dominated American Jewry—the fear that twice in their lifetime the Jewish people would be slaughtered and would be able to do nothing about it."[9] According to Silberman, the American Jewish community thought, during the 1967 war, that "another Holocaust was in the making" and that "it looked and felt as though once again the world would sit idly by while Jews marched to their death." Pointing out, like others, that American Jews had paid little attention to the Holocaust before 1967, he offered the following reasons: "Some, perhaps, felt guilty over their inability to prevent the dreadful event or, failing that, to rescue more than a handful of people; others needed the healing balm of time before they could come to terms with what had happened; most were simply too caught up in their own lives and in the exciting move from the margins of American society to its mainstream." Even after the Eichmann trial in 1961, "which turned the Holocaust into front-page news in American newspapers," he wrote, discussion of the subject was "desultory."[10]

"Desultory," or unmethodical, is perhaps a good description. There were discussions, and even heated arguments among some circles in the Jewish community. For example, Hannah Arendt's vindictive account of the Eichmann trial in *The New Yorker* in 1963 (published the same year as a book, *Eichmann in Jerusalem*) provoked a controversy that lasted throughout the early 1960s. Arendt concluded that Jewish leaders shared in Eichmann's guilt, and that the Jews went to their death like sheep to the slaughter.[11] However, controversies about specific books or events are not the same as an organized effort to institutionalize the Holocaust and its memory as a primary concern of the organized Jewish community. That did not occur until later.

Author and scholar Leonard Fein, too, linked the Six Day War and awareness of the Holocaust, stating that in 1967 "the fear was precise, and 'another Auschwitz' was its name. Back then, no one yet knew how resourceful and how tough and how skilled at war the Israelis had become. So, when some Arab leaders boasted that the Jews would be driven into the sea, the Jews of America felt terror, as Jews."[12] Michael Berenbaum, director of the Research Institute of the U.S. Holocaust Memorial Museum in Washington, concurred on the important influence of the Six Day War. He also mentioned the statements of Arab leaders to "drive the Jews into the sea," and told me: "American Jews felt their vulnerability and pulled out all the stops."[13] Even though Israel was victorious in the 1967 (and then the 1973) war, the fear of annihilation preceding those victories evoked the Holocaust and led the organized American Jewish community to institutionalize its memorialization.

Elie Wiesel is the only authority on the Holocaust I found who does not agree that the 1967 war was the principal cause of the emergence of Holocaust memorialization in the United States. "We worked on it," he told me. "My first book came out here in 1960, which means eighteen years, after all [until Carter intervened]. In the meantime, I was teaching and writing, and other people were. In 1960 nobody read, nobody cared. Then it accumulated. There were television programs, the Eichmann trial in 1960, other trials later on. Things happened. . . . The Israel wars didn't have anything to do with it."[14] When I asked how the idea of Holocaust memorialization had grown so much since 1960, Wiesel responded: "A convergence of events. Between 1960 and 1979 there was a very small group of people who worked on this. Beginning in the 1960s, I would go around literally from conference to conference, from convention to convention, from community to community, to speak about this. Because nobody else did. When other people began, I stopped. For the last twenty years or so, I don't really speak about this subject. But at that time, nobody did it, so I did. I didn't speak about museums or memorials—only about the need to remember." Although Wiesel denies the crucial influence of the 1967 war in Israel, I agree with the others who believe it was precisely the reason that the "very small group of people who worked on this" began to gain a sympathetic ear in the United States.

It is important to emphasize that, prior to 1967, very little material was published here on the Holocaust. In addition to Elie Wiesel's *Night*, copyrighted here in 1960, other early books were *The Diary of Anne Frank* (1952), Gerda Weissmann Klein's *All But My Life* (1957), and Raul Hilberg's *The Destruction of the European Jews* (1961).[15] Although *Night* had already been published successfully in France, Wiesel had great difficulty finding a publisher in the United States.

After the 1973 Yom Kippur War reinforced fears of the Six Day War, concern with commemorating the Holocaust intensified in the organized American Jewish community by the middle of the 1970s. Soon afterward, three unrelated events helped to firmly entrench the issue of Holocaust memorialization in the agenda of the organized American Jewish community. First, Menachem Begin became prime minister of Israel in 1977. More than any previous leader, he used the evocation of the Holocaust to defend Israel's existence and its policies. The major American Jewish organizations, led by the Presidents' Conference, followed suit. Then, in the summer of 1977, the Immigration and Naturalization Services division of the U.S. Justice Department set up a Special Litigation Unit to prosecute alleged Nazi war criminals living in the United States. That same year, Congress requested an investigation to determine whether U.S. government agencies had obstructed investigation and prosecution of alleged Nazi war criminals; and on May 15, 1978, the General Accounting Office of the House of Representatives issued its report.[16] A short time earlier, in April 1978, NBC television broadcast the series *Holocaust*, which—albeit in a kitsch, soap-opera format—brought the subject into living rooms across the country and gave it national grass-roots acceptability.

Perhaps the best evidence of formally placing a domestic issue on the Jewish agenda on a national scale is the *Joint Program Plan* of the National Jewish Community Relations Advisory Council, the national umbrella organization under whose institutional jurisdiction an issue such as memorializing the Holocaust falls. NJCRAC first placed the idea of memorializing the Holocaust on its agenda formally in 1972–73 when it included a section entitled "Interpreting the Holocaust" in its published annual *Joint Program Plan*. This brief section encouraged local community relations organizations to observe the thirtieth anniversary of the Warsaw Ghetto uprising.[17] Although various efforts to commemorate the Holocaust had been undertaken earlier by organizations, local Jewish communities, and survivor groups in the United States, its placement on the NJCRAC agenda institutionalized memorialization nationally in the American Jewish community for the first time. (The recommendation in the 1961–62 *Joint Program Plan* that Jewish community relations agencies "cooperate in studying and assessing all the effects of the Eichmann trial and in interpreting its meaning and its lessons" is NJCRAC's only reference to the Holocaust in program plans prior to 1972.)[18]

Beginning in 1973–74, NJCRAC's *Joint Program Plan* also included a section entitled "Commemorating the Holocaust." Among other recommendations, it suggested that local communities create "visual memorials to the Holocaust, such as permanent exhibits, monuments, plaques [and] signs," and that they develop local archives. These recommendations were reiterated in the *Program Plans* for 1974–75, 1975–76, 1976–77, 1977–78, and 1978–79.[19] Only in 1979–80, after President Carter had appointed his President's Commission on the Holocaust, was there a major shift in NJCRAC's published statement on the Holocaust. It had not previously recommended or even mentioned creation of a national Holocaust memorial in its *Joint Program Plan*. Now that Carter had put the issue on the federal agenda, NJCRAC came out in support of it. From then on, the issue of commemorating the Holocaust appeared annually in the *Joint Program Plan* through 1994–95, with the exception of 1991–92. Depending on the year, the discussion varied from a small "Continuing but Urgent" segment to a major section on "Lessons of Bitburg" (in

1985–86). After the Washington museum opened in 1993, the 1993–94 and 1994–95 *Joint Program Plans* encouraged visits to the museum.

Rabbi Irving "Yitz" Greenberg described the eleven years between the 1967 Six Day War and the 1978 NBC *Holocaust* miniseries as a time of "soaking the ground." "The miniseries never would have been produced or had the reverberations," he said, "but for this ten years before of saturating the ground. It took ten years of saturating the ground, building up a scholarly following, building up a religious consciousness. And then it was like striking a match, when you had saturation with benzene. And it blasted off."[20] (At this point, the groundwork for Carter's President's Commission on the Holocaust commenced.)

Another indicator that memorializing the Holocaust had become timely for the organized American Jewish community is the coverage of the Holocaust in books about the community. When Nathan Glazer wrote his classic *American Judaism* in 1957, he was not concerned about remembering the Holocaust. "Describing American Judaism in the mid-1950s," Jacob Neusner wrote in 1979, "the great sociologist Nathan Glazer managed to write an entire book without making more than passing reference to the destruction of European Jewry. The contrast with the 1970s is striking. Now there is no way to address the Jewish world without referring to 'the Holocaust.'"[21] Even during the 1960s and much of the 1970s, the subject of remembering the Holocaust was absent from most scholarly examinations of the American Jewish community. As Charles Silberman pointed out: "When *Commentary* conducted a symposium on 'the condition of Jewish belief' in 1966, for example, its editors did not so much as mention the Holocaust in the five long questions it sent to the participating rabbis and theologians, nor did more than a handful of the thirty-eight respondents raise the question on their own."[22]

Six years before Neusner's article and seven years after the *Commentary* symposium, in 1973, the American Jewish Committee and the Jewish Publication Society of America jointly published *The Future of the Jewish Community in America*, a book of essays prepared by leading scholars for an American Jewish Committee task force on the future of the American Jewish community. Although Neusner said there was no way to avoid mention of the Holocaust in the 1970s, he was writing in 1979. In

1973 the issue was still hardly noted in a book by leading scholars of the community such as David Sidorsky and Daniel Elazar. Nevertheless, Sidorsky, a prominent professor of Jewish history who edited the book, cited the Holocaust as one of four recent major events "presumably" influencing the formation of identity in the Jewish community: "The first is the Holocaust, and although it may be claimed that memory has dimmed its impact, it may also be true that only now is the realization of the event, which traumatized awareness by its overwhelming enormity, becoming absorbed into consciousness."[23]

Sidorsky therefore recognized that the Holocaust had become important, but he was hedging his bets. Furthermore, the subject was virtually ignored by the other experts on the American Jewish community who contributed chapters to his book. There was only one other reference to the Holocaust in Sidorsky's book, and it commented on the lack of interest in the subject. In an article entitled "Toward a General Theory of Jewish Education," Seymour Fox observed that "the Holocaust is barely mentioned in our classrooms."[24] (This was generally the case in the early 1970s, in contrast to special curricula offered by many school districts beginning in the 1980s and continuing into the 1990s.) In an article entitled "Decision Making in the American Jewish Community," Elazar did not even mention memorialization of the Holocaust as relevant to decision making, although he did refer to the resettlement and rehabilitation of Europe's Jews.[25] Glazer's 1957 book, *American Judaism,* the 1966 *Commentary* symposium, and Sidorsky's 1973 book are typical of virtually all books on the American Jewish community between the end of World War II and the Yom Kippur War: the subject of the Holocaust or its memorialization is not discussed as relevant or important for the organized American Jewish community. Between Sidorsky's writing in 1973 and Neusner's in 1979, there was a giant leap in interest in the Holocaust.

Soon after the 1973 war the picture had changed dramatically. The Israel wars were the catalyst for interest in the Holocaust not only because they evoked the possibility of another Holocaust, another genocide of the Jewish people. There was another side to the aftermath of the Six Day and Yom Kippur wars. Israel's image changed in the minds of many individual American Jews and non-Jews, including decision makers in Washington. Instead of the poor defenseless David, Israel had suddenly become Goliath.

The leaders of the organized Jewish community were able to link the new interest in the Holocaust to their support of Israel's policies: for them, memorialization of the Holocaust was a way of saying, again, that Israel—redeemer of the remnant of Holocaust survivors—was still the victim, and not a victor or aggressor. During both wars, there had been fear that Israel might be destroyed, that a new Holocaust would result in the mass murder of Jews. This fear brought memories of the Holocaust out of the closet, even for people who had no personal recollections. And the organized Jewish community made use of this fear. Linking the Holocaust with Israel helped the organized community hold the interest (and donations) of some American Jews who, in the wars' aftermath, questioned Israel's policies. When questions about the occupation of the West Bank and Gaza Strip, and Israel's treatment of Arabs, got in the way, community leaders could invoke the Holocaust. The Holocaust was easier to "sell" than the idea of an Israeli occupation because the question of victimization was unambiguous.

After the wars, many secular Jews who had considered Israel as their strongest connection to Judaism became disillusioned with Israel's policies and were searching for a new, nonreligious link. Memorializing the Holocaust became their new symbolic affirmation. This substitution of the Holocaust for Israel among some American Jews was not acceptable to the organized American Jewish community, which continued to support Israel and its policies. Therefore, leaders of the community used the emergence of Holocaust memorialization in a way that explained the need for Israel's existence and its policies. In the 1990s, the organized American Jewish community still links the idea of memorializing the Holocaust to the importance of the existence of a strong Israel. Although the community supports peace negotiations between Israel and the Palestinians and neighboring Arab states, hard-liners resisting the idea of "land for peace" cite the Holocaust as a reason for secure borders.[26]

The Holocaust was evoked by the American Jewish community in the 1970s, according to historian Rabbi Arthur Hertzberg, in order to keep in mind anti-Semitism and the vulnerability of Israel: "The Holocaust was a shattering memory. It evoked guilt, compassion, and fear. It said to American Jews, in an essentially optimistic time, that being Jewish is to know that life itself is often about tragedy, suffering, and murderous hatred. Even the new State of Israel, the center of Jewish hope and power, was not merely about glory and triumph; it was endangered by Arab enemies. Jews were called to rally to Israel in the name of the slogan 'Never Again.'"[27] It was widely believed in the 1950s and 1960s that the effort for Israel would somehow keep the next generation of American Jews Jewish. But then, as Hertzberg noted, "in the 1980s, the observance even of the new Jewish *mitzvah*, the commitment to Israel, was becoming more tepid." This cooling process was evident even at the time of the 1973 war. "American Jews were less involved than they had been in June 1967," Hertzberg wrote. "Contributions were just as massive, but there were fewer volunteers among the young. Some American Jews had already begun to question Israel's policies. In 1973, a few hundred Jews had banded together in an organization that was named Breira ('alternative') to insist that Israel should make peace on the basis of a Palestinian state in the West Bank and Gaza."[28]

The major American Jewish organizations did not substitute remembrance of the Holocaust for commitment to Israel; but they used the memory of the Holocaust to gain support for Israel, and they made room in their agenda for institutionalizing Holocaust memorialization. This was complemented, however, by the phenomenon of many American Jews shifting their focus from Israel to the Holocaust. It is difficult to paint a clear picture of this shift, because it had another influence: it happened at a time when Americans in general were searching for and beginning to assert their ethnicity. In 1960, John Fitzgerald Kennedy, an Irish Catholic, was elected president, and, in 1963, Martin Luther King, Jr., had "a dream." Black was becoming beautiful in the 1960s, and other hyphenated Americans were seeking their roots.

At this very time, Israel's occupation of the West Bank and Gaza became painful for many American Jews in the wake of the 1967 and 1973 wars. Thus the prevailing mood of ethnicity in the United States at that time—reinforced by disillusionment with Israel—created both the need and opportunity for the Holocaust's emergence as an issue. As Leonard Fein pointed out: "Along comes the Holocaust, and makes us special. It's not the kind of special we'd have chosen, but there it is, ours by right, and awesomely substantial. If you have the Holocaust, what more do you need?"[29]

Jeshajahu Weinberg, the first director of the U.S. Holocaust Memorial Museum in Washington, told me: "Why the preoccupation with the Holocaust now? It is not enough to say that it was Wiesel, although he had an important role in popularizing the Holocaust in the United States. The issue matured in the mid-1970s. Secular Jews in this country had a problem. During the 1970s, a period of flourishing ethnicity, secular Jews had a problem knowing what their center of ethnicity was." The search for identity helped Jewish ethnicity—increasingly defined by secular Jews around the subject of the Holocaust—to flourish.

An Israeli, Weinberg believes that, since 1948, American Jews "thought that such support for Israel as financial, tourism, sending their children there for programs, created the Jewish content for them. But a few years after the Six Day War, the glory was over and there was the divisiveness of the politics of occupation. . . . The stock of Israel diminished and the Holocaust became the Jewish content for American Jews—a way to remain Jewish as a secular Jew."[30] American Jews had projected all of their ideals onto Israel. In the 1970s they had become aware that Israel was not entirely the idealistic country they had perceived it to be, and they adopted the Holocaust as the symbol of their ethnic identification.

In a 1990 talk, Arthur Hertzberg also connected emergence of interest in the Holocaust to the climate of ethnicity that was part of the 1960s in the United States, and to still unresolved fears of anti-Semitism among the American Jewish community: "The subject was *treyf* [nonkosher] in the 1940s, because American Jews were breaking out of ghettos. They didn't want to appear to be victims. It came on in the 1960s, because the role of Jews in America changed. It was the era of Kennedy, Blacks, Vietnam. It was easier to speak in your own name." The Holocaust is central in the United States, according to Hertzberg, because anti-Semitism is the only way American Jewish consciousness can objectify the Jewish religion. Everything else in Judaism is subjective here. "The only thing alienated American Jews can get hepped up about is anti-Semitism, because it's a threat to life and to their vision of themselves."[31] In sum, because of disappointment with Israel's policies, fear of anti-Semitism, and the climate of ethnicity in the United States, the Holocaust arose as the new symbol of Jewish identity.

The proliferation of "Holocaust centers," beginning in the late 1970s and continuing into the 1980s and early '90s, is evidence of the increased interest in the Holocaust in the United States. According to former YIVO Institute for Jewish Research director Samuel Norich, writing in 1987, of the 84 entities commemorating the Holocaust that were listed in the 1985–86 *Directory of Holocaust Centers, Institutions, and Organizations in North America* published by the U.S. Holocaust Memorial Council, 41 of them did not exist in 1977.[32] In a 1988 edition of the same directory (published after Norich's article), there were 98 listings of Holocaust institutions in the United States, including 19 museums, 48 resource centers, 34 archival facilities, 12 memorials, 26 research institutes, and 5 libraries.[33] In the 1995 *Directory* of the Association of Holocaust Organizations, 101 Holocaust institutions were listed[34]. The Association of Holocaust Organizations was founded in 1985 to serve as a network for organizations and individuals to advance Holocaust-related programming, education, awareness, and research, and began issuing a directory in 1989. Unlike the earlier directories published by the U.S. Holocaust Memorial Council, a listing in the Association directory requires payment of a membership fee. This may partially account for the fact that the number of institutions listed did not increase substantially between 1988 and 1995. History will record whether the proliferation of Holocaust-related organizations peaked at the end of the 1980s and beginning of the 1990s, or will continue to grow in the future. However, it seems likely that in the future new Holocaust institutions will emerge at a slower rate than they did in the 1980s and early '90s.

If the overwhelming institutionalization of memorializing the Holocaust continues, it may, in fact, eventually bring about a weakening in some American Jews' ties to the Jewish community. If many Jews are secular, and the secular ethnic manifestation of organized Judaism emphasizes mass murder and commemoration of the past, will future generations want to remain linked to the Jewish community? As Leonard Fein warned in 1988: "The danger is that we will come (have come?) to see the Holocaust as the most important thing that ever happened to us, even the richest, the one most filled with consequence and implication."[35]

Nor should this view of the Jewish past be the dominant event of Jewish history transmitted to Jews and non-Jews alike. As James Young has pointed out, Holocaust museums are becoming increasingly central for the study of history, fund-raising, and community activism. "Consequently, instead of learning about the Holocaust through the study of Jewish history, many Jews and non-Jews in America learn the whole of Jewish history through the lens of the Holocaust." There are, of course, long-established museums such as the Jewish Museum in New York City, the Hebrew Union College Skirball Museum in Los Angeles, and the Spertus Museum of Judaica in Chicago that present a broader history of the Jewish people. And A Living Memorial to the Holocaust-Museum of Jewish Heritage is designed to teach about the whole span of twentieth century Jewish history, including the Holocaust. However, Young is concerned that Holocaust memorials and museums are inclined to organize Jewish culture and identity around this event, with few other countervailing museums to present the Jewish past and contemporary life in the Diaspora. "As a result, not only will the Holocaust continue to suggest itself as a center of American Jewish consciousness, but it will become all that non-Jewish Americans know about a thousand years of European Jewish civilization."[36] Succinctly summing up this serious concern about the centrality of Holocaust memorialization in the organized American Jewish community, Saul Friedlander asks: "Will this be the core in the future, or can we go beyond it?"[37]

3

Early Attempts To Create a New York City Holocaust Memorial

This is the site for the American memorial to the heroes of the
Warsaw Ghetto battle April–May 1943 and to the six million
Jews of Europe martyred in the cause of human liberty.
—Plaque in Riverside Park dedicated October 19, 1947

The political alliance that was instituted in 1981 to create a Holocaust memorial museum in New York City has a long and complicated prehistory. Although memorializing the Holocaust was not
formally on the agenda of the organized American Jewish community until 1973–74, two significant but unsuccessful commemorative efforts in the city were undertaken in 1946 and in
the early 1960s. They did not succeed primarily because the idea
of memorialization was not then of interest to the organized Jewish community and did not yet have any political value for
American government officials. The first attempt, in 1946, was
initiated by one vigorous and dedicated person who used a small
organization as a power base to try to interest others. Individuals, rather than Jewish organizations, backed the effort.

In the 1960s, by contrast, some major Jewish organizations
joined the spearheading group. However, they did not give the
project priority, and appropriate political alliances were not
forged. Ultimately both projects failed, but they helped to set
the stage for later government intervention in memorializing the
Holocaust. When Mayor Edward I. Koch's administration inter-

vened to "initiate" a memorial in 1981, the idea already had a history of thirty-five years of plans and attempts in New York City. Prior to Koch's tenure, interest groups approached New York City mayors to request a memorial. But Mayor Koch co-opted the idea, made it his own, officially intervened, and approached the Jewish community. He initiated the public/private political alliance that supported the project.

A close look at the attempts to create a Holocaust memorial in New York City before Mayor Koch came on the scene will shed some light on why they did not succeed. Factors that account for the early failures include the inexperience of interest groups in forming political alliances, the political climate, financial problems, lack of interest and other priorities in the Jewish community, the subsequent lack of political benefits for government officials, and the psychological inability of survivors and other Jews to face the issue of the Holocaust, as well as disagreements within the interest group seeking to create the memorial. No mayor of the city intervened in those early attempts because there was no serious interest shown by the organized Jewish community and thus no political gain in co-opting the project. Mayors and other elected officials gave lip service and limited assistance and promised to cooperate, but they did not make the project their own, as Mayor Koch did later on.

The first attempt to create a Holocaust memorial in New York City (and probably in the nation)—in Riverside Park between Eighty-third and Eighty-fourth streets, along the Hudson River—occurred in 1946–47. The effort was coordinated by a group called the American Memorial to Six Million Jews of Europe. Mayor William O'Dwyer was honorary chairman of the National Committee of Sponsors, and Robert Moses, as parks commissioner, was a member ex officio. Mayor O'Dwyer was supportive and designated a piece of city land for the memorial, but otherwise was not closely linked with the project. Powerful Parks Commissioner Moses was also generally supportive of the idea. The list of sponsors was long and prestigious, including many congressmen, professors, and both Jewish and non-Jewish clergymen who lent their names but were not actively involved. Unlike later attempts to build Holocaust memorials in New York City, this project was not officially sponsored by a consortium of Jewish organizations or by the city itself. Nor was the issue "hot."

No coalition of political allies was working together on the project.

This first attempt at a memorial was really a single-handed effort. The initiator and guiding spirit was Adolph R. Lerner, a Polish Jewish refugee who was a journalist and publisher as well as vice president of the National Organization of Polish Jews in New York, a group of refugee professionals.[1] He had fled Vienna when the Nazis took over Austria in 1938, moving first to France and then to the United States. During 1943 and 1944 he worked at the official Polish News Agency in New York, editing bulletins that arrived from the Polish underground. In 1944 he used photographs and documents sent by the underground to publish a history of the fate of the Jews in Europe. He later organized these materials as an exhibit at the Vanderbilt Gallery on Fifty-seventh Street in New York City, under the auspices of the Jewish Labor Committee.

Lerner had enough political savvy to know that he could not create a memorial single-handed, and that he needed an interest group behind him. In January 1946, he presented his idea for a memorial to the National Organization of Polish Jews in New York, suggesting that a memorial "in tribute to the Heroes of the Warsaw Ghetto and the six million Jews slain by the Nazis, be erected in New York City."[2] On February 6, 1946, Lerner used the organization's name to submit a written request to Mayor O'Dwyer for an appropriate site for an "eternal light" memorial dedicated to the fallen heroes of the Warsaw Ghetto. In response, the mayor invited Lerner and a delegation from the National Organization of Polish Jews to City Hall, where they met with Comptroller Lazarus Joseph. Rather than getting involved personally, the mayor delegated his Jewish comptroller. A few days later, Lerner and two other members of his delegation were invited to visit Stuart Constable, chief designer of the Parks Department, who told them that Commissioner Moses had approved the proposal and would be glad to cooperate. At that meeting, Arthur Szyk, a member of the delegation, suggested that Jo Davidson, a distinguished sculptor, would be the best choice for the project.[3] Davidson was not only well-known, but also a friend of Constable's.[4]

On April 18, Lerner received a letter from Moses that read, in part: "Frankly, I am not very sympathetic to the idea of another ETERNAL LIGHT [a light above the Torah ark in synagogues, which was how Lerner had described the proposed memorial to O'Dwyer]. I am sure, however, that you can find a suitable place in one of the parks for a fitting Memorial, if it is to be designed by a first-rate sculptor, assisted by a competent architect. I understand that you have been considering Jo Davidson as the sculptor—you could not find a better man. It is impossible for me to make any final decision on the Memorial, or its location, until I see models and plans of the Memorial. The Art Commission will undoubtedly make the same request."[5] With Moses, who controlled the parks, lauding the committee's first choice of Davidson as the artist, the project seemed likely to go forward. As will be seen, however, Lerner and his committee did not seem to understand how to benefit from their choice of Davidson and push the project through.

On April 27, 1947, "Eternal Light Monument in the City of New York in Memory of Six Million Jews of Europe" became a corporation. Lerner then invested time in trying to shore up his interest group, spending more than a year unsuccessfully seeking the support of the major Jewish organizations. "Individually nearly all the Jewish organizations made me believe that they were wholeheartedly for the project, but finally I came to the conclusion that all my efforts to bring them together for a unified action were in vain," he wrote. "I had several meetings with the representatives of the NCRAC [National Jewish Community Relations Council, which did not then include the "J" in its acronym] member agencies who in general had expressed themselves in sympathy with the sentiment, but many of them felt that they were not directly concerned as organizations."[6] NJCRAC did not place the topic of Holocaust memorialization on its agenda until 1973–74, twenty-six years after Lerner sought its support.

Davidson wrote to Lerner on April 16, 1947, that he would prepare a model, putting "my heart and soul into the creation of this Monument." He continued, "such a monument would be a symbol of the unconquerable spirit of all freedom loving people and a warning to tyranny that we shall not forget." Davidson and Constable chose the site in Riverside Park, between West Eighty-third and Eighty-fourth streets. Scientific analyses of the politics of site selection do not apply here: according to Lerner's account, Davidson said that he and Constable had seen an old bearded Jew standing on that spot in contemplation and decided it was ideal. On May 2, 1947, Lerner received a letter from Moses stating that the site had his approval. He also granted permission for a dedication ceremony.[7] The city, however, retained veto power over the design.[8]

At a meeting on May 20, 1947, the name of the organization created by Lerner was officially changed from the Eternal Light Monument to the American Memorial to Six Million Jews of Europe, Inc., and Lerner was reelected president. Two days later a certificate of the corporation's name change was filed with the secretary of state of New York State. On May 28, at a meeting in Borough President Rogers's office, Lerner reported on plans for dedicating the Riverside Park site on October 19. Efforts to raise funds for the dedication almost ended in failure, until Israel Rogosin, a wealthy acquaintance of Lerner's, joined the group, pledged $1,000, and promised to get most of the rest of the necessary $6,000 from friends.[9]

On September 23, 1947, Moses wrote to Lerner: "You may be sure you will have the full cooperation of the Park Department." In response, Lerner recorded in his papers: "I was very happy about this and felt a deep gratitude and love for [Moses]."[10] Moses has been criticized for being an "anti-Semitic Jew" who did not even want to acknowledge his Jewishness.[11] At this time, however, perhaps moved by the impact of Hitler's genocide of the Jews, he seemed genuinely interested in bringing a memorial to fruition. Despite his expressed support, however, there is no record of Moses trying to push the project through with an iron fist, as he did with so many other projects that he wanted.

On October 19, 1947, a ceremony was held at the Riverside Park site, where a plaque (intended as a cornerstone) was dedicated. Soil from concentration camps and a proclamation from the chief rabbi of Palestine were among items placed in a box beneath the cornerstone. According to newspaper accounts, some 15,000 people attended the dedication ceremony. Lerner, then chairman of the memorial executive committee, was quoted in a September 17, 1947, press release as saying that the memorial "would be a living American symbol of democracy and brotherhood, and would inspire the fulfillment of the world's obligations to those who survived the Nazi holocaust." Lerner had Zionist motives for dedicating the site immediately prior to the United Nations vote on the partition of Palestine. In his press release, Lerner seemed to imply that because of the Holocaust, the world—that is, the United Nations—had the responsibility to create a Zionist state.

Surrounded by a metal fence, the plaque in Riverside Park is still there nearly fifty years later, along with an inscription: "This is the site for the American memorial to the heroes of the Warsaw Ghetto battle April–May 1943 and to the six million Jews of Europe martyred in the cause of human liberty." Lerner's statement and the plaque seem to balance the distinctively Jewish aspect of the Holocaust with a more universal message of "democracy and brotherhood" and "the cause of human liberty." In the political climate of the 1990s, when group ethnicity is proudly displayed and Jews in the United States are less insecure about anti-Semitism, the statement that "the Jews of Europe died in the cause of human liberty" seems not only historically false but unfair to the victims. They did not "die" for "the cause of human liberty"; they were *murdered*, in a rationally planned genocidal national policy, merely because they were Jews. The commemoration effort begun in 1946 never materialized beyond this plaque, but 1994–95 saw a new plan to erect a monument to the Warsaw Ghetto uprising at the same site.

On November 26, 1947, the memorial committee met at the Hotel Roosevelt, with Rogosin elected chairman of the board and Lerner appointed executive director, at a salary of $600 a month. An advisory art committee was established, and a decision was made to launch a fund-raising campaign to raise $600,000. On March 11, 1948, the American Memorial to Six Million Jews of Europe wrote to Jo Davidson, sculptor, and Eli Jacques Kahn, architect, to confirm arrangements for construction of a monument in Riverside Park. Davidson was supposed to deliver a scale model no later than July 1 of that year, which then needed approvals from the New York City Art Commission, the Department of Parks, and the board of directors of the American Memorial committee. Davidson was to receive a maximum of $15,000, of which $5,000 was enclosed. Kahn was to render preliminary architectural and engineering services for a maximum fee of $5,000. Subsequent phases were to be arranged after approvals of the scale model.[12]

In April 1948, the campaign to raise $600,000 for the memorial was announced in a local newspaper.[13] Mayor O'Dwyer wrote to Lerner on July 26, 1948, that "your campaign to obtain funds to erect this monument has my wholehearted approval and I am confident that our liberty-loving and generous citizens will respond to your appeal." He added: "This will not be a monument of bronze or concrete but rather a spiritual citadel inscribed: *It shall not come to pass again!*" Despite this glowing rhetoric, there is no evidence that O'Dwyer helped with fund-raising efforts or made any further commitment to the cause.

On October 20, 1948, a year after the Riverside Park ceremony, the American Memorial to Six Million Jews of Europe organized a first-anniversary ceremony at City Hall. Emphasizing the need for funds was clearly on the agenda, as Lerner said in his address: "With the encouragement of our great mayor and of eminent leaders of our religious and cultural institutions I urge all of you to give us your continued financial and moral support to the end that the magnificent memorial we are planning will rise before many months have passed."[14]

Scale models of the monument by Davidson and Kahn, depicting the April 1943 Warsaw Ghetto uprising, went on exhibit at the Jewish Museum in November 1948. Their design depicted a heroic resistance figure, a religious Jew in supplication, and a man helping an injured comrade, along with a slumping dead figure. This figurative art was to be placed on a pedestal atop a series of steplike blocks.[15] At the time, Lerner had also mentioned that the committee had asked other sculptors to submit models and had not yet made a firm decision.[16] The memorial committee was not pleased that, after months, Davidson's model was no more detailed than "the same little figures which he had in November 1947." The artist, however, insisted that the model be submitted to the City Art Commission. The commission rejected the Davidson design, but Arthur S. Hodgkiss, executive officer of the Department of Parks, later told the *New York Times* that the sponsors did not like the "academic group of statuary" and that his department had tried in vain to "mediate" the dispute.[17]

The reasoning behind the commission's rejection was not revealed, and the memorial committee itself did not seem inclined to encourage the design's acceptance. Possibly the art commission rejected the proposal because it lacked details, as the memorial committee had complained. Other plausible explanations are that the rejection reflected the art commission's disapproval of the sculptor's academic rendering or his specifically Jewish theme. In addition, as with later decisions against other Holocaust memorials proposed for the Riverside Park site, the commission may have decided that the theme was too depressing or brutal for the park.

After this initial impasse, the memorial committee held a competition for design of a memorial. Artists including Davidson, and also Erich Mendelsohn and Ivan Mestrovic, Percival Goodman, William Zorach, Leo Friedlander, and Chaim Gross, submitted proposals. The artists' models were exhibited at the Jewish Museum in October 1949, and at the Museum of Modern Art for one month in January 1950. Goodman's model was "favored" by the memorial committee in October 1949, but Lerner said it had not been finally accepted. Goodman, on the other hand, insisted that the memorial committee had accepted his design, and then dropped it when they learned that Parks Commissioner Moses disapproved of its style. Goodman, a Columbia University architecture professor who had designed modern houses and public buildings, had conceived a 60-foot stone pylon topped by a bronze menorah, with a flagstone plaza and a granite wall at the southern end. The design was ultimately rejected by the parks commission because it "pre-empted too much of the park from public use" and was not suited to Riverside Park. According to parks official Hodgkiss, the department "felt it would take over, rather than fit into, that part of the park."[18]

On June 17, 1951, the art commission unanimously backed the design by modernist architect Erich Mendelsohn and the Yugoslav sculptor Ivan Mestrovic, one of the five designs in the memorial committee's competition.[19] A German Jew, Mendelsohn had lived for a time in Palestine after fleeing Hitler in 1933. His works in Israel include the Hadassah Hospital on Mount Scopus and the Weizmann home in Rehovot. The internationally known Mendelsohn came to the United States in 1941. On July 18, 1951, the American Memorial to Six Million Jews of Europe announced the art commission's approval of this much more universal design. The sculpture was to be an 80-foot pylon of two tablets on which the Ten Commandments would be inscribed, a 100-foot bas-relief wall depicting humankind's struggle to fulfill the commandments, and a giant carving of Moses.

Although Lerner's committee had obtained a site from the city parks commissioner, placed a cornerstone in a public ceremony attended by government officials and thousands of people, engaged a distinguished architect-sculptor team, and received the official approval of the New York City Art Commission, this first effort to create a major Holocaust memorial in the city failed. The main reason for its failure was that the organized American Jewish community, along with the government, had not set an agenda for Holocaust memorialization. There was thus no possibility of forming a strong interest group–government coalition to see the project through, especially after Erich Mendelsohn's death in 1953. According to S. L. Shneiderman, a journalist who was involved in the project, leaders of Jewish organizations at the time urged that any money raised in the American Jewish community be used for rehabilitating Holocaust survivors rather than building a memorial, a position that resulted in fund-raising difficulties.[20] If this report is accurate, the organized Jewish community hindered, rather than encouraged, the effort to create the first Holocaust memorial in New York City.

Lerner complained of always having to scrape for money. He expressed his "disappointment in not succeeding to move the leading Jewish civic and religious organization[s] to a unified participation in the project. Although the leaders of various religious groups of Jewish faiths joined as sponsors of the Memorial project, and also the leaders of various civic organizations became sponsors, I missed the active support of a number of leading civic Jewish organizations of which the attitude was rather aloof."[21] In addition, he referred to disagreements within the committee, such as Rogosin's appeal to a narrow base in fund-raising as opposed to his own wishes for a mass appeal. The contract with Davidson and Kahn, he observed, had become "a source of the most distressing intrigues and quarrels, and has created situations which never ceased to threaten to destroy this whole project."[22] In her book about undertakings that never reached fruition in New York City, Rebecca Read Shanor wrote of the project that it failed because of lack of funds. However, she did not explain why funds were not forthcoming from the organized Jewish community.[23] The fact that memorialization of the Holocaust was not on the community's agenda is, I believe, the main reason no forceful private-public coalition was organized on behalf of the project, nor any successful fund-raising efforts.

One reason that the organized Jewish community did not aggressively support creation of a memorial in the early 1950s was that the Jewish Agency at that time was negotiating with

West Germany to pay reparations to survivors of the Holocaust and to Israel. The community did not want to anger West Germany at a time when Israel was trying to extract hefty guilt payments. In March 1951, Israel prime minister Ben-Gurion had submitted a claim to the four occupying powers of Germany—the United States, Great Britain, France, and the Soviet Union—for $1.5 billion, his price for Jewish property looted and destroyed by the Nazis. When the powers refused to deal with him, instead asking him to deal directly with Germany, Ben-Gurion said he would do so. He then asked Jewish Agency chairman Nahum Goldmann to negotiate with Chancellor Konrad Adenauer of West Germany, and Goldmann was promised more than $800 million. Negotiations also took place with East Germany, but no agreement was reached.

The community may also have been cautious about supporting a Holocaust memorial because of the then pervading political climate of the Cold War. The old ally, the Soviet Union, was now the enemy; and the old enemy, Nazi Germany, was the new ally, in the form of the German Federal Republic, or West Germany. From the end of the war, the United States was secretly bringing into the country known Nazi war criminals—for example, through "Project Paperclip"—in its search for a technological supremacy over the Soviet Union.[24] In the panicky climate of that time, the organized Jewish community was afraid that an anti-Nazi, or anti-German, activity could be construed as being pro-Communist. They may also have been afraid that a memorial would draw attention to the fact that so many resistance fighters and heroes had been Communists. This was not an atmosphere in which the conservative, established Jewish organizations wanted to actively support and raise hundreds of thousands of dollars for a monument that would be both specifically Jewish and anti-German.

The organizations had reason to be cautious, because this was the era when Senator Joseph McCarthy began his infamous investigations of people he considered Communists, and many Jews were high on his list of targets. In March 22, 1947, President Harry Truman issued Executive Order 9835, a program to search out "infiltration of disloyal persons" in the U.S. government. Between that time and the end of 1952, some 6.6 million people were investigated. Meanwhile, external events such as the 1948 Berlin blockade, the 1949 Communist victory in China, the Soviet

Union's explosion of its first atomic bomb, and the beginning of the Korean War in 1950 were portrayed as signs of an international Communist conspiracy. The Truman administration, as Howard Zinn wrote, had "established a climate of fear—a hysteria about Communism—which would steeply escalate the military budget and stimulate the economy with war-related orders. This combination of policies would permit more aggressive actions abroad, more repressive actions at home."[25]

McCarthyism made the Jewish community especially afraid, because it had a decidedly anti-Semitic cast. By the summer of 1950, the prosecution of accused spies Ethel and Julius Rosenberg, who were Jewish, was a major factor in the anti-Communist mood of the country; the Rosenbergs were found guilty of espionage and executed on June 19, 1953. Naomi W. Cohen's history of the American Jewish Committee quotes a 1947 memorandum of that organization which read: "For a number of years, anti-Semitic activists have assiduously promoted the smear that Jews are Communists. They have found this to be the most effective line with which they were left, since the decline of organizational activity. The acceleration of the anti-Communist campaign has come as a windfall to them, and our reports indicate a steady procession of anti-Semitic operators from their regular sphere of activity onto the bandwagon of the general anti-Communist movement." Cohen named Gerald L. K. Smith, Conde McGinley, and Upton Close as among these "hatemongers."[26]

Many of those accused by McCarthy and his supporters were Jewish; and Jewish organizations and individuals were thus extremely sensitive to past and present accusations of "international conspiracy," Communist party membership, and disloyalty. Some major Jewish organizations bent over backward to prove their loyalty, even offering to sell out their suspect members. For example, in 1953 there was a letter of understanding between the House Un-American Activities Committee and such organizations as the Anti-Defamation League, the Jewish War Veterans, and the American Jewish Committee, in which the Jewish organizations offered to draw up dossiers for the committee.[27]

This was the political climate of the United States at the time that the group called the American Memorial to Six Million Jews of Europe was trying to create a Holocaust memorial in Riverside Park. And New York City was one of the cities most affected by the Cold War and McCarthyism. It had a concentration of leftist, socialist, and Communist individuals and organizations, many of them Jewish. Although Mayor O'Dwyer lent his support to the idea of the 1947 project, he would not have dreamed of initiating the creation of a Holocaust memorial or aggressively supporting one: this was not the time to gain political advantage by intervening and placing such a memorial on a government agenda. The major American Jewish organizations themselves were not aggressively supporting the idea or backing it financially. To the contrary, there is evidence that they were opposed, since such a project would take away from fund-raising efforts on behalf of Israel and resettlement of Jewish refugees.[28]

The Holocaust survivors themselves were in no mental or financial condition to organize the creation of a memorial in the decade following the war. Psychologically, it would take many years for some of them to begin talking about their experiences; some would never be able to do so. They were beginning new lives in a strange country with a different language—a feat that is difficult even without having suffered near-death. In addition, as Elie Wiesel explained to me, the survivors were considered "second-class citizens" by the organized Jewish community at that time.[29] Although survivors and survivor groups would be involved in later efforts, their leadership at that time would not have been well received by the community. As new Americans, survivors were also "walking on eggs" to show gratitude to their adopted country and prove that they had no connection with their countries of origin, most of which had become part of the Soviet bloc. They were looking forward rather than backward.

A national fund-raising drive for $500,000 to finance the Riverside Park memorial was not announced until September 1952, five years after the dedication ceremony. There has been no published analysis of why the project failed, and almost everyone active in this first attempt to create a Holocaust memorial is no longer alive. However, from the history of the project, it is possible to understand what factors contributed to its ultimate failure. The memorial committee was operating in the Cold War political climate of the time. The organized Jewish community had financial problems, was not especially interested, and had other priorities. The community's lack of interest was echoed by government officials, who would reap no political benefits. In addition, many survivors and other Jews were psychologically unable to face the Holocaust, and there were disagreements within the interest group seeking to create a memorial. The most obvious practical reason for the failure was the committee's inability to raise sufficient funds. A combination of these factors made it impossible to form a political coalition that might have moved the project forward at that time. A coalition such as the one that followed Mayor Koch's initiation of the 1981 project was not even a gleam in anyone's eye.

The fearful environment stimulated by the Cold War and the related fear of anti-Semitism are likely reasons that statements the committee made about the project were not distinctively Jewish. The universal approach of the group sponsoring the memorial was underscored by Rabbi David de Sola Pool, a member of the advisory design committee to the memorial committee, who wrote: "The monument will seek to express, as only an artist can, the aspiration of man toward the moral law of a universal God and the ideal of brotherhood and love among men." As he wrote in a letter to the editor of the *New York Times*, the Nazi atrocities must not be forgotten, but "the memorial is not 'a strictly Jewish memorial.' It does, indeed, record the sacrifice of the six million Jews who lost their lives under Nazi rule. But the remembrance of them belongs to all men for whom nazism [sic] is repugnant and odious. Many Christians are associated with the memorial. . . ."[30]

4

Memorial Plans Change with the Political Climate

We are in a new state. It is tremendously exciting—one sign of it is that no one person can actually keep up with everything which is going on. . . . "The times they are a-changing," and we are part of it—Richard Flacks, February 16, 1964*

After the failure of the first New York City Holocaust memorial project in 1952, ten years elapsed before a new effort was mounted. Meanwhile, the Cold War continued, but the domestic political scene was changing. In 1954 the Supreme Court had struck down the "separate but equal" doctrine with its *Brown* v. *Board of Education* decision. Rosa Parks sat down in the white section of a bus in Alabama in 1955 and was arrested. This set off a boycott and other actions that resulted, in November 1956, in the Supreme Court's outlawing segregation on local bus lines. In 1960, the first Catholic in American history was elected president. By the summer of 1963, Martin Luther King, Jr., had told 200,000 black and white Americans assembled in Washington, D.C., "I have a dream." In August 1965, President Lyndon Johnson signed the Voting Rights Act into law.[1]

Between 1962 and 1965, in this new atmosphere of civil rights demonstrations and legislation, as well as ethnic pluralism, a second attempt was made to create a major Holocaust memorial in Riverside Park. The new struggles for human rights

---

**Quoted in James Miller, *Democracy Is in the Streets: From Port Huron to the Siege of Chicago* (New York: Simon & Schuster, 1987), p. 192.*

by blacks in the United States and the new climate of ethnicity may have consciously, or unconsciously, influenced this renewed effort to memorialize the violation of the human rights of Jews by the Nazis.

This next effort in Riverside Park was not mounted by the same people who initiated the 1947–52 attempt. In fact, two different groups were trying to erect two different memorials in the park in the early 1960s. Some leaders of Holocaust survivor groups were involved in this second attempt, although the real emergence of survivors as a visible and united interest group did not occur for almost twenty more years. It might be possible to do a rational analysis of competing interest groups to explain why one memorial in Riverside Park was not enough at this point. However, the following classic Jewish joke explains the situation better, by placing it in the irrational context of Jewish communal life: A Jew was shipwrecked on a desert island and built two mud huts. When he was rescued, he explained to his puzzled rescuers why he needed two of them. They were both synagogues, one of which he refused to enter.

Not only were there two memorial committees with two different projects destined for the same site, but both groups engaged the sculptor Nathan Rapoport to design their monuments. Rapoport, who was born in Warsaw in 1911, is famous for his Holocaust memorials, especially his massive and heroic Warsaw Ghetto monument, unveiled on the ghetto site on the fifth anniversary of the Warsaw Ghetto uprising, April 19, 1948. Rapoport's reputation as the creator of the Warsaw monument must have led to his commissions to design the two Riverside Park projects in the early 1960s. The Warsaw monument was reproduced at Yad Vashem in Jerusalem in 1967, and Rapoport later designed the Holocaust memorial sculpture at Liberty Park, New Jersey. Rapoport studied in Paris, but returned to Warsaw in June 1939. After the Germans invaded Poland that September, he fled northeast and spent the war years in the Soviet Union, in Bialystok, Minsk, and then Siberia. He returned to Warsaw, and then to Paris, after the war.[2]

The first, broader-based interest group that contracted Rapoport consisted of Polish Holocaust survivors, the Warsaw Ghetto Resistance Organization (WAGRO), with the backing of thirty-four Jewish organizations; the other group was the Artur Zygelboim Memorial Committee. The WAGRO effort was headed by survivor Vladka Meed, representing WAGRO and the survivors, and Benjamin Gebiner of the Workmen's Circle. Using the WA-GRO organization headed by her husband, Benjamin Meed, as her base, Vladka Meed, along with Gebiner, brought together a coalition of thirty-four major and minor Jewish organizations, most of which were minor survivor organizations, to create the Memorial Committee for the Six Million Jewish Martyrs and Heroes.[3] Rapoport's design for this WAGRO-sponsored coalition, submitted to the group on October 13, 1964, was a Torah scroll, with bas-reliefs of Holocaust episodes. According to the artist, "On this scroll is written in sculptural language the history of the Jews. It tells of martyrdom, fight, and of liberation."[4]

On November 12, 1964, WAGRO and twenty-five representatives of Jewish organizations met with Mayor Robert F. Wagner and his parks commissioner, Newbold Morris, to request that a memorial be erected. As with Mayor O'Dwyer, a group approached the mayor rather than his approaching the group. Besides the mayor, this group had already sought other political support in the state legislature. New York State Senate minority leader Joseph Zaretzki accompanied them and spoke on their behalf. However, there is no further record of his involvement, and a triangular political coalition that included the state legislature never evolved.

Nathan Rapoport was present at the meeting with the mayor and gave him a photograph of the planned Torah scroll monument. At about the same time, WAGRO announced that pianist Artur Rubinstein would assume chairmanship of its memorial committee, the Memorial Committee for the Six Million Jewish Martyrs and Heroes.[5] As is common for Jewish and other causes in New York City, a famous superstar had been enlisted to add glamour and gain publicity. This did not, however, give the group enough clout to carry out its project.

In December 1964, WAGRO retained Rapoport to create a sketch and scale model of the sculpture, based on earlier diagrams and illustrations. The clay scale model was to be completed in approximately three months, and payment was to be $2,000. On January 19, 1965, WAGRO called a meeting at the Statler Hotel in New York, which was attended by almost eighty representatives of Jewish organizations and chaired by Dr. Joachim Prinz, president of the American Jewish Congress. The purpose of the meeting, according to Prinz, was "to create a broad organizational and moral basis for the efforts to erect the memorial." There were memorials in Warsaw, Israel, Paris, Amsterdam, and a new one in Philadelphia, he pointed out, but not in New York, the largest Jewish community in the world.

Vladka Meed, who spearheaded the project for WAGRO, reported on the group's warm reception by Mayor Wagner on November 13. The mayor had pledged his full support and reiterated the city's promise of the Riverside Drive site. There were, however, powerful opposing forces. She was concerned about the position of Parks Commissioner Newbold Morris, who had recently written to Rapoport that "a public park is a place for enjoyment and recreation and not for exposing users of a park to the tragedy and horrors of one of the most dreadful chapters of human history." But it was WAGRO's "unshaken belief," she noted, that the united Jewish organizations would be able to overcome these difficulties. (The major Jewish organizations were not, however, "united" in giving this project priority financial or political backing.)

At this meeting, Rapoport unveiled his model. It was to consist of two scrolls cast in concrete, 26 feet high and 40 feet wide. In addition to bas-reliefs representing the Holocaust, the names of camps, ghettos, and sites of Jewish resistance would be inscribed. There would also be provision for an auditorium, a museum, and a library. (As early as 1964, it should be noted, the concept of a Holocaust memorial in New York City included a museum.) The estimated cost was $1 million (which seems too low), and members of WAGRO pledged the first $100,000.

The following resolution was adopted by the conference: "Representatives of thirty-two major Jewish organizations assembled on the nineteenth of January, 1965, at the Statler Hotel, New York City, express their full support and devotion to the idea of a proper Memorial for the Six Million Martyrs and Heroes of the Holocaust, in New York City. This resolution is subject to the ratification by the respective organizations." The conference authorized Dr. Joachim Prinz and WAGRO to form a steering committee from among the member organizations and to present to the steering committee a detailed program of further action.[6]

The group that sponsored the second proposal for a Holocaust memorial in Riverside Park in the early 1960s, the Artur Zygelboim Memorial Committee, had a much narrower base and was supported by some Jewish labor groups. The Zygelboim committee's proposal, which had been commissioned in 1962, was for a monument of a figure with outstretched arms, engulfed in flames and thorns. Its theme was much more specific than that of Rapoport's design for the WAGRO coalition. This sculpture, also by Nathan Rapoport, commemorated the heroic suicide of Artur Zygelboim, a Jewish Bundist labor leader who was a member of the Polish parliament-in-exile in London. When he learned about the death camps and his family's fate in 1943, he killed himself to protest the world's indifference to the mass destruction of Polish Jewry and the defeat of the Warsaw Ghetto fighters.[7]

Vladka Meed had warned the WAGRO committee about the negative attitude of the parks commissioner, and soon the art commission followed suit. At the New York City Art Commission's January 28, 1965, meeting at the home of its president, Arnold Whitridge, the commission unanimously rejected both of Rapoport's designs for Riverside Park.[8] The minutes show that submission 10894—Riverside Park, Manhattan, Warsaw Ghetto Monument Certificate 10803 (represented by exhibits 2287-AV and AW) and submission 10895—Riverside Park, Manhattan, Zygelboim Memorial Certificate 10804 (represented by exhibits 2287-AX and AY) were not approved.[9]

Eleanor Platt, a sculptor who was an art commission member, was a forceful opponent. She wrote to other commission members before the meeting: "The [Zygelboim] figure is depicted in so tragic a posture that it does not seem to be appropriate for location on park land intended for recreation and relaxation. It does not seem to be desirable to confront children with sculpture of such distressing and horrifying significance, worthy as it might be in a more relevant place. I can reach no other conclusion than that a public park is not a proper place for it." She noted that the Torah scroll sculpture was "excessively and unnecessarily large." Platt also thought that placement of either of the memorials "would set a highly regrettable precedent" because it might provide an opening for other "special groups" to erect memorials on public land. As she put it, "How would we answer other special groups who wanted to be similarly represented on public land? In an attempt to treat all equally we could well end up with a profusion of such memorials and become responsible for a progressive violation of the basic concepts for park land use."[10] An editorial in the *New York Times* supported the art commission's decisions, on the grounds that city parks are not the proper place for monuments. "Each new installation brings one more invasion of the open land that was carefully landscaped and preserved by men of vision as long as a century ago," the editorial argued.[11]

Dr. Emanuel Scherer of the Zygelboim committee protested that his committee would continue to press for the monument. After the art commission's rejection, however, the Zygelboim group transferred its effort to creation of a memorial in the New Mount Carmel Workmen's Circle Cemetery in Brooklyn, where Zygelboim's ashes had been brought from London and interred on September 24, 1961. (In April 1972, a memorial stone engraved with a flame motif was unveiled there.) The statue that Rapoport had designed for the WAGRO committee ultimately found a home in Israel in 1971, at the apex of Martyrs' Forest in the Judean hills near Jerusalem.

The leaders of the Memorial Committee for the Six Million Jewish Martyrs and Heroes continued to pursue their goal. Mayor Wagner was sent a telegram of protest by the executive committee of the Workmen's Circle, drafted at a special meeting. The telegram asked the mayor to intervene, reverse the commission's decision, and "immediately to call a public hearing to determine whether the Municipal Arts Commission should not be reversed and censured."[12] Dr. Joachim Prinz, chairman of the steering committee for the memorial committee sponsored by WAGRO and the thirty-four other Jewish organizations supporting construction of the scroll sculpture, sent a telegram to Mayor Wagner expressing "profound shock" and urging the mayor to intervene.

Rabbi Max Schenk, president of the New York Board of Rabbis, also sent a letter to the mayor in reference to Platt's description of the memorial backers as a "special group." "We Jews who live in New York do not consider ourselves a 'special group,'" he wrote. "We happen to be almost three million inhabitants of this city of eight million, an integral part of the warp and woof of America's greatest community."[13] The WAGRO-sponsored memorial steering committee met on February 15 at the Wellington Hotel to discuss its next step. That turned out to be a February 24 meeting between Mayor Wagner and the steering committee, headed by Rabbi Harold H. Gordon of the New York Board of Rabbis.

Eleanor Platt had really stepped on sore toes when she referred to the Holocaust memorial committees, that is, the Jews of New York City, as a "special group." They considered themselves an integral and influential part of the city's power structure, and they expected speedy and adequate intervention from Mayor Wagner to reverse the situation. The mayor's response, however, was typically weak, trying to appease the Jewish groups without making a definite commitment or criticizing the art commission. In a March 6, 1965, statement, he labeled the WAGRO-sponsored committee as "distinguished," and acknowledged his understanding that the group was willing to accept a different design or location for its project. He emphasized his deep personal interest, recalling that in 1947 he had represented his father, U.S. Senator Robert F. Wagner, in dedicating a plot of ground for building a memorial in Riverside Park. He also reminded the memorial committee that he was one of the first supporters of WAGRO's current project.

Following this personal declaration of support for a memorial, Mayor Wagner made a "motherhood and apple pie" statement against Nazism and in favor of *a*, but not *the*, memorial: "What happened during the Nazi period is unparalleled in the annals of mankind. The Six Million destroyed were part of all mankind. We fought a world war to defeat a government that made such horrors not only possible, but a reality. The world cannot afford to forget the Six Million. A memorial to these Six Million would serve to remind all of us of our share in the guilt of indifference and our responsibility to prevent a repetition."[14]

Mayor Wagner next addressed the "special group" issue, without acknowledging that New York City's Jewish community was of distinctive importance to the city. "All New Yorkers are proud of our varied population and the major faiths to which they adhere," he continued. He then universalized the project, by noting that "while the representatives of one of the major faiths seek the funds to establish the memorial, I believe that it is a project in which the entire community should—and would want to—share." Pointing out that he had been assured by the memorial committee that it would be responsible for raising the necessary funds, he implied that he was not giving city funds to a "special group." He further justified his support for the concept of a memorial by citing precedents of similar memorials "erected in prominent places" in Paris, Philadelphia, and Warsaw. In conclusion, he assured "the distinguished committee" and his "fellow citizens" that "the City of New York will provide the appropriate site for this very necessary memorial in a location readily accessible to millions of residents and visitors."

Mayor Wagner's weak reaction is evidence that once again a memorial committee did not have its political forces aligned and ready to move the project forward. Wagner clearly was not ready to put himself in the forefront of efforts to create a Holocaust memorial in New York City. In making this statement, which never mentioned the unfavorable action of the art commission, Wagner supported the general idea of a Holocaust memorial in the city and promised the steering committee that the city would still provide a site. He made it clear, however, that funding would be private, and that a Holocaust memorial would be beneficial for the whole city, not only for the Jewish interest group that had approached him. He also made it clear that the location and design of the memorial were still unspecified. Dr. Prinz, chairman of the steering committee, made the best of the mayor's statement, telling the *New York Times* it was a confirmation "that a monument will be built in an appropriate and accessible place in our city." A spokesman for the art commission told the newspaper that sponsors of the memorial would have to resubmit plans after a site had been confirmed with the mayor.[15]

On February 24, 1965, the same day that the steering committee met with Mayor Wagner, Adolph Lerner, originator of the 1946 project, wrote from Rome to his colleague Emil Shneiderman. Lerner had read in the international edition of the *New York Times* that new models of a memorial had been submitted to the New York City Art Commission. Lerner asked that Shneiderman inform Dr. Prinz "of all details about the history of the [first] Memorial project and without waiting and struggling for a new approval by the Art Commission, he should go ahead with building of a monument based on the [Mestrovic-Mendelsohn] models already approved."[16] He added, as though asking Shneiderman to do this for him: "If I would have the documents that I left with you, I would write to Mayor Wagner and remind him that the model of Mestrovic and Mendelsohn has already been accepted and therefore there is no necessity for new models." There is no further documentation to indicate whether Lerner's idea was pursued.

In his 1965 letter Lerner also asked Shneiderman a pointed

question: "I would be grateful if you inform me how it happened that suddenly the Jewish organizations became interested in the erection of the Memorial—when I struggled for seven years to get their help the answer I got was 'it is more important to care for the living.'"[17] Lerner could not know then that this attitude was still unchanged and would continue to hinder efforts to create a Holocaust memorial for many years.

However, 1965 marks a new phase in the history of attempts to create a major Holocaust memorial in New York City. The city government, that is, the City Council president and mayor, did intervene for the first time, both in site selection and in design of a memorial. But unfortunately, this was not cooperative intervention at the request of an interest group that had formed an alliance with the government. Nor was it a step that won the organized Jewish community's favor. In fact, the reactions of both the community and the memorial committee were vehemently negative at one point.

Following the art commission's rejection of both Rapoport memorials and its aftermath, there was a brief and problematic interlude of government intervention by the city. First the city suggested and then reneged on a new location on Times Square. Then the city endorsed a new design for a memorial in yet another location, across from Lincoln Center, without consulting the memorial committee. The intervention became official and two-pronged on September 1, 1965, when Mayor Wagner supported the suggestion of City Council president Paul Screvane that Times Square replace Riverside Park as the site of the Holocaust memorial. Screvane had suggested a paved mall between West Forty-fifth and Forty-sixth streets, south of the mall with memorials to Father Duffy and George M. Cohan. "A suitable memorial, at the crossroads of the world," Screvane had urged, "can be a constant reminder that unless each generation of Americans not only jealously safeguards, but enlarges, its inheritance of personal liberty and dignity, a retrogression to bigotry, intolerance and human degradation can occur."[18] (Ironically, nineteen years later the *Wall Street Journal* would suggest that George Klein, cochairman of the New York City Holocaust Memorial Commission and developer of Times Square through the Urban Development Corporation, build a Holocaust memorial there rather than in Battery Park City. If the journalist knew this early chapter in the history of site selection, he did not mention it.[19])

This was not a decision made as the result of an interest group–government alliance of any kind. Instead, it was a case of the mayor and City Council president telling an interest group what the government had decided without even the group's input. Leaders of the WAGRO-sponsored Memorial Committee for the Six Million Jewish Martyrs and Heroes were reportedly pleased with the idea of locating a Holocaust memorial on Times Square in 1965, even though they had not participated in the decision-making process for its relocation. Rabbi Max Schenk, president of the New York Board of Rabbis, noted that "we feel this is ideally located." Rabbi Harold Gordon, also with the Board of Rabbis, noted that the committee was studying new sketches for submission to the art commission and that it expected to work closely with the commission to get an idea of what kind of memorial would be satisfactory.[20] However, by November 1965 the city had shifted the promised site to the northern end of Lincoln Square Park, across from Lincoln Center at Columbus Avenue and West Sixty-fifth Street. On November 23, the committee wrote to Mayor Wagner and formally accepted this site.

Then, in December, for the first time the city intervened in design selection, choosing the theme of Cain and Abel for the memorial without consulting the committee. The memorial committee was appalled to learn that the art commission had proposed a design for the Lincoln Square Park site that had not been approved by the committee and was deemed completely unsuitable. The committee objected to both the design's theme and the lack of participatory process. The interest group had not even been offered the opportunity for input or review.

The committee met for three hours on December 30 to discuss the art commission's proposal. As Dr. Joachim Prinz, chairman of the memorial committee, told the *New York Times* after the meeting, "We are against the theme, not the art." The proposed memorial was a 30-foot-high slab of granite or marble, designed by sculptor Neil Easton, on which would be a scene in bronze depicting Cain slaying Abel. The grounds for the committee members' objections were twofold: they did not believe that the Nazis and Jews were brothers; and they considered Cain's murder of Abel a universal symbol, and therefore not suitable for memorializing the Nazis' particular genocidal plans for the Jewish people. By stating that they were not opposed to the art, Prinz was clarifying that the committee was disputing not the aesthetic quality of the design but its content.[21]

On December 30, Prinz released a statement about the design proposed by the art commission, clarifying that it had never been approved by the Memorial Committee for the Six Million Jewish Martyrs and Heroes. "This Committee represents thirty-four national and local Jewish organizations that have joined hands in the effort to erect a fitting monument to the Jewish martyrs of 1933–45," he explained. "The cost will be borne entirely by the Committee. The campaign for the erection of such a memorial was originated by the Committee. It seems reasonable, therefore, that the City Art Commission should consult closely with the Committee for the Six Million, and that together a fitting tribute to be erected in this city be agreed upon jointly."[22] According to Prinz, many member organizations of the committee had rejected both the design and theme when the art commission released them to the press earlier in the month, and the committee planned to conduct its own international design competition.

After its rejection of the art commission's Cain and Abel motif for a Holocaust memorial near Lincoln Center in December 1965, the memorial committee more aggressively sought to create a Holocaust memorial at another site. But there still was no alliance with city government regarding a memorial. By March 16, 1966, Benjamin Gebiner, then acting chairman of the steering committee, told the press that the committee was "wrestling with the Manhattan Borough President's office and the Parks Commissioner regarding a suitable location."[23] These officials had feared that the Lincoln Center location would obstruct traffic, and again wanted to change the site. The committee, meanwhile, had decided that the Riverside Park site was "hidden in the bushes," and it wanted a more prominent location.

Benjamin Gebiner hoped to meet soon with Borough President Constance Baker Motley and Parks Commissioner Thomas Hoving or their representatives to resolve the question of a site, after which, he added, there would be a design contest and fund-raising drive for the project. The committee also was planning a "memorial shrine" to house documents and artifacts. "We are in the initial stages of our project," said Gebiner. "But we are confident of struggling through these conflicts and achieving an appropriate memorial." Gebiner, an attorney and officer of the

Workmen's Circle, and Secretary Vladka Meed, a survivor representing WAGRO, wrote in a letter to the City Art Commission on
March 22: "Our committee did not authorize any person or any
group to submit in our behalf for your consideration any model
for the erection of a monument commemorating the six million
martyred Jews, annihilated during the Nazi period. We call to
your attention that a sculptor's model for such a monument, on
the theme of Cain-and-Abel, was rejected by our committee." The
letter asked for cooperation in erecting an appropriate monument.[24] This was late in the game to begin building political
bridges.

5

The Holocaust Memorial Endeavor Continues

The Six Day War and other events of the sixties released the Holocaust genie from the bottle in which it had been trapped for over twenty years. But once the genie was out of the bottle, it could not be recaptured and stuffed back in.
—*Aviva Cantor, 1995*

The years 1966–1974 brought a period of startling change with regard to the organized American Jewish community's interest in the Holocaust. In 1966, prior to the 1967 Six Day War, the Holocaust was still not on its agenda. By 1974, after the 1973 Yom Kippur War, the topic was seen as increasingly relevant, and, for the first time, commemorating the Holocaust had been officially placed on the community's agenda in 1973–74 (see Chapter 2).

In August 1966, Vladka Meed and Benjamin Gebiner wrote from the Memorial Committee for the Six Million Jewish Martyrs and Heroes to its affiliated organizations to bring them up to date. (The letterhead now entitled the group the "Committee to Commemorate the Six Million Jewish Martyrs.") They seem to have made progress in forging alliances that would move the project forward. The letter announced that the steering committee had chosen, from a number of possibilities suggested by the city, a site in Battery Park at the southern tip of Manhattan. During the past few months, Meed and Gebiner had been discussing a suitable site for the proposed memorial with the New York City Department of Parks. They had met both with Parks

Commissioner Thomas Hoving, who was "most cooperative and understanding," and with Borough President Constance Baker Motley, who had suggested the Battery Park site. In their letter, they note that the steering committee had already accepted the Battery Park location: "It was pointed out to us, that the previously assigned corner of Lincoln Center on 66th Street and Columbus Avenue, is a very small and noisy triangle with heavy traffic; a danger to any public gathering and unsuitable for a memorial. The several sites available in New York were considered by the Steering Committee at a series of meetings before the choice was made of Battery Park, on the basis of its unique historic significance and because it looks out on the Statue of Liberty and is visited daily by thousands of tourists and New Yorkers."[1] Almost the same wording as the last sentence was used, some twenty years later, to encourage acceptance of and then to describe the site of the Living Memorial to the Holocaust-Museum of Jewish Heritage, which the New York City Holocaust Memorial Commission began to plan in adjacent Battery Park City during the 1980s. Like the earlier attempts to create a major Holocaust memorial in New York City, the effort undertaken in 1965 failed.

Gebiner and Meed's August 1966 letter advised participating organizations that the Committee to Commemorate the Six Million Jewish Martyrs was organizing its own art committee of "prominent citizens." Rabbi Moshe Davidowitch, chairman of the National Council of Art in Jewish Life, was to be its coordinator and David Lloyd Kreeger, a Washington attorney, Jewish community leader, and arts patron, was to be chairman. This was a belated but smart move: the committee was actively asserting its own expertise in selecting a design by appointing leaders whose art credentials would impress the City Art Commission. In the same letter, Leon Jolson, a "prominent industrialist," was named chairman of a new financial committee, and participating organizations were reminded to pay their dues of $100 for administrative purposes.[2] The fact that both Kreeger and Jolson were prominent and wealthy should have improved the committee's prestige, giving it more clout with both the organized Jewish community and elected officials.

Although the participation of Kreeger and Jolson did not lead to successful implementation, after they became involved the committee did have more say in the decision-making process.

(This may have been coincidental.) On October 13, 1966, Arthur Rosenblatt, design consultant to Parks Commissioner Hoving under Mayor Lindsay, sent Gebiner a map of the suggested site for a monument. "I think the site is a proper one as it is also adjacent to the Emma Lazarus memorial tablet, and I suggest your committee consider it," he wrote.[3] Following a reply from Gebiner, on November 21, 1966, Rosenblatt sent him a letter of agreement regarding the site. He enclosed a site plan of Battery Park, marking the exact dimensions of the site, and proposed a meeting to discuss the choice of an architect and sculptor, as well as methods of financing the project. As he reminded Gebiner, the total cost, as well as perpetual maintenance, would be borne by the committee.[4]

On February 18, 1967, the committee issued a press release announcing David Lloyd Kreeger's chairmanship of the art committee, which consisted of seventeen architects, art historians, museum curators, and others prominent in the art world.[5] According to the press release, this committee would commission the design of the memorial in consultation with "leading Jewish historians and religious and cultural personalities." The press release also announced an educational and fund-raising campaign "to gather support for whatever proposal is finally approved." Kreeger was quoted as saying that New York, "the world's political, business, and cultural center, with the largest Jewish population in the world, will at last have a suitable memorial for our generation and future generations."[6]

Records of this effort indicate that it was much more sophisticated and organized than the earlier ones, as well as more savvy in public relations, dealing with government officials, and raising money. However, an event intervened that changed the project's prospects for success: the June 1967 Six Day War. Thus the very event that nearly every scholar credits with creating an atmosphere in which the idea of Holocaust memorialization could take root in the United States also took away the potential funding that would make such memorialization possible. Under the direction of the United Jewish Appeal, a massive fund-raising effort was mounted in an emergency campaign to support Israel during and after the war. In the wake of such crucial financial needs for Jews who were still living, the idea of a monument to Jews who were dead seemed frivolous to communal leaders. The Six Day War raised consciousness of the Holocaust, but this new consciousness encouraged the organized Jewish community and individual American Jews to give money to support Israel—and not to a project memorializing the Holocaust.

Despite the dry financial prospects for its project, the memorial committee carried on its business throughout 1967–68. A meeting was called for December 27, 1967, at the Wellington Hotel, where architect Louis Kahn of Philadelphia presented his design to the participating organizations. Because of David Lloyd Kreeger's association with the project, the committee was able to interest this great architect. (At some time in 1967, the umbrella group's name on its letterhead changed from "Committee to Commemorate the Six Million Jewish Martyrs" to "Memorial to the Six Million Jewish Martyrs, Inc." This was intended only to simplify the name, and was not a reflection of any substantive change in the committee.[7]) August Heckscher, the new Department of Parks commissioner, wrote to Benjamin Gebiner on March 22, 1968, formally advising him of the department's approval to erect a monument in Battery Park. His letter referred to an informal presentation that Kahn had already made to the Municipal Art Commission.[8]

On the same date, Gebiner and Meed wrote to representatives of participating organizations, that Kahn's model had been delivered to Heckscher and to the New York City Art Commission for approval. A meeting was called for April 10, 1968, at the Wellington Hotel "at which time detailed reports will be rendered about our accomplishments up to now and plans for the future will be made."[9] The letter mentioned that final arrangements would be discussed for a ground-breaking ceremony to be held at Battery Park on April 21, although the date was later given as May 5, 1968.

This time the committee had made a conscious effort to win the required government approvals. The decision to select Kahn as the designer was not only aesthetic but also political, according to Vladka Meed. She told me that Kahn's abstract design, which was both sculptural and architectural, did not satisfy all of the survivors, some of whom wanted something more graphic. But with an abstract design by a renowned architect such as Kahn, the committee thought it would have a better chance of gaining approval by the City Art Commission. It therefore decided to go ahead with it.[10] (It is important to note that the art commission had approved the Mestrovic-Mendelsohn design for

Riverside Park in 1951, although the project was never executed. Approval by the art commission did not guarantee successful completion of the memorial.)

The memorial was formally approved by the art commission in March 1968, and by October of that year a six-foot scale model was on display at the Museum of Modern Art. (The project architect for the Kahn design was Marshall Meyers of Philadelphia.) A museum press release describes the design as follows: "It consists of seven glass piers each 10' square and 11' high placed on a 66' square granite pedestal. The center pier has been given the character of a small chapel into which people may enter. The walls of the chapel will be inscribed. The six piers around the center, all of equal dimensions, are blank." The minimalist design of the proposed memorial prefigures Maya Ying Lin's Vietnam memorial in Washington, D.C. The *New York Times'* architecture critic Ada Louise Huxtable characterized the design as "beautiful, and chilling." "There is about it a silent, almost frozen formality, a crystalline sense of the eternal emptiness of death," she wrote. "This is architecture and, at the same time, sculpture, and it is symbolism of the highest order, timeless and contemporary."[11]

This new committee was operating in a political climate quite unlike that of 1947—a climate that should have nurtured the concept of a Holocaust memorial. Civil rights and anti–Vietnam protests reverberated throughout the country during the 1960s. The My Lai massacre on March 16, 1968—which, on a smaller scale, was not unlike such Nazi massacres as Babi Yar or Ponar—may have increased at least subliminal consciousness of the Holocaust. In addition to the civil rights and peace movements, other groups were standing up for their rights, such as a women's movement, a prisoners' movement, a Native American movement. As Howard Zinn wrote of this era, "There was a general revolt against oppressive, artificial, previously unquestioned ways of living. It touched every aspect of personal life: childbirth, childhood, love, sex, marriage, dress, music, art, sports, language, food, housing, religion, literature, death, schools."[12] These movements, particularly those bringing ethnicity to the forefront of American consciousness, should have provided fertile ground for creation of a memorial that could be described as a symbol of Jewish ethnicity in the United States.

Within this political mood of civil rights movements, assertion of ethnicity, and struggle to understand the brutal war in Vietnam, the art commission in March 1968 approved the design of the Committee to Commemorate the Six Million Jewish Martyrs. The leaders of this effort to create a Holocaust memorial do not recall making any connections between the civil rights struggles, revelation of Vietnam war horrors, and their own project, nor do their limited available records provide such evidence. Benjamin Gebiner told me that the upheavals of the 1960s had nothing to do with the committee's work.[13] However, these crucial issues, which affected both the consciousness and conscience of all Americans at that time, could not have been absent from the minds of the committee members.

Copies of correspondence show that the commemoration effort was organized as follows: A committee of participating Jewish organizations was nominally behind the effort, including major national organizations, survivor groups, and the New York Board of Rabbis. Twenty-eight organizations are listed on the letterhead, whereas the 1947 letterhead listed only individuals. The return address of the Memorial to the Six Million Jewish Martyrs, Inc., is that of the American Jewish Committee, demonstrating that this memorial committee, unlike a previous one during the 1940s and '50s, was linked to major Jewish organizations. Nevertheless, this appearance of a broad and unified interest group of major Jewish organizations was more window dressing than reality. Correspondence reveals that crucial decisions were made by the steering committee, mainly by Gebiner (representing the Workmen's Circle) and Vladka Meed (representing WAGRO and, from 1968, the Jewish Labor Committee), with strongest secondary support from the American Jewish Committee and the American Jewish Congress. The other components of the "broad base" of participating organizations received news such as site selection as a fait accompli.

The theme of the memorial was described as follows by art committee chairman Kreeger in a letter to architect Louis Kahn: "The monument is envisioned as one which will reflect and evoke the emotional, psychological, and historical impact of the tragedy of the period. . . . It should also deal with man's struggle to retain his dignity under the most horrendous of circumstances, and express hope for a better future, where man will not merely survive but prevail."[14] The theme was thus to be both particularistic and universal. Kreeger could not have known that an appropriate compromise for presenting these opposing viewpoints would be heatedly debated among Holocaust historians and museum creators for decades.

With the cost of the memorial projected to be at least $1 million, the dedication ceremony originally scheduled for April 1968 never took place. Asked why, Gebiner told me: "We were confronted with a terrific budget. . . . It pertained to the question of raising millions of dollars. And it didn't move." Not only was the New York Jewish community unsuccessful in voluntary efforts to raise the money needed for creation of a monument, but he also faulted the Holocaust survivors who lived in the city. "I also accuse the survivors who had among them many people of great means who talked a lot about monuments and the Holocaust, but when it came to brass tacks there was no response," he said. "And it began to peter out little by little, and that's all."[15]

Gebiner's analysis is not fair to the survivors he accused, because the memorial was not simply their responsibility but also that of the larger organized Jewish community. They were only a small part of the larger community, and others with equal or greater wealth contributed substantially to Jewish causes but not to this one. The most significant reason for failure to raise funds was probably the Six Day War. Gebiner added something, however, that was more to the point: "Every major organization that participated in this committee had their own problems for raising money for their own causes and own organization." This statement highlights two problems: it was extremely difficult for a new organization to come on the scene and raise funds for a new cause, in competition with the highly structured Jewish communal organizations that were already in place. And the latter, although they allowed their names to appear on a letterhead, had other priorities for which they were already raising funds. Gebiner singled out the American Jewish Committee as the only organization that contributed a considerable amount of money to the memorial; but they paid only part of Kahn's fee of some $17,000. The reasons the memorial failed, Gebiner concluded, were lack of money, self-sacrifice, and devotion. In other words, it failed because the interest group behind it was very narrow and the major Jewish organizations had no real commitment to promote it. Without the backing of the organized Jewish community, memorialization held no political value for elected officials; and it was therefore difficult for the small interest group to build the public-private coalition necessary for successful implementation.

Insufficient funding was clearly a major issue. On October 23, 1968, Jerry Goodman, then of the American Jewish Committee, reported to Bertram Gold, the organization's executive vice president, on a small meeting of memorial committee members. Raising a sum of $1.5 million had been discussed, and an appeal for large gifts had been suggested (with a small number of people underwriting the entire project). This would be supplemented by a public subscription campaign.[16] Soon afterward, Louis Kahn presented the memorial committee with his bill, for a total of $17,687.93, some of which had been owed to him for more than a year.[17] Kreeger wrote from Washington to Gebiner on December 3, 1968, of his embarrassment at the delay in paying Kahn's bill. He urged that each of the constituent organizations contribute from $500 to $2,500 in the next two weeks, and he suggested that a committee chairman should be selected "who has been active in Jewish and philanthropic affairs in the New York area."[18] His suggestions were not followed.

By July 18, 1969, not much had happened in the fund-raising arena. Jerry Goodman wrote to Kreeger on that date about a meeting of "some of the national [Jewish] agencies involved, or interested," observing that "at that meeting the problem was put squarely on the agenda and while several ideas were analyzed, the most concrete proposal was made by Bert Gold. While it is very tentative, he has succeeded in interesting a few leaders of the Federation of Jewish Philanthropies in New York to discuss the project and see if it can be connected to their work, and their fund-raising. At the present stage there is no commitment, merely a willingness to talk. . . . At the same time, Ben Gebiner has been urged to secure money from several of the agencies to settle the short-range debt to Lou Kahn."[19]

The idea of the Federation's involvement did not seem to get anywhere. The leaders of Federation would consider such a project competitive with their ongoing local programs and related United Jewish Appeal commitments to Israel. As previously explained, the Holocaust was used to raise funds for Israel and immigration, not for a memorial. In June 1971, Kreeger and the American Jewish Committee were still corresponding about where to find the relatively small amount of money to pay Kahn. Between May and November of 1971, Gold wrote to all of the

major American Jewish organizations, asking them to contribute
to the memorial, especially in order to settle the bill with Kahn.
In the end, Gold received some money from them, and the American Jewish Committee paid the balance due.

By December 16, 1971, Kahn had finally been paid and the
memorial committee tried to go forward. At a meeting that night,
a fund-raising campaign task force was set up under Julius
Schatz of the American Jewish Congress. Schatz reported that
someone associated with the Bergen-Belsen survivors had
pledged $25,000 and WAGRO had promised to match the sum.
The Farband Labor Zionist Order, an educational and philanthropic organization, had promised to try to raise $50,000, and
the *Daily Forward*, a Yiddish newspaper, had also committed itself to the campaign. The major Jewish organizations, none of
which had made a promise, would be "approached for a financial
commitment."[20] The projected date for completion was April
1973, the thirtieth anniversary of the Warsaw Ghetto uprising.
All of this scrambling for funds never produced the necessary
financial backing, however, because the major American Jewish
organizations had other priorities. The limited funds promised
by the smaller groups could not get the job done. According to
Gebiner, Israel was always the first priority, and the memorial
could not compete with it for financial attention.

Vladka Meed concurred that Israel was the first priority. "The
momentum for the Kahn project ended with the 1967 war emergency campaign," she told me. "Then we started again, and again
there was an emergency in 1973." She did not, however, blame
the major Jewish organizations for the project's failure. "You
can't accuse the organizations," she said. "To create such a project, you need individuals with money. You need a group of dedicated people with financial resources to complete the project."
(A survivor herself, she did not say, as Gebiner did, that those
individuals should be survivors.) Meed also pointed out that the
project was not really underway prior to the Six Day War. "When
the Jewish community faced other priorities and the construction of the memorial hadn't really started," she told me, "there
were emergency campaigns and none of the national organizations were able to undertake financing the memorial."[21]

While meager fund-raising efforts continued until the end of
1971, Benjamin Gebiner and Vladka Meed had already written
to Mayor John Lindsay on May 18, 1971, thanking him for his

cooperation but calling a halt to their activities. They told him that the Jewish community had other priorities since it was "confronted with the responsibility of standing by the side of Israel and Soviet Jewry." Because the organized Jewish community was "rendering every possible assistance" to these two causes, it was necessary "to desist at present from any other major fundraising." They then asked that "the City of New York, and you as the mayor, publicly announce that this site will be reserved for the above project, so that at a future date, when the crises are lifted, and hopefully it will be soon, we can resume our sacred work to create a remembrance and a reminder that our six million Jews did not die in vain."[22]

Ten days later, Marvin Schick, Assistant to the Mayor for Intergroup Relations, replied to Gebiner and Meed: "As your letter indicates, the Mayor believes that Battery Park is a suitable site for the Memorial. In view of your decision not to proceed right now with the project, we believe that it would not serve any purpose for the Mayor to make a public statement now." Nevertheless, he expressed his availability to meet with them about "this noble endeavor which is so much needed to remind our people of what happened a generation ago and also to teach them of the evil that can result from group hatred." Mayor Lindsay clearly did not want to make a public statement in support of a moribund project, and he had assigned his liaison to the organized Jewish community to smooth things over for him. At that time, strong support for a Holocaust memorial would not have given him much credit with the organized Jewish community. When I asked Schick about the episode nearly twenty years later, he said he did not remember any details.[23]

Thus, in an era of ethnic and human rights movements, the "movement" to memorialize the Holocaust did not succeed. Yet Benjamin Gebiner, Vladka Meed, and others active on the committee did not seem angry or bitter about past failures. When they spoke with me in 1990, they were looking forward to the completion of Holocaust memorials in Washington, D.C., and New York City.

Julius Schatz, who, representing the American Jewish Congress, was involved with the memorialization effort during the 1960s, was one of those who mentioned the Six Day War as a major reason for the failure of fund-raising efforts. He also recalled ongoing heated discussions about the benefits of a monument versus a museum. Finally, there was an agreement to "go for whatever was possible in terms of money."[24] At that point, financial circumstances demanded a monument rather than a museum.

An undated and unsigned draft letter, which seems to have been written in 1973 or 1974 and addressed to representatives of participating organizations, recommended that fund-raising cease. After noting that the committee had tried for a year and a half to launch a $1 million fund-raising campaign to construct the monument, the letter asked what had happened. Then it answered its own question: "During these crucial months Israel has been attacked by the Arab world supported by the Soviet Union. Every dollar and every tangible support have been expended to keep Israel alive and to preserve the security of her 2 1/2 million people. America has been in the midst of a severe financial crisis, and a stock market which has been heading into a tailspin."[25] Because of these "unforeseen crises," the steering committee "unanimously recommended a suspension of the campaign to raise a million dollars for the monument. To do otherwise would be an interference with the massive efforts to ensure Israel's urgent requirements for defense and survival."

The draft then presented an alternative suggestion, to "favor at this time a decision to launch a more modest campaign to create a museum and center which would encourage research, exhibits, visitation and remembrance." But the letter then pledged "to fulfill the sacred task of remembrance of our 6,000,000 martyrs and we further pledge that at such time when Israel's existence is ensured, we will then reactivate our campaign to build a monument in New York City worthy of the heroism and sacrifice of our 6,000,000."

A letter dated May 1974 may be the final version of this draft. This letter, addressed to "Dear Friend and Colleague," recapitulated the history of the ten-year effort, beginning with Nathan Rapoport's rejected design for Riverside Park in 1964. A broad coalition of Jewish organizations had decided to pursue two goals: a suitable monument on a desirable site and a memorial center offering activities and programs to study and commemorate the Holocaust. The committee had tried to raise $1.5 million for the Kahn memorial in Battery Park but had failed. (This was not a "huge" sum, as the letter said. In fact, it was a small sum to pay for a major work of public art.) The letter mentioned the difficulty of raising even the $17,000 owed to Kahn for his preliminary work, noting that only four organizations helped to pay the sum: the American Jewish Committee, WAGRO, the American Jewish Congress, and the ILGWU (International Ladies Garment Workers Union), which is not even listed as a participating organization on the letterhead.

The letter went on to reiterate the reasons for the failure to raise funds for the memorial: "the worsening economic situation, cost estimated for the monument increased as inflation mounted. Israel's struggle for survival in recent years (The Six Day War, War of Attrition, and Yom Kippur War) and the crisis of Soviet Jewry." It also noted another setback: Louis Kahn had died on March 17, 1974.

But, unlike the draft, the letter did not call for suspension of the fund-raising campaign. Instead, it said the committee was stalemated. "We are unable to proceed further without the firm commitment and financial help of the organized Jewish community toward a monument or memorial center. Nevertheless, it is our hope that you will give serious thought to alternatives and arrive at practical ideas to help create a project which will memorialize the heroism and martyrdom of the Six Million in a dignified and meaningful manner." The letter was signed by the Executive Committee: Benjamin Gebiner, Chairman; Vladka Meed, Secretary; Julius Schatz, American Jewish Congress; David Geller, American Jewish Committee; and Joseph Mlotek, Workmen's Circle.[26]

After the committee had given up on Battery Park because of the lack of funds, Schatz told me, they approached the Jewish Museum on Fifth Avenue with architectural designs for a Holocaust library to be built above an addition to the museum. The museum, or its parent organization, the Jewish Theological Seminary of America, never acted on the proposal.[27] A memorandum dated June 13, 1972, verifies that the committee contacted Dr. Gerson Cohen, then chancellor of the Jewish Theological Seminary, about this idea.[28] People associated with the seminary said the idea was rejected because the seminary wished to remain an autonomous institution.

6

The Players Change but Still No Progress

The days when people held their breath at the mention of the Holocaust are gone. As are the days when the dead elicited meditation rather than profanation.—Elie Wiesel, A Jew Today, *1975*

By the time Mayor Edward I. Koch interceded in the issue of Holocaust memorialization and announced his Mayor's Task Force on the Holocaust in July 1981, there was no interest group in New York City actively seeking to create a memorial. The Memorial to the Six Million Jewish Martyrs, Inc., the last such group, had dissolved itself three years earlier. Vladka Meed's and Benjamin Gebiner's May 1974 letter had not definitively killed the memorial committee, but on June 29, 1978, it was officially dead. On that date, the Warsaw Ghetto Resistance Organization (WAGRO) wrote to the memorial committee (attention: Vladka Meed) that "unfortunately, we were not successful, although we know that honest and sincere attempts were made by your committee. As matters have developed lately, we know, an overall national committee will be created to establish a permanent memorial under the auspices of President Carter. . . . Therefore, we think, the work of the Memorial for the Six Million Jewish Martyrs should be concluded."[1] Nevertheless WAGRO was looking forward to working with Vladka Meed or the memorial committee, the letter concluded, to establish a permanent memorial in the United States.

This letter from WAGRO is signed by Robert Born, Treasurer,

and Hirsh Altusky, Executive Secretary. It could have been signed by Benjamin Meed, who is Vladka's husband and also president and founder of the organization. When WAGRO headed a coalition of Jewish organizations attempting to create the rejected Rapoport memorial in Riverside Park, Vladka Meed was secretary of the project and representing WAGRO. After 1968, she worked for the Jewish Labor Committee and considered that entity, rather than WAGRO, the Jewish organization with which she was most closely affiliated. Now WAGRO, as a participating organization but no longer the spearheading one, was writing to her as executive secretary of the Memorial to the Six Million Jewish Martyrs, Inc. The illusion of the "broad base" of support had come full circle. While the major American Jewish organizations had given the project lip service, most of the real work was done by Vladka Meed and Benjamin Gebiner, with Julius Schatz of the American Jewish Congress and several staff members of the American Jewish Committee the only representatives of major Jewish organizations who gave consistent support. As detailed in Chapter 5, the American Jewish Committee was also the main source of limited emergency money for the project.

It is significant that the 1978 letter terminating the memorial committee implies that the idea of a major memorial in New York City was shelved because President Jimmy Carter had announced his President's Commission on the Holocaust. This indicates a relationship between the Washington and New York projects as early as 1978. President Carter's intervention on a national level already had an indirect effect on the effort to create the memorial designed by Louis Kahn for Battery Park: it was the final death blow to an already dying project.

But prior to Carter's intercession in 1978, there were yet other Jewish community efforts to create a major Holocaust memorial in New York City during the 1970s. WAGRO itself—not the committee called the Memorial to the Six Million Jewish Martyrs, Inc.—tried to establish a Holocaust memorial in New York City at that time. An undated WAGRO memorandum states that "it is high time that the city which is the home of the largest Jewish community in the world should have a permanent shrine and museum of the Holocaust to serve as a reminder to the world that the impossible and unspeakable could happen again if we do not teach future generations of the horrors of the Nazi era."[2] The memorandum proposes that a building for sale by New York

City be acquired for this purpose. The building (parcel no. 18, section no. 1, block 197, lot 1), located on the northeast corner of Lafayette and White streets, was a three-story former firehouse, Engine Co. 31. The memorandum aimed to "involve in this project the entire Jewish community of New York. Above all, this museum should serve to present a warning to future generations that the atrocities of World War II must not be repeated against any people, regardless of race, color or creed." The closing paragraph appeals to "all men of good will who sympathize with our objectives to lend us their support. We are urging the people of the City of New York and the entire Jewish community to help us realize this dream."

By the time of this undated memorandum, which was most likely written in 1975, commemorating the Holocaust was already on the agenda of the National Jewish Community Relations Advisory Council (NJCRAC). The 1973 Yom Kippur War had reinforced the Holocaust consciousness that emerged with the 1967 Six Day War. However, nothing ever developed regarding this proposal, according to WAGRO's files and president Benjamin Meed. One important reason may be that it was perceived as a narrow-based effort led by a survivors' group. As Elie Wiesel later observed, until President Carter placed the issue of Holocaust memorialization on the agenda in 1978, major Jewish organizations did not consider survivors an important interest group within the greater Jewish community.[3]

Meanwhile, WAGRO soon initiated yet another attempt to obtain space for a Holocaust memorial center, this time at the New York Cultural Center at Columbus Circle. On December 9, 1976, Benjamin Meed wrote to Charles G. Bluhdorn, chairman of the board of Gulf & Western Industries. He congratulated him for buying the Columbus Circle building and donating it to the City of New York, but expressed "sadness" that WAGRO was "undercut" in its own attempts to obtain the building. "Within the last two months the abovementioned building was called to our attention [as a site for a Holocaust center] and we visited it several times," he wrote. "We met with Mr. John J. Rowan, Vice President of New York Urban Servicing Co., Inc. Meetings were held on several levels within the Jewish community to work out plans of purchasing and maintaining such an institution. Naturally, our basic obstacle was obtaining the necessary funds and we are afraid we missed a unique opportunity."[4] Meed asked

Bluhdorn to include "our project of remembrance" in the cultural center. A copy of this letter was sent to Mayor Abraham D. Beame.

Meed tried to form a political alliance with Mayor Beame to achieve his goal. He actively tried to gain the mayor's ear and approval, but neither he nor his WAGRO group had enough power or influence to win the mayor's support. At that time, along with the copy of the letter to Bluhdorn, Meed sent Beame a letter with a "special appeal" to include WAGRO as a "participating group" in the New York Cultural Center. "I feel that if you agree in principle, the details should be worked out in conference," he wrote. He requested a meeting with the mayor or his representative, and with the commissioner of cultural affairs.[5]

Michael Mehlman, then administrative officer for the Department of Cultural Affairs, answered Meed's letter on December 29, 1976. This respondent's position in the Beame administration indicates that the issue was not high on the mayor's agenda. Mehlman replied that it was premature to make decisions about public use of the building at the present time, and that the interest of WAGRO would be considered in due time ("Don't call us, we'll call you").[6] In response to a letter and phone call, Meed received another letter from the Department of Cultural Affairs on January 19, 1977, this time from Deputy Commissioner Janet Langsam, who reiterated Mehlman's stance on the issue: "There are, fortunately, many other attractive real estate opportunities in the City of New York which I am sure you can explore and I hope the fact that you were not successful in acquiring the New York Cultural Center will not dampen your enthusiasm for a most worthwhile endeavor."[7] This was a polite "goodbye" to Meed from the Beame administration ("Don't call us, and we *won't* call you"). The political alliance WAGRO sought then with Mayor Beame never went anywhere.

At about the same time, a powerful new organization arrived on the Jewish communal scene in New York City: the Jewish Community Relations Council of New York (JCRC). This umbrella and coordinating body was created in 1975 and officially established in 1976. The lineup of players was a formidable list of New York City "heavy hitters." The first president was Richard Ravitch, a developer who later became chairman of the Metropolitan Transportation Authority (MTA) and head of Mayor Koch's Charter Revision Commission. Real estate developer Jack

Weiler was honorary president, and developer George Klein (who later would head Koch's Task Force on the Holocaust) was a vice president. Other vice presidents included Maxwell M. Raab, Daniel S. Shapiro, and Laurence A. Tisch. Irvin D. Husin was secretary and Irving Silverman, treasurer. Malcolm Hoenlein, a masterful political entrepreneur who went on to run the Conference of Presidents of Major American Jewish Organizations, was the executive director. The purpose of the JCRC, as officially stated, was "to serve as the central coordinating and resource body for the metropolitan-area Jewish community." By 1990, as the umbrella agency for sixty-two major civic, communal, educational, and religious organizations, the JCRC set an agenda of Jewish activities, issues, and programs that reflected the concerns, needs, and aspirations of the Jewish community of New York. The broad range of issues addressed by the JCRC includes "Israel and international concerns, domestic and urban affairs, government relations, intergroup relations, anti-Semitism and discrimination, Jewish security and neighborhood stabilization."[8]

One of the unofficial, unstated purposes of JCRC was to serve as a power base for the politically ambitious Hoenlein and his wealthy and well-connected backers, who were, for the most part, real estate developers. These developers who backed the founding of JCRC in 1976 became more powerful in the city after Ed Koch won the mayoral election in 1977 and took office in 1978. After Koch took office, only three years after the depth of New York City's 1975 financial crisis, as Jim Sleeper and others have detailed, he made deals and formed alliances with developers that caused them to become one of the most influential groups of "movers and shakers" in the city. Most of these developers are Jewish, and were appointed by Mayor Koch to the New York City Holocaust Memorial Commission when he created it in 1982.

One hallmark of the Koch administration was its giveaways to developers. Sleeper describes the Koch era as reflecting "abdication of government's legitimate 'police powers' over burgeoning development" and "abandonment of any civic mission broader than what 'development' might define."[9] Between the beginning of the development boom in 1981 and 1987, about 45 million square feet of new commercial space was built in Manhattan. The Koch administration made it easy for real estate developers to become enormously wealthy and powerful by offering tax incentives ($1.3 billion in 1981–87), zoning variances (such as greater building density and height in exchange for public amenities), and sale of city property to the highest bidders without regard for planning. Developers, in turn, were among the largest contributors to Koch's electoral campaigns. For example, in 1985, half of the $9 million in campaign gifts to Koch and the other members of the Board of Estimate (that is, the comptroller, City Council president, and five borough presidents) came from 175 donors, most of them developers, brokerage houses, and their attorneys.[10]

One of the real estate developers who backed the creation of Hoenlein's JCRC, its first vice president George Klein, soon emerged as an important force among developers in New York City. His office building at Fifty-ninth Street and Park Avenue, begun in 1977, was the first new office building constructed in New York City in five years (following the financial crisis of 1975). Hoenlein and Klein began to seek power in the Jewish community and influence in City Hall at around the same time, and found an open door after Koch was elected mayor in 1977. As someone close to the situation put it, Klein and Hoenlein helped each other get ahead politically in New York's organized Jewish community. The close reciprocal relationship between Klein and Hoenlein enabled them to help each other build a pyramid of power in the established organized Jewish community and in their dealings with the mayor's office. Klein became Mayor Koch's personal friend, and Herbert Rickman, Koch's liaison to the organized Jewish community, was also closely associated with Hoenlein and Klein.

JCRC soon got into the act of creating a Holocaust memorial in New York City. At a March 24, 1977, press conference, JCRC president Ravitch listed, among issues of concern for the Jewish community of New York, a serious effort to commemorate the Holocaust. (JCRC was an affiliate of the NJCRAC community relations umbrella, which had been promoting the concept of memorialization since 1973–74 in its *Joint Program Plan*.) In 1977, JCRC comprised twenty constituent member organizations and fifty others with applications pending. S. L. Shneiderman, who had worked on the 1947 Holocaust memorial ceremony in Riverside Park, was present at the press conference. He brought up the fact that he had records of earlier attempts to establish a

Holocaust memorial, and, he interjected, "some of the organizations you [JCRC] represent killed it."[11]

On April 7, 1977, Ravitch sent letters to Shneiderman, Benjamin Meed, and "a selected group of individuals" to meet at his
home on Park Avenue on April 18, to hear Gideon Hausner, chairman of Yad Vashem in Jerusalem (and prosecutor at the trial of
Adolf Eichmann). The purpose of the meeting was to "discuss
the conceptual framework and preparatory steps for initiating a
'living' [Holocaust] memorial." In his letters, Ravitch observed,
somewhat incorrectly, that New York City was "the only major
Jewish community in the world without a commemoration of
the Holocaust." Ravitch went on to place the memorial project
on the agenda of the JCRC: "Recognizing the unique opportunity
presented by the creation of the Jewish Community Relations
Council and the fact that the passage of time mitigates against
the possibility of this long sought dream becoming a reality,"
Ravitch wrote, "representatives of the Survivors' organizations
and other concerned persons approached the JCRC to undertake
this project. The General Assembly of the JCRC authorized the
President to appoint an organizing committee to explore the possibilities and develop plans."[12]

This meeting raises a number of questions: Which representatives of which survivor organizations had approached JCRC?
Or did JCRC, in fact, approach the survivors? Was JCRC's take-
over of the project approved by the Committee to Commemorate
the Six Million Jewish Martyrs, which did not officially cease
functioning until a year later? Was JCRC stepping in to institutionalize the effort and render powerless any potential attempts
by smaller groups (such as WAGRO or the earlier Zygelboim committee)? Was JCRC, then a new umbrella group, using the issue
of memorializing the Holocaust, which had recently become
timely, as a means of gaining greater prominence in the Jewish
community and with respect to the city government? Was any
informal discussion already taking place between JCRC and Ed
Koch, who was to run for mayor that coming fall?

No files, archives, or interviews provide concrete answers.
However, there is an unconfirmed report that, when Koch ran
for mayor for the first time in 1977, the creation of a Holocaust
memorial in New York City was on his general list of items of
interest to the organized Jewish community. Manny Behar, who
worked on the 1977 campaign, told me that he wrote this item

into the campaign platform, but no evidence is available. Behar did not, however, remember any connection between the idea and JCRC's project.[13] If Koch did in fact make mention of a Holocaust memorial in 1977, he then shelved the idea until 1981. Insisting he did not remember, Hoenlein refused to discuss with me JCRC's early history regarding a Holocaust memorial. Nor were the organization's 1977 files accessible.

The presence of Yad Vashem chairman Hausner at the spring 1977 meeting sponsored by JCRC is an indication that Ravitch took the idea of a memorial seriously. Of all of the Holocaust memorials in the world, Yad Vashem Martyrs' and Heroes' Memorial Authority in Jerusalem has been recognized as *the* memorial, complete with exhibitions, historical and art museums, archives, shrines, artifacts, and a sacred aura. Yad Vashem is a government museum, established by law in 1953 for the purpose of commemorating "the disaster and its heroism and to promote a custom of joint remembrance of the heroes and the victims."[14] Because of its vast archives and its status as a quasi-religious shrine, Yad Vashem has been the most important Holocaust memorial museum, not only in Israel but in the world. (This was certainly true in 1977; after April 1993, the U.S. Holocaust Memorial Museum in Washington, D.C., became a formidable contender for this title.)

Ravitch recalled that the idea of a Holocaust memorial for New York City came up when one of the survivor groups joined the newly formed JCRC; based on the history of this issue, it is likely the group was WAGRO. Ravitch agreed that JCRC should do something in New York, which led to the meeting in his apartment. "There was a city-owned site on Forty-third Street and First Avenue," he told me. "I remember that in a relatively compressed period of time I had an architect by the name of Davis, Brody do some sketches. I also had a meeting with Dr. [Yitzhak] Arad of Yad Vashem, and we got [Ernest] Michel very much involved. I even remember flying to Florida once with him to try to solicit a major contribution from a wealthy guy in Miami. We were on the verge of some very serious fund-raising for this. All we wanted from the city was the conveyance of that property."[15]

German-born Ernest Michel, a Holocaust survivor who for many years headed Federation–United Jewish Appeal's (UJA) fund-raising operation in New York City, remained active into the 1990s in efforts to create a memorial. He served as cochairman of development of the New York commission launched by Mayor Koch. Ravitch was a member of Koch's original task force, but was not active on this issue after he became MTA director in 1981. In 1993 he was highly critical of the newest effort to create a Holocaust memorial museum in New York.[16]

The timing of the meeting in Ravitch's home should have been conducive to the success of a Holocaust memorial project. On April 7, 1977, the very day Ravitch sent out invitations to the April 18 meeting, Yitzhak Rabin announced his resignation as prime minister of Israel. On May 17, 1977, Menachem Begin's Likud coalition became dominant in the Israel Knesset, and Begin formed a cabinet in June. Much more than the previous Labor government, Begin used Holocaust rhetoric to validate the existence of Israel and to defend its policies. His election, combined with the 1961 Eichmann trial and the 1967 and 1973 wars, can be considered a turning point in increasing awareness of the Holocaust in the organized American Jewish community. Furthermore, Malcolm Hoenlein, the JCRC director, was close to Begin's Likud party. This combination of circumstances, however, was not enough to make the JCRC initiative successful.

S. L. Shneiderman, who attended the meeting in Ravitch's home, reported on it to Richard Cohen, then public relations director of the American Jewish Congress. Shneiderman had been invited as correspondent for the Israeli newspaper *Al Hamishmar* and the Yiddish *Daily Forward* in New York, but he also seems to have been "spying" for the American Jewish Congress. According to Shneiderman, the meeting was "devoted to a project of establishing a 'Living Memorial to the Six Million Jewish Martyrs.'" About thirty people attended, including representatives of survivor groups and religious organizations, and "probably potential contributors to a fund of about 25 million dollars for the erection of a building, preferably in the vicinity of the United Nations."[17] Ravitch had outlined the project as an institute for research on the Holocaust, with archives, a library, a museum, exhibits, and auditoriums. Shneiderman added that, as far as he knew, no representatives of the American Jewish Committee, the Anti-Defamation League of B'nai B'rith, or YIVO attended the meeting. (This information was important for the American Jewish Congress, which, no doubt, was keeping tabs on potential competing organizations.)

A political analysis of Shneiderman's report demonstrates

that the various participants at the meeting were seeking to protect their own special interests. For example, Benjamin Meed, whose WAGRO ran yearly Holocaust commemorative services on Yom Hashoah (a day of Holocaust commemoration designated by the Israel government as the twenty-second day of the Hebrew month of Nissan), suggested that the projected memorial have a meeting room for 30,000 people to house his commemoration. Eli Zborowski, a resistance group survivor who heads the International Society for Yad Vashem, suggested the new institution be called Friends of Yad Vashem. Both proposals were rejected. Writing about the civic controversies in Chicago during the 1950s, political scientist Edward Banfield noted that conflicts arise because of the "maintenance and enhancement" needs of formal organizations: "The heads of an organization see some advantage to be gained by changing the situation. They propose changes. Other large organizations are threatened. They oppose, and a civic controversy takes place."[18] Thus, controversy occurs, according to Banfield, when the changes proposed by a competing organization seem to threaten the "maintenance and enhancement" of another organization. In this context, it would seem that a prime concern of representatives of Jewish organizations at this meeting was the "maintenance and enhancement" of their respective organizations.

Shneiderman wrote that Michel was attending in a private capacity, as a survivor. When asked if UJA would directly support a fund-raising initiative for a Holocaust memorial, according to Shneiderman, Michel had answered with a categorical "no."[19] Thirteen years later, Michel told me that he never had a negative response from the leadership of Federation-UJA about building a Holocaust memorial, and that some leaders of Federation-UJA have been major supporters of the current project.[20] However, this is not the same as Federation's placing the issue on its agenda and making an allocation for it—something that did not happen in New York City.

In his report to Richard Cohen, Shneiderman noted that completion of the 1947 monument was blocked by "active opposition" from the UJA and the Federation of Jewish Philanthropies, then separate organizations. Then he mentioned Jewish Agency representatives hinting that David Ben-Gurion was opposed in 1947, because a Holocaust memorial would hamper fund-raising efforts for Israel. Although no empirical evidence to prove or disprove these allegations has been found, such a stance would have been in keeping with Ben-Gurion's belief that creating and maintaining the State of Israel was always the first priority. The Jewish Agency functioned as the government of Israel before the state was officially declared in 1948. When he told meeting participants the "painful" story of the Riverside Drive attempt in 1947, Shneiderman reported, most of those present were "astonished." At the end of the meeting, Ravitch announced that he would immediately open a bank account for the JCRC project, and hinted that first seed money would be a seven-figure sum.[21]

By the fall of 1977, the JCRC and its executive director, Malcolm Hoenlein, were clearly in the lead in efforts to establish a Holocaust memorial in New York. This was when Ed Koch first ran for mayor and won, but no records or interviews substantiate any collaboration between Koch and JCRC on this issue at that time. On September 26, 1977, Ravitch invited Benjamin Meed, as one of "a few key individuals," to a meeting in Ernest Michel's office to discuss the concept and design of a proposed Holocaust memorial. Ravitch would be reporting on developments of the past few weeks "in hope that we can then develop plans to bring this to fruition."[22]

On November 6, 1977, Yad Vashem chairman Arad wrote to Hoenlein at JCRC, outlining how he thought JCRC should proceed with respect to the memorial. Responding to a request by Ravitch, on December 12, 1977, John Zuccotti of the law firm of Tufo, Johnston, Zuccotti and Allegaert reported on the state and city regulations that would affect JCRC's proposal to build a Holocaust monument and museum. The proposed site was on city-owned land at the southeast corner of First Avenue and East Forty-second Street. In addition to outlining the complicated process of demapping and Uniform Land Use Review Procedure (ULURP), Zuccotti warned of organized opposition that he predicted would come from the community, objecting to the loss of playground space, and from the United Nations, over loss of potential development space. (Kurt Waldheim, whose own Nazi past was later exposed, was then UN secretary general.)

Zuccotti analyzed the situation with a keen understanding of the project's political implications. "In addition," he wrote to Ravitch, "the opposition may invoke the argument that the monument is a mere give-away of City land to a special interest group. Notwithstanding its lack of merit, the argument may have some impact on the relevant political actors. This is because they will be sensitive both to the suggestions of local ethnic or religious groups that the City provide them with land for some pet project, regardless of its merit, and to the constraints imposed on the City by the fiscal crisis. JCRC should take exceptional care, both in the land disposition agreement and in its public relations effort, to elaborate the importance of the monument to the intellectual and cultural life of the City and to its tourist industry, and to articulate fully the value of the consideration being given for the land."[23]

Zucotti's political sense is impressive. This is the earliest documentation that a Holocaust memorial committee in New York City was aware of the project's possible effect on other interest groups. This is not a case of worrying about anti-Semitic reactions, as happened in the attempt that began in 1946. Rather, it is a case of being sensitive to the interests of competing groups—both those that would not want the memorial intruding into their neighborhoods and those that would want the city to give them the equal opportunity to build their own commemorative projects. JCRC was proposing changes which could threaten other institutions and lead to controversy. Zucotti was warning JCRC to avoid such problems.

The next month, Ed Koch took office as mayor of New York, and a new chapter was about to begin in the long saga of efforts to create a Holocaust memorial in the city. At this point, however, the New York City story took a detour through Washington, D.C. When Richard Ravitch learned that the President's Commission on the Holocaust was to be formed, and that Elie Wiesel would be chairman, he concluded that it was "absolutely silly" to try to compete with a presidential commission that was planning a national memorial. "I thought we'd never raise the money in competition with what they were doing, and the project was sort of aborted," he told me. "The last thing I remember is having a conversation with Elie Wiesel, and saying the symbolism of having the memorial across the street from the United Nations was overwhelming, and that's what I thought the presidential commission ought to recommend."[24] After this discussion with Wiesel—which must have taken place in 1978—according to Ravitch, the JCRC dropped the idea of pursuing a Holocaust memorial. There is no evidence that the JCRC tried to form a political alliance with Mayor Koch, once he took office in 1978, in order to carry the project forward.

Richard Ravitch, however, was not the only New Yorker who thought the President's Commission on the Holocaust should recommend that the national memorial be situated in New York City. On September 29, 1978, Mayor Koch wrote to President Jimmy Carter, offering him full support for creation of a national Holocaust memorial. Mayor Koch then asked President Carter to consider locating the memorial in New York City, enumerating the reasons why this would be a good idea. First of all, according to Koch, families of many New Yorkers were personally touched by the Holocaust and would give enthusiastic support to a national memorial located in New York City. He also pointed out that New York had the largest Jewish and survivor communities outside of Israel, and that most national Jewish organizations were headquartered in the city. Then, going beyond narrow Jewish interests, Koch reminded Carter that New York was the diplomatic capital of the world. He added that the city had a reputation as a haven for the oppressed. "In short," Koch wrote, "a Holocaust Memorial located in New York City would not only serve as a reminder of the world's past indifference to human rights, but as a visible symbol of continuing efforts to protect and promote human dignity and rights." Then, with typical Koch chutzpah, he announced that he had "taken the liberty of enclosing a list of people who, in my opinion, would be particularly helpful in planning and realizing the Memorial."[25]

No response from President Carter was found, but history records that the national Holocaust memorial was destined for Washington, D.C., not New York City. In order to better understand how Mayor Koch created his own Holocaust commission in New York, we need to examine the genesis of its precursor, the President's Commission on the Holocaust.

7
Holocaust Memorialization on the U. S. Government's Agenda

The Holocaust memorial was born out of politics and it was born out of domestic political crisis.—Presidential Aide Mark Siegel, March 16, 1990

In 1977–78, President Jimmy Carter was in trouble with the organized Jewish community. The efforts of his high-level staff members to mend fences after his hard-line statements and decisions on Israel led to his intervening on the issue of Holocaust memorialization and subsequently creating the President's Commission on the Holocaust in 1978. By the time President Carter put the issue of Holocaust memorialization squarely on the agenda of the U.S. government that year, there was already a history of thirty-two years of failed attempts to create a memorial in New York City, the center of Jewish life in America.

President Carter's problems began on March 9, 1977, only two months after his inauguration. That afternoon he stated at a town meeting and press conference in Clinton, Massachusetts, that a Palestinian homeland was a major component of peace in the Middle East, and that U.S. policy called for Israel's return to its pre–1967 borders with insubstantial changes. The Conference of Presidents of Major American Jewish Organizations (Presidents' Conference), which claims to speak for the organized Jewish community, expressed its displeasure to the Carter administration both publicly and privately.[1]

As a result of the organized Jewish community's profound indignation about his comments at the town meeting, Carter named Mark Siegel as his liaison to the Jewish community. Siegel, who was deputy to Chief of Staff Hamilton Jordan, assumed this additional responsibility. "That spring, I was determining in a very systematic way how the community could be involved in the decision-making process with respect to the Geneva peace conference," he told me. "I laid out a lot of political steps so that the Jewish community would have trust and confidence in the president and the administration because, at some point in this process, faith would be required. It was not going to be easy. I sequenced a lot of things. One of the things I said the president should push for was passage of the Genocide Treaty, as a confidence-building measure. Other measures were regular meetings with the community, with major Jewish organizations."[2]

At this stage, Siegel hit upon an idea that was to make history and ultimately have a crucial effect on efforts to create a Holocaust memorial in New York City and Holocaust memorialization in general. "I was aware that the United States was the only Western country that did not have an official memorial to the victims of the Holocaust," he recalled. "I suggested in a memo to Hamilton Jordan that went on to the president that it was long overdue, and that it would be well received in the community." When they both responded favorably, Siegel asked Ellen Goldstein, who was working for Chief Domestic Policy Advisor Stuart Eizenstat, for a briefing memo on the subject of memorials. She responded quickly that many countries had memorials but the United States did not, adding that none was being planned or publicly discussed and that it would be a novel idea. "She proceeded to do a good deal of research on it, talking about the kinds of memorials that existed around the world," Siegel said.[3] The idea was then shelved until March 1978.

Meanwhile, Rabbi Alexander Schindler, then chairman of the Presidents' Conference, on June 7, 1977, expressed concern with what appeared to be an "erosion" of Carter's "commitment to Israel." American Jews were "worried about the expectations Carter is raising in the Arab world," he said.[4] Three days later, the *New York Times* reported, in an article by Bernard Gwertzman, that Carter was "stung" by the criticism of American Jews and was taking steps to repair the relationship. His creation of the President's Commission on the Holocaust the next year was part of his attempt to do so.

On July 6, 1977, President Carter met with more than fifty American Jewish leaders to discuss his views on Israel and peace in the Middle East. Afterward, Rabbi Schindler, speaking as chairman of the President's Conference, said he was reassured. On August 8, 1977, however, Carter announced that the United States was in contact with the Palestine Liberation Organization (PLO), and that the PLO would be an acceptable participant in the Geneva peace talks. All that Carter required of the PLO was that it announce its recognition of United Nations Resolution 242. This resolution, adopted on November 22, 1967, affirms that fulfilling the principles of the UN charter "requires the establishment of a just and lasting peace in the Middle East."[5] Carter also stated that he considered the Palestinians more than just refugees. The Presidents' Conference reported that it was "deeply disturbed by this deterioration in the American position."[6] On October 1, 1977, the situation deteriorated further. The Carter administration and the Soviet Union released a joint statement on the Middle East, calling for Palestinian representation at the Geneva peace conference, and speaking of the "legitimate rights of the Palestinian people" (an idea that was then anathema to the Presidents' Conference). Rabbi Schindler sent a telegram to President Carter, noting he was "profoundly disturbed" at "a shocking about-face of the President's public pledges."[7]

In early 1978, President Carter announced his proposal to sell jet warplanes to Israel, Egypt, and Saudi Arabia as a package. Then, at a White House press conference on April 25, 1978, he stated that if Congress rejected the sale of planes to any of the three countries, he would withdraw the entire package.[8] Siegel told me that in early 1978 he was growing increasingly uncomfortable with his role as liaison to the Jewish community. "It was my clear opposition to the sale of the F-15s to Saudi Arabia, and it was expected of me to sell this sale to the Jewish community, and it became untenable for me," he said. "Ultimately in March 1978 it led to my resignation, which unlike most resignations of public figures was not an exchange of happy letters. I laid out my views in a resignation that was quite public. At that point there had been great tension developing within the Jewish community on a range of issues—a Palestinian homeland, the Geneva peace conference, the sale of F-15s to Saudi Arabia, and there was a real crisis in relations between the White House and the American Jewish community." Siegel was, as he put it, "afraid my resignation fueled that fire," because it seemed to prove people's fears about the administration. After Siegel left in early March, relationships between the Carter administration and the organized Jewish community worsened.

Siegel considers that "the politics of the Washington Holocaust memorial" originated at this time, March 1978. He had put forth the idea almost a year earlier, but there had been no action on it. "As the situation [with respect to the Jewish community] continued to deteriorate in March and April, 1978, apparently what happened in the White House was to decide what to do to repair this hemorrhage," he told me. "And the idea of the Holocaust memorial was resurrected at that point. And I must say I was not pleased, because what was done was at the height of the battle with the Senate over the F-15s, a very ugly battle with [Carter's national security advisor Zbigniew] Brzezinski making a number of unfortunate comments [for instance, that he would "break the back" of the Jewish lobby on Capitol Hill] that some people determined to be anti-Semitic."[9]

A memorandum from Ellen Goldstein to Stuart Eizenstat, dated March 28, 1978, corroborates Siegel's recollections. "Some time ago," she wrote, "Mark Siegel asked me to research a question he had concerning a U.S. memorial for the victims of the Nazi holocaust [sic]. The results of my research are contained in the attached memo [from Goldstein to Siegel, dated June 21, 1977]. While many countries outside of Eastern Europe have memorials or plans for memorials, there is in the United States no official memorial or plans for a memorial. Even though some of these countries had no concentration camps within their borders, many of their citizens are survivors of such camps. The United States certainly has its share of Nazi survivors as well."

In her memo, Goldstein noted that a newspaper column by William Safire on March 27 dealing with Nazis in Skokie, Illinois, had reminded her of Siegel's original request. "I have no idea how far Mark's idea or proposal, if indeed he had one, travelled [sic] in the White House, but I bring it to your attention now," she wrote. "If the Administration were to advance, in some way, the construction of a memorial built with private and/or public moneys, it might be an appropriate gesture in honor of Israel's thirtieth anniversary and a symbol of the United States' support of Israels' [sic] birth and continued life. The idea deserves consideration on its merits, although such a move might appear to some people to be glib public relations."

Eizenstat wrote by hand on the memo that it was an interesting idea and that he wanted to discuss it.[10] Thus it is possible to pinpoint the date when a national Holocaust memorial became "an idea whose time has come" and was placed on the federal government's agenda. It is also possible to document that the idea was initiated for political purposes. As John W. Kingdon has observed with regard to agenda setting, patterns of public policy are determined by what gets on the agenda. Why, after many years, he asks, does a particular time prove right for an issue to emerge? He then lists four stages in the process: an agenda is set; alternatives from which a choice will be made are specified; an authoritative choice is made (for example, by legislative vote); and there is implementation. Participants (parties, elected officials, staff, and media) and processes (problem recognition, generation of policies, and politics of reelection) affect both agenda settings and alternatives.[11]

According to Kingdon, we need to know what made the soil fertile rather than the seed's origin. In the case of a national Holocaust memorial, the soil was made fertile for at least four reasons. First, President Carter desperately needed a positive issue to mend fences with the Jewish community. Second, the idea of memorializing the Holocaust had recently emerged as a pertinent issue in the organized American Jewish community. In addition, the idea had become "Americanized" by its popularized airing to a mass audience of the miniseries *Holocaust* on NBC television at about that time; and the number of books being published on the topic had also increased. Finally, the issue of the presence of Nazi war criminals in America had been placed on the national agenda in 1977 with the creation of a Special Litigation Unit in the Immigration and Naturalization Service. Systematic denaturalization and deportation hearings of accused Nazi war criminals (some of whom had worked for the U.S. government) had been initiated.[12] A memorial was a much less embarrassing way for the government to address the Holocaust.

Kingdon's model views the processes of federal agenda setting as originating in three separate "streams"—problem recognition, policy formulation and refinement, and politics. These three processes operate largely independently, but coalesce at critical junctures: a problem is recognized; a solution is available; and the political climate is right for change. There is an opportunity to push a proposal—what is called a policy window—at the time that an issue suddenly "gets hot."[13] Policy entrepreneurs willing to invest resources in the hope of future return then go into action. This is related to a "tipping point" in coalition building, when people and groups join for fear they will be excluded from possible benefits.

This theoretical model can help us to better understand the practical dynamics of the Carter administration's decision to memorialize the Holocaust: in 1978, the issue "got hot." A policy window had opened, and the "streams" came together: the *problem* of addressing the Holocaust in a way that would divert attention from a much more volatile item already on the agenda (beginning investigations of government use of Nazi war criminals) and from foreign policies that had enraged the organized Jewish community; the *policy* of Holocaust commemoration; and the *politics* of reelection, of finding a domestic issue that would appeal to Jewish voters, whose support for Carter had badly eroded. The need for such an issue had been placed on the agenda, policy entrepreneurs went into action, a Holocaust memorial in Washington was chosen from the alternatives, an official act created the President's Commission on the Holocaust, and the implementation phase began.

Following Ellen Goldstein's memorandum of April 4, 1978, Stuart Eizenstat wrote a note by hand to "B," mentioning that the idea of a memorial should be discussed with Hyman Bookbinder, the American Jewish Committee's Washington representative, and others "to make sure it will be well received."[14] This further illustrates that the purpose of the project was to appeal to the Jewish community, with whom President Carter was having problems. The Carter administration thus initiated the creation of a political alliance with the organized Jewish community around the issue of Holocaust memorialization for the purpose of winning its support.

Eizenstat, with White House counsel Robert Lipshutz, next wrote a memorandum to President Carter on April 25, 1978, on the subject of a "Holocaust Memorial." There was no official American Holocaust memorial, the memo stated, and stronger support than ever for its creation "among many Americans—

not just Jewish-Americans."[15] The reasons they gave included the recent television program *Holocaust;* the creation of memorials in other countries; and the aging of the "thousands of concentration camp survivors in this country." Only the first reason would probably make "many Americans" amenable to the idea, and even this cannot be proven. Nevertheless, these were Eizenstat's rationalizations to Carter. He added that there would soon be a White House celebration of Israel's thirtieth anniversary, and that creation of the State of Israel was closely linked to the Holocaust. "If you are interested in pursuing an official U.S. memorial to the Holocaust victims, that date would seem an appropriate time to announce plans for such a memorial," Eizenstat wrote. "The memorial would serve not only as a reminder to all Americans of the millions who died in the Holocaust, but also of the birth of Israel and its continued life."

As noted in the memorandum, there were still questions to be resolved about the content of the memorial, where it should be located, how it should be funded, and the role of the federal government in sponsoring or maintaining it. Eizenstat recommended that a fifteen-member committee of "distinguished Americans, both Jewish and non-Jewish" be appointed by the president to resolve those questions and to make recommendations within six months. There should be "sufficiently wide support," the memo concluded, so that private funds could be used to pay for the building and, in whole or in part, for the maintenance. "We do not believe that any federal dollars will need to be expended. However, for other reasons, we might want to have the government contribute toward the memorial, if not through direct expenditures then at least through the gift of land." (It would follow from the project's history that these "other reasons" might be to please the alienated organized Jewish community.) There is a handwritten notation on the memorandum: "I concur—and so does Cy, Z.B.," indicating that Zbigniew Brzezinski and Secretary of State Cyrus Vance were consulted and approved of the plan.

The idea of a President's Commission on the Holocaust, Eizenstat told me, came to his attention through Ellen Goldstein, who got the idea from Mark Siegel. "As one who lost relatives in the Holocaust," he said, "it seemed compelling to me. I mentioned it to President Carter and sent him a memo. The president's major concern was financial. It didn't take a lot of arm twisting. We talked about the idea of a commission and a suitable memorial. He asked who should be the chairperson, and I said that only one person, Elie Wiesel, was suitable. I called Wiesel, and he was out of the country. When I found him, he was very excited, agreed, and came to see the president."[16]

Wiesel, who later resigned as chairman, told me that the commission was created for political purposes. From the beginning it was a political act, he told me, because President Carter wanted to ingratiate himself with the Jewish community and realized that this was an important issue. Carter's desire to get the Jewish vote was behind the idea, Wiesel said, and Eizenstat was the person who engineered it.[17]

Asked whether the purpose of creating a Holocaust commission was political, Eizenstat hedged, remarking: "Every decision has political and substantive aspects. Sometimes you make a decision that is not political, or you try to minimize the politics. This, to me, was long overdue, because of revisionism, lack of records, and survivors dying. I felt it was extremely strong substantively, or I would not have recommended it even if it had good political aspects. Politically, it showed the president's sensitivity to Jewish concerns at a time when some Jews were still not comfortable with a Southern Baptist. It was not done for political reasons, but we knew it should be popular in the Jewish community."[18]

Mark Siegel was more direct about the political implications of the President's Commission on the Holocaust: "The Holocaust memorial was born out of politics and it was born out of domestic political crisis. I know that's the case. I know that's what happened," he told me. He added that it went on to do very good things, he was happy it was being built, and "every time I go by that site I feel wonderful." Nevertheless, it was created for political purposes.[19]

As Eizenstat had suggested in the April 25 memorandum to Carter, the president announced, at the celebration of Israel's thirtieth anniversary on May 1, 1978, at the White House, that he was appointing a commission to recommend an official American Holocaust memorial. He followed Eizenstat's lead in tying memorialization of the Holocaust both to Israel and to the United States, as well as to a broader symbol of human rights violation. At the May 1 ceremony, which was attended by Israeli prime minister Menachem Begin and one thousand invited guests (most of whom were American Jewish community leaders, government officials, and rabbis), Carter referred to the Holocaust as "the ultimate in man's inhumanity to man." The six million Jews murdered by the Nazis died in part "because the entire world turned its back on them," he stated, and a memorial would "insure that we in the United States never forget." He added that "we will never waver from our deep friendship and partnership with Israel and our total, absolute commitment to Israel's security."[20]

The creation of a President's Commission now moved quickly, especially since Senator Wendell Anderson (D-Minn.) had introduced a bill during the last week of April to establish a national memorial to victims of the Holocaust. This bill would have authorized the president to appoint an eleven-member commission to develop plans for design, construction, and location of a memorial. There is evidence that the president's staff wanted to "beat the Senate to the punch" so that credit would not be diluted. This is shown most obviously in a July 20, 1978, memorandum from Eizenstat and Lipshutz to Tim Kraft, the appointments secretary, which included the following paragraph: *"We would like to get a memo to the President shortly after his return from Bonn* [emphasis in original]. Senator Anderson, who had introduced legislation to form a similar commission before the President's announcement, is getting pressured to pursue his legislation because of apparent White House lack of interest. David Rubenstein and Ellen Goldstein from Stu's staff will be available to assist you and your staff in preparing a memo for the President."[21]

An earlier memorandum from Goldstein to Eizenstat on May 2, 1978, also indicates pressure to initiate the implementation phase. Handwritten across the top is a note (most likely by Eizenstat): "Ellen: Please set up [a staff meeting] ASAP. Let's move on this." This memo, too, takes note of the proposed Anderson legislation. Goldstein urged the staff to "move quickly and wisely" to fulfill Carter's "public commitment" to create a Holocaust memorial.[22] A day earlier, the day of the White House ceremony, Eizenstat had written to Carter that he had spoken with several senators and congressmen who agreed that announcement of a Holocaust commission was a good idea and appropriate at that time. On the bottom of this memo, Carter wrote by hand: "Stu, Bob—Be careful *not* to make any promises—JC."[23]

The president was thus willing to make vague commitments, but not ready to back them with concrete action.

President Carter's staff, however, was ready to move ahead with specific action. They began to create a political coalition, under their control, that would get the project started. On May 10, 1978, Ellen Goldstein wrote to Stuart Eizenstat, presenting a "rough agenda" of issues that needed to be resolved before the commission could be named and start its work. She was concerned about the choice of commission members, noting: "Clearly, the most important issue to settle is whether the Commission is to be a 'blue-ribbon' panel, but there are also other issues about Commission members that must be resolved: Jewish and non-Jewish proportion, bipartisan participation, federal arts officials, etc."[24] She included a list of potential candidates. As a possible chairman, she suggested Arthur Krim, president of Orion Films, because of the following qualities: "keen political skills, articulate moderator, Democrat, consummate fund-raiser, and he is highly regarded and respected." Political considerations were thus clearly spelled out in black and white. Furthermore, Eizenstat's recollection that Wiesel was the "only person" considered "suitable" for the chairmanship—which is generally accepted as a fact—was not accurate.[25]

Goldstein then implied that the administration staff, rather than the commission, would be making some crucial decisions: "We may want to further influence the Commission's decision concerning what the memorial should be, where it should be located and how it should be funded. Many believe that, in order for it to be an 'official' memorial, it must be in Washington. It is also accepted that the memorial should not be just a marble statue, but educational as well. However, the Commission must be careful not to add further to the competition and rivalry, both for funds and recognition, in this area." Funding would be private, she reiterated, but the government "must have a significant role in this effort."[26] Goldstein did not explain what she thought this "significant role" should be.

By July 20, 1978, the project had moved forward. Eizenstat and Lipshutz wrote a memorandum to Tim Kraft, informing him that they had contacted members of the Jewish community about the choice of Elie Wiesel as chairman of the commission: "Wiesel is the undisputed expert on the holocaust [sic] period and his appointment would be without controversy, but his political and fund-raising abilities are not clearly established." Again, the considerations were political. Also included was a list of recommendations for advisory board members, and for the commission itself, which, they suggested, should include camp survivors, a rabbi, and recognized leaders, including representatives from the arts. They also pointed out that they had recommended four women and a black.[27]

On September 9, 1978, Eizenstat and Goldstein sent President Carter another memorandum, recommending that he sign a congressional resolution (H.R. 1014) that designated April 28 and 29 as "Days of Remembrance of Victims of the Holocaust." They suggested that the President's Commission on the Holocaust, which he had promised to appoint on May 1, be announced at the same time.[28]

On September 18, Lipshutz and Eizenstat sent President Carter a memorandum including their list of twenty-four recommended commission members, with Wiesel as chairman. (Coincidentally, the Camp David accords providing a framework for peace between Israel and Egypt were signed the day before.) Then, on November 1, 1978, Goldstein sent Eizenstat, Lipshutz, and Ed Sanders (then liaison to the Jewish community) a memorandum referring to political considerations regarding public announcement of the new commission. The announcement would be on Monday, at the recommendation of the Press Office; Monday is a usually a slow news day, and thus good for getting press coverage. Courtesy calls would also be made to congressional offices. Goldstein's memo also cited possible roles for the religious press and the Washington Jewish community. Elie Wiesel was announced as chairman of the commission and Rabbi Irving "Yitz" Greenberg as its executive director. The commission's thirty-four members included survivors, Holocaust scholars, elected officials, and other prominent Jews and non-Jews.[29] (Elie Wiesel told me that Carter's commission continued to be political after its creation, because there was not a single Republican on it.[30] However, at least one member, Congressman S. William Green, was a Republican.)

On November 1, 1978, President Carter signed Executive Order 12093, officially establishing the President's Commission on the Holocaust. Its charge was to submit a report "with respect to the establishment and maintenance of an appropriate memorial to those who perished in the Holocaust, to examine the feasibility for the creation and maintenance of the memorial through contributions by the American people, and to recommend appropriate ways for the nation to commemorate April 28 and 29, 1979, which the Congress has resolved shall be 'Days of Remembrance of Victims of the Holocaust.'"[31]

By signing this executive order, which created an interest group and specified a memorial designated by both the president and Congress, Carter created an "iron triangle" with a twist. Political scientists designate as an "iron triangle" the solid trilateral bond formed by an interest group, its advocates in Congress, and an executive branch agency. Government policies emerge from this closed triangle of interests, with members of Congress passing favorable legislation, agency bureaucrats implementing these mandates, and special-interest groups supporting the helpful elected officials (with votes and campaign contributions).

President Carter's Holocaust memorialization "iron triangle" had a twist in that Carter created the interest group, and the executive sought out alliances both with the interest group and with Congress. According to political scientist Harold Seidman, the relationship between a government agency and an interest group is based on mutuality of concerns, generally established by provisions of laws enacted by Congress.[32] In the case of the Holocaust commission, the dynamics of the iron triangle were somewhat different. Here, the president, rather than Congress, initiated the legal means for uniting forces to accomplish his goal. He even created an interest group, and then included ten members of Congress as part of the thirty-four-member commission, which was the interest-group "angle" of the triangle. As we will see, the political coalition behind the New York Holocaust museum project also includes a blend of elected officials as interest-group members.

The main purpose of the commission, whose first meeting was held on February 15, 1979, in Washington, was to recommend to President Carter a suitable memorial. As commission member and congressman Stephen J. Solarz told his constituents, "There are no constraints on what we may recommend other than the limits of our own imagination and the requirements of good taste. We are free to recommend that the funds for such an endeavor be public or private or both. If a physical structure—be it a monument or a museum—is going to be constructed, we can suggest that it be built in Washington or New York or any other location we deem suitable."[33]

On March 25, 1979, Solarz held a public hearing in his Brooklyn district to hear what his constituents recommended as an appropriate memorial. On April 6, 1979, another member of the commission and of Congress, Representative S. William Green, conducted a similar hearing in his Manhattan district. Herbert Rickman, Special Assistant to Mayor Koch, testified at the Green hearing that the national memorial should be in New York City. "We fought against having it in Washington. We fought to have it here in New York," he told me. "I remember testifying for the city and organizing others to testify for the city at a hearing in New York by the President's Commission. We made a very telling argument that this is the largest Jewish city, largest survivor city in the United States—that it really belonged here. Also because of the heavy tourist concentration, that it belonged here. When we went down to defeat on that, then we began in earnest to plan for it [a separate memorial] in New York City."[34]

Records of the two hearings reveal that most of the scholars, authors, religious and organizational leaders, and survivors who testified did not address the issue of location. Because they were testifying before a presidential commission, they seem to have taken for granted that the site would be Washington, D.C. There are only three people whose available recorded testimony made a "pitch" for New York City as the site of the proposed memorial. Rickman's is the strongest, as noted in his prepared remarks for the March 25 Solarz hearing, speaking on behalf of Mayor Koch: "How appropriate such a memorial would be in the city which is the center—symbolically and factually—of immigration to the United States," he said. "New York City is also the center of Holocaust research. Nowhere else can one find resources such as those of our academic and intellectual communities and our great libraries and archives. Nowhere else are there centers such as the YIVO Institute, Leo Baeck Institute, Yeshiva University, or the Oral History [archive] of the [Brooklyn] Center for Holocaust Studies. . . . Not only does New York have the largest Jewish community of any city in the 4,000-year history of the Jews; among our residents is also the largest group of Holocaust survivors. Obviously, New York is the place where such a living memorial belongs, in a setting both appropriate and enduring."[35]

According to handwritten notes from the April 6 Green hearing, Rickman presented similar remarks there. Notes from the April 6 testimony of Malcolm Hoenlein, then executive director of the Jewish Community Relations Council of New York (JCRC), reveal that he, too, advocated New York as the site. Among his reasons, he cited New York City as the major center of scholarship on the Holocaust, the country's media center, business capital, and focus of tourism with 17 million visitors per year. He added that the mayor's commitment was matched by that of the entire Jewish community, and that Jewish groups were ready to join the effort.[36] Congressman Marvin Greisman, who then represented the Lower East Side, sent a letter to Congressman Green outlining his proposal to establish a Holocaust Memorial "both in the nation's capitol [sic] and in New York City—the heart of America." More specifically, he said the memorial should be on the Lower East Side.[37]

In all of the testimony available from the 1979 hearings, only Rickman, Hoenlein, and Greisman advocated a national memorial in New York City. All three of them had an obvious vested interest: it would have been a real coup for the mayor and for the head of the umbrella of local Jewish organizations, and, of course, for the congressman representing a heavily Jewish district. For many others who testified—for example, heads of other Jewish institutions, most with their own Holocaust education programs—a new major institution could be viewed as competition. They therefore would have had no desire to push for its location in New York City.

It is significant to note that George Klein did not testify or submit a written statement at either hearing, according to the records of the U.S. Holocaust Memorial Commission. There is no documentation, but it is common knowledge in Jewish communal circles in New York City that Klein and Hoenlein were extremely close. Klein was a founding vice president of the JCRC, which Hoenlein created as a power base for himself and its founders, many of whom were real estate developers. Klein was also close to Mayor Koch, who described him as an "old friend."[38] Rickman, Koch's political liaison to the organized Jewish community, was in a position to bring together Hoenlein, Koch, and Klein to launch the Mayor's Task Force on the Holocaust, after the national project selected Washington as its site. It is likely that Hoenlein encouraged Klein to become involved with the Mayor's Task Force on the Holocaust in 1981, although no one seems able or wishes to recall the exact circumstances through which this occurred. Because of the close connection between these people, Rickman's and Hoenlein's appearance at the 1979 hearings could be said to be setting the stage for Klein's entrance on the scene two years later. JCRC had dropped the idea of creating a New York City Holocaust memorial in 1978, after President Carter announced the national project. Now both Mayor Koch (and Rickman) and JCRC wanted the national project to be located in New York City, where they could have a piece of the pie.

Although Rickman said he tried hard to have the federal Holocaust memorial located in New York City (and Mayor Koch wrote to President Carter on behalf of a city site), this possibility apparently was never realistic. Rabbi Yitz Greenberg, the first director of the President's Commission, told me: "I don't think it's correct that New York was considered. I wasn't privy to the first conversation that Stuart Eizenstat had with President Carter, but the idea of New York City as an alternate to Washington for the federal memorial was never seriously discussed." He said the idea of a national memorial in New York "didn't make any sense at all." Greenberg explained that, in the thinking of the President's Commission, "the federal government was Washington, close to the White House, and New York was a different constituency, if you will."[39]

Hyman Bookbinder, a member of the commission, recalled that the idea of New York City as a location was quickly dismissed. "At the very first meetings, there was a question of location," he told me. "But this was one of the first things decided and is in the minutes. The decision was made that the memorial was national and should be in Washington."[40] Eizenstat concurred: "I think it was always assumed the memorial would be in Washington, but it was up to the commission, which was monitored by presidential staff."[41] At its second meeting on April 24, 1979, the President's Commission recommended that the memorial be in Washington, and it approved this decision at a third meeting on June 7. On September 27, 1979, the President's Commission presented its official report to President Carter, stating "Location: The Commission resolved that the memorial should be built in Washington, D.C., the capital of the country and the seat of government, for the materials to be presented by it affect all Americans."[42]

On October 7, 1980, Public Law 96–388 was enacted by the

Ninety-sixth Congress, establishing the United States Holocaust Memorial Council, which would "plan, construct, and oversee the operation of, a permanent living memorial museum to the victims of the Holocaust" as well as "develop a plan for carrying out the recommendations of the President's Commission on the Holocaust in its report to the President of September 27, 1979."[43] The government was to provide the site, but funding was, for the most part, to be private. This law set in place the federal plan to create a Holocaust museum.

8

Mayor Koch's Holocaust Memorial Task Force

George Klein is an old friend, he's a very proud Jew, he's a very rich man, and he was an immediate candidate to be involved—by virtue of all of that.
—Edward I. Koch, May 18, 1990

The complex coalition of political forces attempting to create a Holocaust memorial museum in New York City during the late 1980s and early 1990s had its roots in a unilateral act by Mayor Edward I. Koch in 1981. Unlike President Jimmy Carter's 1978 initiative, the start of Mayor Koch's involvement with Holocaust memorialization is difficult to pinpoint. There is no "smoking gun" of staff memoranda in the Municipal Archive (where they should be, if they existed). Staff memoranda in the Carter Library make it possible to trace the allegedly step-by-step political thinking behind the creation of the President's Commission. In New York, where the original cast of players was much smaller (mainly Mayor Koch and his special assistant, Herbert Rickman, along with probable behind-the-scenes maneuvering by the head of the Jewish Community Relations Council, Malcolm Hoenlein), the absence of such documentation is evidence that decisions were informal and oral. A high-level JCRC staff member who worked with Rickman confirmed that there would be no written records, as there are for the Carter administration, documenting the genesis of such a project in New York City.

It is also difficult to pinpoint the source of the idea for three other reasons: The President's Commission, and even the U.S. Holocaust Memorial Council that succeeded it, had been set in place before Koch announced the creation of his task force in July 1981. The federal project, by virtue of its very existence and other factors discussed here and in Chapter 7, influenced and sometimes intervened in the New York City process. Furthermore, because New York City may be considered the Jewish "capital" of the United States, housing headquarters of most of the national Jewish organizations and the largest number of Holocaust survivor groups outside of Israel, the concentrated Jewish communal life often creates a complex web. For more than a century, this city has been the center of Jewish American culture. This abundance of Jews and things Jewish has generated a density and diversity of minor and major Jewish organizations that are often in competition, with their leaders jockeying for position and acknowledgment. In addition, unlike Washington, D.C., New York City had a record, dating back to 1946, of unsuccessful attempts to create a memorial. Thus Mayor Koch, unlike President Carter, was not starting with a "clean slate." Although this was the first time a mayor of New York created a Jewish interest group to implement a Holocaust memorial project, similar interest groups had tried to influence five mayors prior to Koch. Historically, Jewish communal activists seeking a memorial had been initiators; with respect to the Koch administration, they were reactive. Unlike his predecessors, Koch made memorializing the Holocaust his own idea.

The recollections of Herbert Rickman, the political entrepreneur who created Koch's Holocaust task force and commission, do not fit the chronology of the documentable facts. "Elections were in 1977 and Koch was elected," Rickman told me. "During the transition, I had a firm commitment in my own mind that we were going to create a memorial. I reached out to the survivors, such as Ben Meed and others. No one was encouraging at the time, because of their bitterness over earlier experiences. They said it would take a miracle. The mayor had given me the tacit okay to go ahead, although he was not very involved. The idea was that it had to be Jewish and not just bricks and mortar. The concept from the very start was a living memorial." In other words, the memorial would be a museum rather than a monument, and the historical framework of the museum and its component educational programs would have a particularistic Jewish approach to the Holocaust. "We then began in the early days of the administration, in 1978," Rickman added, "to assemble people, ideas, talking to leaders of the community, to gauge the support."[1]

There is no evidence that such early discussions took place. Neither the files of the Warsaw Ghetto Resistance Organization (WAGRO), the Municipal Archives, nor available files in the JCRC office or elsewhere show any record of a meeting between Rickman and Meed, the JCRC leaders, or other survivors or community leaders at this time. Although there are no staff memoranda documenting the creation of a Holocaust memorial during the early Koch years (before April 1981), copies of letters should be on file, especially with WAGRO, if such a meeting had taken place. If Rickman had written to or spoken with Ben Meed (who heads WAGRO) in 1978, there is no record of it. Even if all communication was oral and informal, Meed's first specific recollection is of a June or July 1979 meeting. The first letters on file are from Meed to Koch on June 26, 1979, and to Rickman on July 17, 1979. Since the written record in Meed's archives shows that Meed corresponded with elected officials about this issue for many years, the absence of records of such correspondence with Koch or Rickman before June 1979 probably indicates that Rickman's recollected chronology is not accurate. If informal oral discussion had taken place, no one but Rickman remembers it. Although it is possible and even likely that such a topic could have been discussed, no person or available record can corroborate it.

The only other person with an early recollection of the subject is Koch's 1977 mayoral campaign aide Manny Behar, who said the idea of a Holocaust memorial was part of the "Jewish laundry list" in mayoral candidate Koch's Jewish New Year message that year. Behar, who was a college student when he worked on the campaign, told me that he placed the idea of Holocaust memorialization there, without first discussing it with Koch.[2] However, there is nothing to substantiate this claim. Moreover, if Behar's memory is accurate, Koch seems not to have been involved in the decision to make Holocaust commemoration part of his Jewish agenda in the 1977 mayoral race.

The first available record of Ed Koch's public expression of support for a memorial dates from April 1979, one and a half years after his election and two years before he set in place his Holocaust memorial task force. At the commemoration of the thirty-sixth anniversary of the Warsaw Ghetto uprising, sponsored by WAGRO on April 22, 1979, Koch said in front of thousands of participants, "Yes, Mr. Meed, a living, permanent memorial to the victims of the Holocaust must rise here in New York City. It belongs here. And *here* it will eventually be built. I support this undertaking as a Jew, as a New Yorker, as mayor of this city, and as a human being who, with all of you, is totally committed to commemorating the searing inhumanities of the Holocaust, so that never again will they befoul and shame the history of mankind."[3]

WAGRO's annual Holocaust memorial service, which has drawn thousands of participants each year, may have helped to convince Koch that creating a memorial was a good idea politically. According to Meed, Koch became involved with the idea of a memorial because of his annual participation in the WAGRO commemoration. "I think the commemoration had a tremendous influence on Koch," he told me.[4] Meed was referring to the emotional impact of the event, which may have influenced Koch. However, the huge attendance—standing room only and thousands of people listening via outside loudspeakers—would also influence an astute elected official such as Koch. Those who attended the WAGRO memorial service were potential voters and political contributors, and they were committed to commemorating the Holocaust.

Shortly after the 1979 WAGRO memorial ceremonies, then comptroller Harrison J. Goldin stepped briefly into the picture. In a letter to Ben Meed on June 14, 1979, he mentioned telling Mayor Koch about Meed's idea of using the Cultural Center at Columbus Circle for a Holocaust memorial. Koch suggested that Meed send the city a written proposal, Goldin wrote.[5] (Meed had originally presented this idea to the Beame administration in 1976, as detailed in Chapter 6.) On June 28, 1979, Meed sent such a proposal to both Mayor Koch and New York governor Hugh L. Carey. "The purpose of this memorandum is to present a proposal for the establishment of a suitable memorial in New York City to the Jewish victims of the Holocaust in World War II," he wrote. He pointed to the precedent of the President's Commission, reminding the mayor and governor that "the significance of commemorating the victims of the Holocaust recently has been given an added recognition by the President and Congress of the United States in establishing, on November 1, 1978, the President's Commission on the Holocaust and its Advisory Board." Himself a member of this advisory board, Meed reminded Mayor Koch and Governor Carey that the commission had "expressed itself in favor of setting up a living institutional memorial which would contain meeting spaces, archives, libraries, exhibitions, and other educational facilities related to the Holocaust." He then pointed out that the federal memorial "most likely" would be created in Washington and that, WAGRO believed, "a similar memorial should also be created in New York City, the site of the United Nations as well as the site of the largest single Jewish urban community in the world."[6]

WAGRO had "conducted an extensive review of the different opportunities in New York City for the implementation of the proposal to establish a suitable memorial," the letter noted, and had concluded that the New York City Cultural Center at Columbus Circle was "the most promising opportunity." Meed closed by indirectly promising the mayor and governor the kind of acclaim that had already been given to the president: "Recently we have congratulated President Carter for taking the initiative in establishing the President's Commission on the Holocaust. Similarly, we are now looking toward Governor Carey and Mayor Koch in expectation of their support and leadership in establishing a Holocaust memorial in the city of New York."[7] Meed's appeal to both the mayor and the governor could be seen as a clue to the way the issue would develop in 1986, with both Mayor Koch and Governor Cuomo heading the coalition responsible for building a memorial.

In a letter dated two days earlier, June 26, 1979, Ben Meed had written to Mayor Koch asking for an appointment to discuss the New York Cultural Center at Columbus Circle as the site for a permanent Holocaust memorial.[8] This idea was later vetoed by the donor of the building. On September 21, 1979, the president of the Gulf & Western Foundation, which was about to give the Cultural Center property on Columbus Circle to the city, wrote Koch that the company refused to have it used as a Holocaust memorial. According to the foundation president, Samuel J. Silberman: "As worthy as such a memorial might be, it would be a complete perversion of the reason we bought the building in the first place," which was for use as a cultural center.[9]

Although, according to Herb Rickman, the Koch administration was thinking about a Holocaust memorial from the very beginning of his first term, which began in January 1978, there is no substantial evidence of Koch's interest in a memorial until his April 22, 1979, speech and his response to Meed's June 26 and June 28 letters. Meed's letters that year may have planted the seed, following President Carter's intervention on the issue a year earlier, but Koch still did not act for two more years. Furthermore, Ben Meed was not a major player in the organized Jewish community in 1979. His power base, WAGRO and the annual commemoration of the Warsaw Ghetto uprising, was connected with but not particularly important to the community. After he headed the first International Gathering of Holocaust Survivors in Jerusalem in 1981 and the first American Gathering of Jewish Holocaust Survivors in 1983, he became more prominent. Thus in 1979, Koch did not feel pressured to act in response to Meed's suggestion that he create a Holocaust memorial. When Mayor Koch did initiate a memorial project in 1981, it was not at the request of Meed or of other leaders of the organized Jewish community. When he finally acted on the issue, he took the lead, co-opted the idea, and made it his own at a time that was politically expedient. Rather than asking a survivor such as Meed to head his effort, he chose George Klein, a major developer who was his close friend, political ally, and a founding officer of Malcolm Hoenlein's JCRC.

Meanwhile, in response to Ben Meed's 1979 letter about Columbus Circle, a meeting with Herb Rickman evidently took place on July 16. On July 17, Meed then wrote to Rickman, thanking him for the meeting of the day before, at which they had discussed "the proposal for a holocaust [sic] memorial in the city of New York." This letter is the first available written evidence that the mayor's office was thinking about creating a New York City Holocaust Commission. "I should also like to refer to the proposal to establish a Mayor's Commission on the Holocaust," Meed wrote. He then tried to protect his own and his organization's interests, suggesting that survivors, including WAGRO members, be part of the commission; and he offered to recommend specific names.[10]

Koch's intervention in 1981, with his creation of a Holocaust task force and subsequent commission, was beneficial both to the organized Jewish community and to Koch himself. It initiated a

Approximately fifteen thousand people attended the Riverside Park dedication ceremonies for the anticipated first Holocaust memorial in New York City on October 19, 1947.

Photograph by John D. Schiff. Courtesy of YIVO Institute for Jewish Research.

During the ceremonies on October 19, 1947, Mayor William O'Dwyer holds a bronze casket containing soil from a Czechoslovakian concentration camp as he stands in an excavation on the site where a Holocaust memorial was to be erected on Riverside Drive. Rabbi Israel Goldstein of Congregation B'nai Jeshurun hands O'Dwyer a scroll written by Dr. I. Herzog, Chief Rabbi of Palestine, to be deposited with the casket under the cornerstone of the memorial. Also pictured here *(foreground)*: Borough President Hugo E. Rogers; Rabbi Goldstein; Jurai Slavak, Czechoslovakian Ambassador; Henri Bonnet, French Ambassador; Adolph Lerner, chairman of the memorial committee; The Rt. Rev. S. Harrington Littell; Msgr. Francis W. Walsh; Dr. J. Thon, President of the National Organization of Polish Jews.

Courtesy of AP/Wide World Photo.

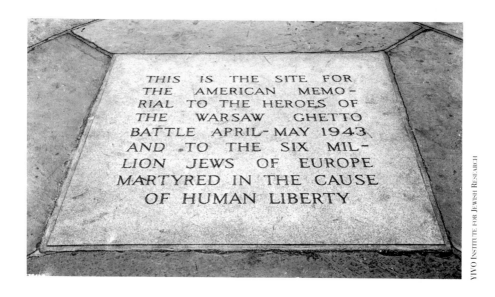

THIS IS THE SITE FOR
THE AMERICAN MEMO-
RIAL TO THE HEROES OF
THE WARSAW GHETTO
BATTLE APRIL-MAY 1943
AND TO THE SIX MIL-
LION JEWS OF EUROPE
MARTYRED IN THE CAUSE
OF HUMAN LIBERTY

Two views of the cornerstone of the original Riverside Park Holocaust memorial project dedicated on October 19, 1947.

Installation view of the exhibition "American Memorial to Six Million Jews of Europe, by Percival Goodman" (January 17–February 22, 1950). Goodman's model of a sixty-foot stone pylon topped by a bronze menorah was favored by the memorial committee in 1949 but was rejected by Parks Commissioner Robert Moses.

Photograph © 1995 The Museum of Modern Art, New York. Courtesy of The Museum of Modern Art, New York.

The memorial design for Riverside Park by Eric Mendelsohn and Ivan Mestrovic, approved by the New York City Art Commission in 1951, was to include an eighty-foot pylon of the Ten Commandments, a 100-foot bas-relief, and a large carving of Moses.

Courtesy of YIVO Institute for Jewish Research

Nathan Rapoport's design for the Riverside Park site commissioned by the Zygelboim Memorial Committee in 1962, a figure with outstretched arms engulfed in flames and thorns, was rejected by the New York City Art Commission.

Courtesy of YIVO Institute for Jewish Research

Nathan Rapoport's design for Riverside Park, which consisted of a twenty-foot concrete Torah scroll with bas-reliefs and inscriptions related to the Holocaust, was submitted to the Memorial Committee for the Six Million Jewish Martyrs and Heroes in 1964, rejected by the New York City Art Commission, and eventually installed in Israel.

Courtesy of Alan Schneider, Director, B'nai B'rith World Center, Jerusalem.

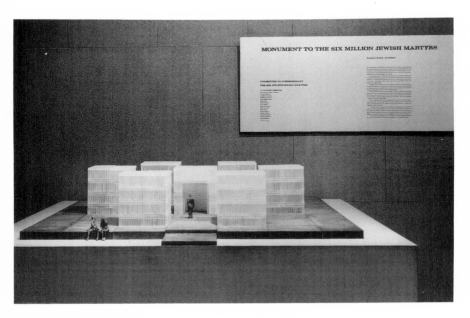

Installation view of the model by Louis Kahn for a memorial featuring seven glass piers each ten feet square and eleven feet high placed on a sixty-foot square granite pedestal. The model was approved by the New York City Art Commission in 1968 and was to be installed in Battery Park at the southern tip of Manhattan. The Museum of Modern Art exhibition, "Memorial to the Six Million Jewish Martyrs," displayed the model from October 17 through November 17, 1968.

Photograph © 1995 The Museum of Modern Art, New York. Courtesy of The Museum of Modern Art.

The U.S. Custom House, located in lower Manhattan and which currently houses the Museum of the American Indian, was approved as the site for the New York City Holocaust Memorial Commission's proposed museum in 1984 prior to the decision to move the project to Battery Park City.

Photograph by Jeffrey Tinsley © 1994 Smithsonian Institution, photo no. 91-8296 6A. Courtesy of the Smithsonian Institution.

Rendering of the Museum of Jewish Heritage and Memorial by James Stewart Polshek & Partners was originally planned for Battery Park City in 1986 and included a residential tower.

Courtesy of James Stewart Polshek & Partners and the Museum of Jewish Heritage, New York. Artist: Mona Brown.

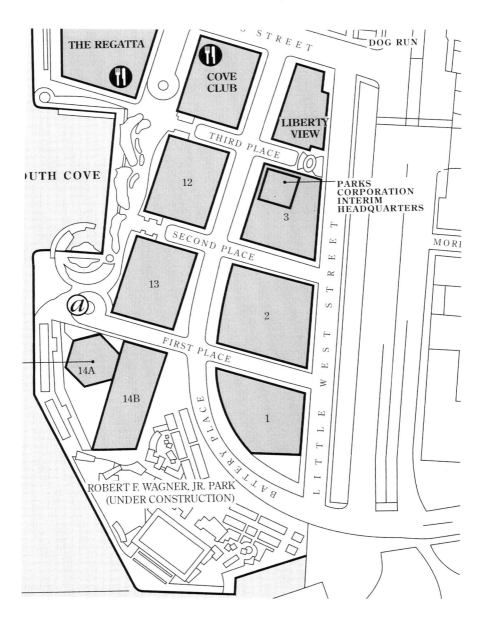

A map of the southern portion of Battery Park City, the site of A Living Memorial to the Holocaust - Museum of Jewish Heritage. The museum (Site 14A) is adjacent to the esplanade along the Hudson River, south of First Place and north of the South Gardens.

Courtesy of the Battery Park City Authority.

The skyline of lower Manhattan from the Hudson River, with a circle indicating the site of the Museum of Jewish Heritage in Battery Park City.

An early model of the Museum of Jewish Heritage designed by architect Kevin Roche to rise eighty-five feet in the air on Site 14A of Battery Park City, and displayed at the October 16, 1994 ground-breaking ceremonies.

Courtesy of Kevin Roche John Dinkeloo Associates and the Museum of Jewish Heritage, New York.

Elected officials and leaders of the Museum of Jewish Heritage project initiate construction at Battery Park City with a ground-breaking ceremony on October 16, 1994. George Klein (*wearing hat*) is in the center and Mayor Rudolph Giuliani and Governor Mario Cuomo are on his left.

Courtesy of Peter Goldberg and the Museum of Jewish Heritage, New York.

The most recent architectural model of the Museum of Jewish Heritage designed by Kevin Roche, which became a reality with the ground breaking —and a projected 1997 opening date.

Courtesy of Kevin Roche John Dinkeloo Associates and the Museum of Jewish Heritage.

The foundation outlining the hexagonal shape of the Museum of Jewish Heritage, under construction by late 1995, with the Turner Construction Company as general contractor. By the spring of 1996, the steel frame of the building had been erected.

Courtesy of Peter Goldberg and the Museum of Jewish Heritage, New York.

coalition of political forces that changed over time, with these changes and unforeseen external conditions resulting in years of impasse. However, in its initial stage, the coalition represented a reciprocal political contact between the organized Jewish community of New York City and the mayor. The community, especially chairman George Klein and the survivor groups, gained prestige from this recognition by the mayor of the importance of a major memorial project. Even the organized Jewish community had treated survivors as "second-class citizens," whether out of guilt or fear of their being different.[11] Suddenly these survivors became first-class. Klein gained a visible and prominent role as the Jewish community's leader for the project. And Mayor Koch, by intervening and making the memorial an official project of his city government, also gained prestige among his constituents in the organized Jewish community. Thus Koch's intervention in Holocaust memorialization was mutually beneficial for him and Jewish communal leaders.

In his classic study of the dynamics of influence and power in Chicago during the 1950s, political scientist Edward C. Banfield analyzed how government sometimes intervenes and creates its own interest group to advocate its ideas. Often the situation is a "two-way street": Organizations that want something from the government use "civic leaders," or civic groups, as their intermediaries in dealing with political leaders; and political leaders similarly use "civic leaders" as intermediaries, for example, by appointing them to commissions (such as Koch's Holocaust commission). Often political leaders make up their minds in advance with regard to a commission's decision, and they use these "intermediaries for other purposes than those that are publicly announced"—to obtain campaign contributions, for example. Political leaders use these civic leaders for a variety of purposes, according to Banfield, among them to communicate or negotiate with constituent groups, to create a favorable climate of public opinion, to legitimate plans, and to disarm criticism by directing it away from themselves.[12]

Banfield's analysis can be applied to Mayor Koch's Holocaust memorial project to an extent. In the case of the New York City project, however, there is another dimension to the reciprocity, or "two-way street." Herb Rickman's decision to encourage Koch to support a Holocaust memorial task force and subsequent New York City Holocaust Memorial Commission was not only based on Rickman's determination that this was a preference of a powerful constituent group—the organized Jewish community. Rickman and Koch went one step further: they crafted from this larger interest group, the organized Jewish community, a task force and then commission that included powerful and wealthy Jews—real estate developers and attorneys—whom they were also courting for another purpose.

Thus the reciprocity between Koch and members of the commission who were involved in real estate development operated on two levels: in one sense, they initiated a project to help each other memorialize the Holocaust; and, on a second level, they were working together to become wealthy or more powerful. Koch gave the developers tax incentives and zoning concessions, and they gave the mayor the bulk of his campaign contributions. As Jack Newfield and Wayne Barrett wrote of Koch's connections to Klein and other real estate developers: "The dollars rolled into the 1981 Koch campaign coffers in the millions, primarily from the very real estate interests that had gotten fat on the tax abatements granted by his administration. It didn't hurt that the man collecting contributions as Koch's campaign finance chairman was the former deputy mayor who'd awarded the abatements, Peter Solomon."[13] Nevertheless, despite their project's political expediency, both Herb Rickman and Mayor Koch told me that they both were personally committed to memorializing the Holocaust.[14]

While there is no written record of how the idea of the task force originated, both Rickman and Ben Meed stated that the idea came from Rickman, on behalf of Koch. Meed told me: "I met with Herb Rickman. I remember it was in a coffee shop near City Hall, and we discussed the creation of such a commission. Herb Rickman was the man who kept the contacts. He came to me." Meed does not remember the date of the meeting to which he referred.[15]

Subsequent to the correspondence between Rickman and Meed in July 1979, I found no records regarding the creation of a Holocaust memorial commission or task force until April 22, 1981, an election year. The idea seems to have fallen between the cracks for two years. When questioned about this lapse, Koch told me: "If you're the mayor of the city of New York, you have to be bouncing a thousand different things in the air at the same time. Then it depends on what the pressures are, who talks to you, whether something suddenly becomes predominant because the editorial writers are writing about it. I cannot tell you what the pressures were at that time. I only know that there were several things that I've always wanted to be identified with, as having been instrumental in creating them. One was the Holocaust museum, doing it here in New York City, I thought it was very important. The second one I always wanted to do something about was a ticker tape parade for the Vietnam veterans and a monument to them. I did both the ticker tape parade and monument, and the Holocaust museum—at least I moved them along."[16]

Rickman told me he was "hazy" on the details and had not looked at the files in years. He blamed Jimmy Carter's announcement of the creation of his President's Commission on the Holocaust for "sidetracking" the New York project. "I know the community knew we were doing it and there was excitement about it," he said. "And then, lo and behold, word came that there was a commission that had been created by Carter to determine where this would take place—and we got sidetracked because we then tried to get the [national] memorial in New York."[17]

Carter made his initial announcement on May 1, 1978. The first proof of *preliminary* discussions between Herb Rickman and Holocaust survivors is the correspondence of June–July 1979 with Ben Meed; and the task force was not formed until two years after that. This discrepancy in timing cannot be accounted for. It is evidence that Mayor Koch's creation of a Holocaust memorial task force was not placed on the agenda as early as Rickman claims. It was not, in fact, publicly announced until July 1981, perfect timing to help Mayor Koch in his bid for reelection that fall. Given Koch's political shrewdness, it would follow that his decision to create the task force was determined in part by what he thought his Jewish constituents wanted, which in turn would be most effective in arousing and mobilizing public opinion on his behalf.

After Mayor Koch's political entrepreneur, Herb Rickman, had been influenced by what he thought were the wishes of the organized Jewish constituency, he finally began, by April 22, 1981, to set the agenda for a Holocaust memorial task force. This is the date of the first available memorandum on the subject.[18] This memo has neither a "to" or "from" on it, but its placement in Rickman's section of the Koch records at the Municipal Archives

indicates that he was at least involved. Since the subject is a
meeting with George Klein, and both Rickman and Koch give
Rickman credit for asking Klein to head the project, it is likely
that the memo is from, or possibly to, Rickman.

The memorandum proposes the creation of a task force for a
duration of four to five months, beginning with a target date for
its announcement on May 3, 1981. The scope of its activities
would be to determine the nature, site, and financing of a Holocaust memorial, and to recommend a permanent body for developing the memorial. A press conference was planned for
May 3, with clearance needed from all members before the public
announcement. George Klein wanted political officials to be included as members "to demonstrate the seriousness [and political clout] of the task force." These elected officials were to be
listed as "ex officio," in contrast to the task force of "lay members." An executive committee would be designated to do much
of the work. According to this memo, Klein seemed to think he
had much influence in initiating the task force. He not only asked
for inclusion of political officials, but requested that its first
meeting be held at Gracie Mansion, the mayor's home. However,
Klein was also mentioned in another section of the memorandum
labeled "Issues to be cleared with the Mayor." The issue needing
clearance was Klein's "involvement with [Republican] Richard
Rosenbaum's campaign," which demonstrates that the task force
indeed touched on political concerns.

"Klein wasn't anyone's idea but mine," Herb Rickman told
me. "And it wasn't because Klein was a developer. At that time
'developer' was not a nasty word, and Klein was not the developer that he is now. He was only a beginner. It was because Klein
was a survivor. He certainly had a passion and a commitment.
It was not an easy sell in those days—no one wanted it. And we
very much wanted access into money, and we thought that he
would give us that access. And the survivors felt strongly about
him. They knew him, they knew his reputation. And I checked
very carefully. There were no negatives on him. In that period,
he did not have the stature that he has now. And he certainly
was not a major figure in the development community, as he is
now. If we did not have his expertise in building and development, lord only knows how much it would have cost us in the
long run."[19]

Mayor Koch explained the choice of George Klein much more

succinctly: "He's an old friend, he's a very proud Jew, he's a very rich man, and he was an immediate candidate to be involved—by virtue of all of that."[20] Koch had chosen his rich "old friend," a prominent developer closely tied with the JCRC and the organized Jewish community, instead of Ben Meed, whose influence and power base were limited to survivor organizations.

Klein is a survivor (as Rickman had described him) in the broad sense of the word. He was born in Vienna, and immigrated to the United States with his parents as a small child, in the aftermath of *Kristallnacht*, the Nazi-incited riots against Jews and Jewish property that took place on November 9–10, 1938. Klein's family made its fortune from Barton's kosher chocolates. His credentials among leaders of survivor organizations stem from his father's involvement in Orthodox rescue efforts, the Vaad Hatzalah, during the Holocaust. George Klein is prominent in the Orthodox religious establishment in New York City and among Jewish financial backers of Republican politics. Rickman said Klein was not a "major figure in the development community" in 1981, but in fact he was a major figure from at least 1977. His office building at Park Avenue and Fifty-ninth Street, which he started constructing that year, was extremely important to the future of real estate development in New York City. This project gave Klein prestige as an important developer, because it was the first new office building that commenced construction in Manhattan in five years.[21]

On July 6, 1981, Koch sent out letters of appointment to the Mayor's Task Force. As political scientist Robert Dahl once explained regarding New Haven Mayor Lee's creation of a Citizens' Action Committee for urban redevelopment, Koch's task force was supposedly a structure of citizen participation, but it was deliberately created by a mayor to endorse his proposals.[22] In other words, one function of Koch's task force was to sell the project to the community in order to assure its acceptability.

Koch said Herb Rickman was responsible for task force appointments: "Probably Rickman did that," he told me. "These are leading New York Jews." The twenty-eight "leading New York Jews" were invited to Gracie Mansion on July 22, 1981, for the first meeting of the Holocaust memorial task force. Task force members included George Klein, chairman (president, Park Tower Realty Corp.); Elie Wiesel, honorary chairman; Rabbi Chaskell Besser (Agudah Israel and close to Klein); Kenneth J.

Bialkin, national president of the Anti-Defamation League of B'nai B'rith and attorney (partner, Wilkie Farr & Gallagher); Leonard David (founder and a director, Colonial Penn Group); Dr. Yaffa Eliach, Holocaust scholar (Center for Holocaust Studies, Brooklyn); Murray Finley (president, Amalgamated Clothing and Textile Workers' Union); Judge Marvin Frankel (managing partner, Proskauer Rose Goetz & Mendelsohn); Alan Greenberg (chief executive officer, Bear Stearns & Co.); Rabbi Irving Greenberg (director of the National Jewish Resource Center and ZACHOR Holocaust Resource Center); Judah Gribetz (partner, Mudge Rose Guthrie & Alexander); Ludwig Jesselson (president, Phibro Corp.); Leonard Lauder (president, Estée Lauder, Inc.); Benjamin Meed (president, WAGRO); Bess Meyerson; Ernest Michel (campaign director, UJA-Federation); Rabbi Israel Mowshowitz (former president, New York Board of Rabbis); Richard Ravitch, past president of JCRC (chairman, Metropolitan Transportation Authority); Rabbi Alexander Schindler (president, Union of American Hebrew Congregations); Irving Schneider (executive vice president, Hemsley-Spear Corp.); Rabbi Arthur Schneier (chairman, World Jewish Congress—American Section); Beverly Sills (general director, New York City Opera); Bernice Tannenbaum (immediate past national president, Hadassah); Laurence Tisch, president, JCRC (chairman of the board, Loews Corp.); Peggy Tishman (past vice president, Federation of Jewish Philanthropies of N.Y.); Marvin Traub (chairman of the board, Bloomingdales); Walter Weiner (president, Republic National Bank of New York); and Solomon Zynstein, president of American Federation of Jewish Fighters, Camp Inmates and Nazi Victims (president, Zynn Fashion). The Advisory Council consisted of Rickman; Henry Geldzahler, commissioner of the Department of Cultural Affairs; Malcolm Hoenlein, JCRC executive director; Karl Katz, director of the Metropolitan Museum of Art's Office of Film and Television; and Howard Rubenstein, president of the public relations firm of Howard Rubenstein Associates.

With few exceptions, none of the people named to the task force was expert in Holocaust education. Only Elie Wiesel (whose position was merely honorary), Dr. Eliach, and Rabbi Greenberg were teaching and writing about the Holocaust. Yaffa Eliach, Ben Meed, Solomon Zynstein, and Ernest Michel were survivors, with Michel also heading the UJA-Federation's fund-raising operation in New York City. Rabbis represented each of the three major branches of Judaism. Other than that, the members were mainly men who were wealthy and well connected in the Jewish as well as the business, financial, real estate, or legal communities. (When the ensuing commission was formed, many more developers were appointed by Mayor Koch.) Only five of the twenty-eight task force members were women. In addition to the famous and glamorous Bess Meyerson (not yet cultural affairs commissioner) and Beverly Sills, Yaffa Eliach was a scholar and survivor, and Bernice Tannenbaum and Peggy Tishman were communal leaders, the latter also a member of a prominent family of real estate developers.

President Carter's political entrepreneurs who initiated the national project in Washington, D.C., had insisted that the President's Commission on the Holocaust include non-Jews. Koch, on the contrary, appointed only Jews to his task force. When asked why he made this decision, he told me: "This is the Jewish Holocaust. The museum in Washington is not." He said there were no pressures from other groups to be included, and that the project's funding was entirely private.[23] He did not mention that the possibility of using city land, which has monetary value, would, in effect, give the project public funding.

Rickman insists there was nothing political about the appointments or about the timing of the task force's creation. However, during the months preceding the 1981 mayoral election, any such action was political per se. Koch's creating a Holocaust memorial task force at that time and appointing these prominent and mostly rich members of the Jewish community could only have helped him win the 1981 election with 75 percent of the vote, including 73 percent of the Jewish vote.[24] It is also likely to have helped him obtain campaign contributions from wealthy members of the organized Jewish community, although there is no study of any correlation between announcement of the task force and contributions. (Board of Elections records on campaign contributions are destroyed after five years.) George Klein was at the very top of Ed Koch's list of contributors when he ran for election for mayor in 1981 and for governor in 1982.[25]

Following the task force's Gracie Mansion breakfast meeting on July 22, a press release the next day announced that Mayor Koch had named a committee to develop a plan for creating a permanent Holocaust memorial; according to the press release, Koch had "acted at the request of a number of Jewish groups and communal organizations in announcing the formation of the task force at that time." There is no evidence to support such a statement. It was, in fact, Rickman who launched the project on Koch's behalf. Koch's Holocaust project was initiated by the mayor, and was then eagerly embraced by the organized Jewish leadership. They did not come to him with the idea.

According to the July 23 press release, Mayor Koch had asked the task force to report to him by December 1, 1981, with recommendations on the nature of the memorial, its location, how to raise funds to build it, and how to continue the work of the task force and carry the project forward. It concluded with a quote from Koch: "The city of New York, which has the largest Jewish community of any city in the 4,000-year history of the Jews, also has the largest group of survivors of the Holocaust outside Israel. Here we must have a living memorial to the Jewish victims of the Holocaust, a place in which to pledge a renewal, a reaffirmation of the oath: never again."[26] This was not a bad "campaign pitch" in what he himself had just described as the city with "the largest Jewish community of any city in the 4,000-year history of the Jews."

George Klein and the other New York City real estate developers who became members of the Holocaust commission and major contributors to Mayor Koch's campaigns were in a position to effectively use their political influence and to build on this strength to gain even more influence and power. Some members of the commission, and especially Klein, used their political resources to the fullest. The members of Koch's task force had the political resources to influence government and the political savvy to use these resources to further increase their influence.

The creation of the Holocaust memorial task force and subsequent Holocaust Memorial Commission gave Herb Rickman, Ed Koch, George Klein, and others the opportunity to use the issue of Holocaust memorialization to increase their potential influence in the organized Jewish community and with New York City's developer community (which often overlap). They used their political resources efficiently to promote the idea of a memorial museum in the community and with elected officials. At the same time they were able to increase their own prestige in the community and in the political arena by associating themselves with the project. Leadership of the task force gave them more status as "players"; and as professional political players, they knew how to take advantage of untapped but available resources. A political resource is only a potential source of influence, and most citizens hardly use their resources, as political scientist Robert Dahl noted.[27]

At the suggestion of Rickman, Koch had appointed George Klein as chairman of the task force. Klein was then in a position to encourage his friends, other wealthy developers, to be generous both to the effort to create a Holocaust memorial and to Koch's mayoral campaign. Klein was later to get, with Koch's backing, millions of urban-renewal dollars for his Times Square redevelopment project. Klein thus had the opportunity to use slack resources with high efficiency, gaining influence with the mayor and the Jewish community, and thus further enhancing his own political resources through his association with the community, the mayor, and, of course, through his development projects. Koch told me that many developers were named to the Holocaust Memorial Commission (that succeeded the task force) because of Klein's connections. He said of the heavy developer involvement: "That's for money. You have to raise a lot of money for this. And George Klein is a developer, so they would be his personal friends."[28]

While Koch made use of the task force and later memorial commission for his own political ends, Klein and some of the members who had the skills of political players were able to use their appointments to build up and upon their own resources. For example, in addition to Klein, Ben Meed also used his connection with the New York project to increase his political resources in the Jewish community. As the head of WAGRO, a chief organizer of the 1981 World Gathering of Holocaust Survivors, and a member of the U.S. Holocaust Memorial Council in Washington, Meed was able to use his task force affiliation to increase his power among survivor organizations. He also was able to make use of the new prominence given to survivor organizations by all of these activities to increase the power of survivor organizations in the organized American Jewish community. By 1987, the American Gathering/Federation of Jewish Holocaust Survivors, which grew out of the World Gathering, was a member of the Conference of Presidents of Major American Jewish Organizations.

Two advisory council members, Malcolm Hoenlein and Howard Rubenstein, are other political players who used the task force to expand their political resources efficiently. As executive director of JCRC and a close ally of (JCRC vice president) Klein's in the Jewish community, Hoenlein volunteered to provide staffing and temporary office space for the new task force. He was thus able to work behind the scenes and recommend appointments to the subsequent commission through Klein. This increased his power in the organized Jewish community. Rubenstein's public relations firm had the Koch campaign and many developers (including George Klein's Park Tower Realty) as important accounts. His association with the mayor increased his power with the developers, and vice versa. His firm's volunteer public relations work for the task force and subsequent Holocaust commission gave him a vehicle for further associating himself with the interests of all of these clients, and his power increased. He later became a cochairman of the Holocaust memorial commission.

As chairman of the task force, Klein, guided by Rickman and Hoenlein, proceeded with the next step in this newest attempt to create a Holocaust memorial. On October 2, 1981, he wrote to task force members that "we want to proceed with all deliberate speed to carry out the mission of the Mayor's Task Force on the Holocaust Memorial."[29] Klein's letter recommended dividing the work into four committees: Content of the Memorial, Location, Funding and Budget, and Inventory of Resources (to avoid duplication of what was already available in New York City). He then announced that volunteers had already agreed to chair three of these committees: Judah Gribetz for Inventory of Resources; Rabbi Irving Greenberg for Content of Memorial; and Irving Schneider for Location. It was perhaps a preview of the fundraising problems that were to ensue that the funding slot was not filled. Klein's Park Avenue office would be the temporary mailing address for the task force. The use of this address, as well as the language of the letter, may inadvertently point to another problem that was to follow. "I am discussing with some members the Chairmanship of the Funding Committee," the typed letter states. The "I am," however, is crossed out by hand and "we are" is substituted. The use of "I am," changed to "we are" only at the last minute, is an indication that Klein's first impulse was to take charge. Most commission members I interviewed did not want to be quoted but told me that a major problem in the history of the memorial museum was George Klein's failure to delegate responsibility and his view of this as "his" project.

After the October 1981 letter, no correspondence is found until a letter dated January 20, 1982, informing task force members of a public hearing to be held on February 1, 1982, at the request of Mayor Koch, regarding the creation of a memorial. Notices of the hearing had been sent to "every Jewish organization, community and Holocaust group in the City," this letter stated. Members were also informed that the draft report, which was to have been finished by the end of 1981, was almost complete, and would be sent for comments "shortly."[30] The only report available from this time is entitled "Mayor's Task Force on the Holocaust: Ideas for a NYC Holocaust Memorial Center." Dated December 1981, it appears to be a report of the committee headed by Rabbi Greenberg, which was to have explored content of the memorial. The report recommends that a Holocaust memorial center address the culture of European Jewry that was destroyed, give a detailed factual account of the destruction of European Jewry (including resistance), and explore how this could have happened in "the supposedly civilized twentieth century." It also calls for an exhibition center for the general public, a scholarly archive that would become "America's Holocaust scholarship center," and a survivors' space, with personal taped memoirs and memorabilia, arguing that "only through a sophisticated holistic approach can this museum fully realize the idea of uniting the scholarly and the popular."[31] This modest preliminary proposal eventually became a grandiose project that encompassed a complicated and changing political alliance; intricate real estate deals; the hiring of sophisticated fund-raising, public relations, and design professionals; and a projected budget of more than $100 million (which was later substantially reduced).

The Mayor's Holocaust memorial task force held hearings on February 1, 1982, in the Board of Estimate chamber at City Hall, with George Klein as chairman. In his opening remarks, Herb Rickman referred to the purpose of the hearings as soliciting "opinions from all concerned New Yorkers on this vital memorial." He made it clear, however, that this memorial was not for "all" New Yorkers, but for the Jewish community: "It is our hope that this memorial to the Jewish martyrs of the Holocaust will encourage other groups who perished through genocidal campaigns during this century to establish memorial task forces along similar lines, and we will be proud to work with them as we have with the Jewish community."[32] This was a politically polite way of excluding Armenians, Gypsies, homosexuals, Poles, Ukrainians, and any other group that may have wished to be part of this exclusively Jewish memorial.

After the hearing, which had given interested parties the opportunity to present their ideas, and thus added a veneer of "participatory democracy," the task force moved forward and recommended the establishment of a permanent Holocaust Memorial Commission.

9

The New York City Holocaust Memorial Commission

There is not anybody I know who is opposed to a museum of the Holocaust in New York City. [But for] an enormous neo-Renaissance palazzo—dedicated to a manifestation of power, money and nothing but money—to be transformed into a museum of the Holocaust is displeasingly, offensively ironic.—Brendan Gill, New York Times, *August 2, 1984*

On September 14, 1982, Mayor Edward I. Koch's intervention in the effort to establish a Holocaust memorial in New York City was formalized. This effort, which had been attempted unsuccessfully by Jewish community groups and individuals since 1946, was now officially a "permanent" project of the government of the City of New York. At this time, Mayor Koch was fully in control of the project, for which he created the interest group and chose or approved its cochairmen and members. At this initial stage, the political coalition was still uncomplicated: Koch and his political entrepreneur Herbert Rickman formed a political alliance with an interest group they had originated for the purpose of creating a Holocaust memorial museum. The chairman of the interest group was developer George Klein, who received political favors for his development projects from Koch (as did other developers) and returned these favors in the form of major campaign contributions.

During the last week of August and the first week of September, 1982, Koch sent letters to prospective members and officers of the New York City Holocaust Memorial Commission to announce the creation of a permanent commission, upon recommendation of the temporary task force. The letter stressed the importance of New York City as the site of a major memorial because, as Koch put it, "New York City is regarded by all as the cultural and spiritual nucleus of American Jewry and is home to the largest number of Holocaust survivors." "It is tragic that the city with the largest Jewish population in the world outside the state of Israel," the letter pointed out, "still does not have a fitting memorial to the six million martyrs lost in the Second World War[1]."

The first meeting of the commission was scheduled for September 14 in City Hall, to be followed by a press conference with the mayor. Koch's special assistant, Herb Rickman, coordinated invitations and plans for the meeting. According to Rickman, the mayor's office "had always said from the beginning that we did not want the dollars and cents to come from government. It had to be privately raised. We were very clear on that. What the city was offering was our services, help in the selection of a site, and the imprimatur of the administration—plus the help in putting together the task force. And as we put together the task force, we also prepared to put together the commission." Except for the possibility of using city-owned land and the time put in by Rickman and others while on the city payroll, it is true that no public money was involved.

But developer George Klein, who had headed the task force, informed Rickman that he could not continue alone at this stage and wanted a cochairman. Rickman then began to search for one. At that time, the late Henry Morgenthau, the father of Manhattan district attorney Robert M. Morgenthau, was being hailed as having been the only Jew in government during World War II who spoke up about saving the Jews of Europe from extinction, Rickman told me. The elder Morgenthau had been President Franklin D. Roosevelt's secretary of the Treasury and had played an important role in urging rescue efforts. As I have mentioned, Klein's father, too, had played an important role in rescue efforts, through the Orthodox Vaad Hatzalah. Ironically, Klein and Morgenthau had in common, as qualifications for cochairmanship of the commission, both their fathers' past histories and their current political support for Koch.

The YIVO Institute was not interested in merging, and the Brooklyn Center did not do so until 1990, after serious financial problems made independence impossible. Cooperation with the Washington, D.C., Holocaust memorial project turned to competition for artifacts and funding. Some key staff people also moved from one project to the other. For example, New York consultant Jeshajahu (Shaike) Weinberg became the director in Washington, and New York project director David Altshuler came to the New York commission from Washington. In September 1982, however, none of these developments (nor the fall of commission members Bess Meyerson, Ivan Boesky, associate chairmen Donald Manes and Stanley Simon, and finally of Mayor Koch himself) were foreseen. The project was only at the start of its tortuous path through more than twelve years of impasse.

With the exception of associate chairpersons, who were all current or past city, state, and federal elected officials (and many of whom were coincidentally Jewish), all of the appointees named to the New York City Holocaust Memorial Commission were Jewish.[7] The associate chairpersons were appointed by virtue of their offices, and not as individuals. As Rickman remarked, "We labored long and hard to create a very balanced commission, and I'm very proud of that because we did most of the work in our office." He did not add that this work was done on government time, and on behalf of an interest group that the government had created. "We made certain that we had representation from the survivor community," Rickman added, "and from every major sector of the Jewish community—Zionists, non-Zionists, Reform, Orthodox, left wing, right wing. It truly reflected the community as a whole—even geographically. We strove to have representation from the outer boroughs as well. They were appointed by the mayor, but I worked on them with George [Klein] and then we submitted them to the mayor and we had no problem with any of them."[8] According to Rickman, he and Klein chose the people to serve on the commission, with Mayor Koch's approval.

The commission was not as "balanced" as Rickman stated. The sixty-six members appointed to the original commission (not including the associate chairpersons) can be divided into four categories: high-level officers and philanthropists of the organized Jewish community; developers, real estate attorneys, and high-level members of the financial sector (with these two categories often overlapping); fewer than ten Holocaust survivors; and only three Holocaust scholars. The first category included Morris B. Abram, Julius Berman, Rabbi Chaskell Besser, Kenneth J. Bialkin, Ivan F. Boesky, Rabbi Gerson Cohen, Dr. Saul Cohen, Rabbi Alfred Gottschalk, Judah Gribetz, Marvin Josephson, Rabbi Norman Lamm, Herman Merkin, Paul Milstein, Richard Ravitch, Abraham Ribicoff, Judge Simon Rifkind, Felix Rohatyn, Howard J. Rubenstein, Lewis Rudin, Dr. Raymond Sackler, Irving Schneider, Rabbi Arthur Schneier, Daniel Shapiro, Leonard Stern, Bernice Tannenbaum, Herbert Tenzer, and Peggy Tishman. With the exception of the rabbis, most of these people are also part of the second category. Other New York "movers and shakers" included union leader Barry Feinstein, close Koch associates Kenneth Lipper and Bess Meyerson, Brooklyn College president Dr. Robert Hess, and Beverly Sills. Survivors included Sam Bloch, Jack Eisner, Dr. Yaffa Eliach, Ernest Honig, Leon Jolson, Benjamin Meed, Ernest Michel, and Eli Zborowski, along with Menachem Rosensaft, who was a founder of an organization for children of survivors (and also Bloch's son-in-law). The scholars of the Holocaust were Dr. Henry Feingold, Rabbi Irving Greenberg, and survivor Yaffa Eliach. Only seven members were women, a reflection of the fact that positions of power in politics and in Jewish organizational life in the United States are male-dominated.

The vast majority of the commission consisted of Jewish men who were rich and/or well connected to Jewish money (especially in the real estate development and financial sectors) and to establishment Jewish organizations in New York City. The survivor community was not as well represented, and many of the appointed survivors, themselves, were wealthy and/or well connected. Scholars of the Holocaust, who should have been prominent in such an undertaking, were scarcely included. (One of the three, Yaffa Eliach, could triple in the categories of scholar, survivor, and woman. She was the only female scholar and the only female survivor on the original commission.)

Not only was the commission not nearly as broad-based as Rickman stated, but the "left wing" he spoke of was nowhere in sight (unless he considered "liberal" to be leftist). The members were, in fact, very linked to the generally conservative established Jewish organizations and Koch supporters. Rosensaft, a Labor Zionist who was later criticized for meeting with Palestine

Liberation Organization leader Yassir Arafat, could be considered somewhat "left wing," but he was invited as head of the network of children of survivors, which was not at all a left-wing organization.

Because it was made up of so many powerful and rich New Yorkers in general and members of New York's established Jewish community in particular, and because it was officially empowered by the mayor (who was also part of the interest group), the New York City Holocaust Memorial Commission was seemingly in a position to move government and accomplish its goal of creating a memorial. The relationship to government was one of tacit mutual co-optation: high-level leaders of the Jewish community were getting the mayor to build them a Holocaust memorial, and the mayor was getting these leaders to back him politically and financially. The leaders and the mayor could pretend that the idea of the Holocaust memorial museum was pure, noble, and above politics, whereas in fact it was an integral part of the mayor's political outreach to the community. The structure of this political alliance, at this stage, was still a mutual admiration society, or a reciprocal two-way street.

By the spring of 1983, Mayor Koch's commission was in full swing. Not unrelated was the first American Gathering of Jewish Holocaust Survivors, which took place in Washington, D.C., on April 11–14. The presence of President Reagan and the surrounding publicity for an event at which thousands of survivors met for the first time in the United States made the idea of a Holocaust memorial even more acceptably "American," legitimate, and important. Moreover, since this event specifically heightened attention for the national memorial being planned in Washington, it is likely that Herb Rickman and George Klein realized their own New York project needed an immediate boost of publicity.

On May 3, 1983, before consultation with or approval by the commission, Klein wrote to Gerald Carmen, administrator for the General Services Administration (GSA), requesting that the federal Custom House in lower Manhattan be the site of a memorial. The letter, which began on a first name "Dear Gerald" basis, referred to a recent informal discussion between Klein and Carmen regarding the Custom House. "I am at this time formally requesting, on behalf of the New York City Holocaust Commission, the use in whole or in part of the Old Customs [sic] House located at Bowling Green," Klein wrote. "As you know, our Commission, initiated by Mayor Edward I. Koch, seeks to establish in New York City a museum and memorial dedicated to the millions of victims of the Holocaust. I am certain that you agree that such memorial is appropriate and would surely be welcomed by many people as a fitting tribute." The commission would "abide by all applicable federal standards related to the use of the building and are prepared to submit a formal proposal in the near future," Klein added. Copies of the letter were sent to senators Moynihan and D'Amato, Congressman Theodore Weiss, local GSA director William Diamond, and Commissioner Richard Hasse.[9]

By trying to win support from congressional allies and an executive agency, Klein was attempting to form an "iron triangle" on a federal level so that the commission could achieve the local political goal he was seeking: the Custom House as a site for a Holocaust memorial museum. As we have seen, an iron triangle is the trilateral bond created by an interest group and its supporters in both Congress and an executive agency. In this case, the interest group component of the triangle—the Holocaust commission—was rather cumbersome. The commission was a local interest group, but it was also connected to city government. To complicate the case further, senators D'Amato and Moynihan, who were approached as the congressional component of the triangle, were also commission members.

As was often the case, according to many commission members, George Klein acted first (in consultation with Rickman or Koch) and then asked for rubber-stamp approval from the commission. This approval was formally granted at a meeting of the commission that took place in City Hall on June 8, 1983, with the presence of Mayor Koch and fifty-three members and associate chairpersons or their representatives. Klein presided, with co-chairman Morgenthau sending his regrets because of "unavoidable circumstances." In addition to Koch, a number of powerful elected officials attended. Former mayors Wagner and Beame (commission associate chairmen), Council President Bellamy, Bronx Borough President Simon, Comptroller Goldin, and Governor Cuomo's representative, Rabbi Israel Moshowitz, pledged their support of the commission's activities. Their endorsement was then on the record for the campaign to obtain the Custom House.

By the time of this meeting, progress had been made regarding the status of the commission. The State Department of Education had approved its incorporation as a not-for-profit corporation on June 3, and procedures were expected to be completed and filed with the Secretary of State by June 17, 1983. Dr. David Blumenfeld had been appointed as executive director of the commission, which was now headquartered at the offices of the Jewish Community Relations Council (JCRC). In addition, the Law Department of the City of New York had ruled that the commission was "an official city commission," entitled to use the seal of the City of New York on its letterhead. The fact that the commission was granted use of a city seal and was headquartered at JCRC reflected its ambiguous private-public status.

Klein's report on the Custom House was the most significant item on the agenda. "A number of sites were given consideration, but it was determined that the Old Customs [sic] House located at Bowling Green would best serve the requirements of a memorial museum," he stated. (Who did the "determining" is not addressed.) The U.S. Custom House had been vacated by the federal government in 1973 when customs service operations were moved to the World Trade Center. Built in 1907, it is considered one of the finest examples of Beaux Arts architecture in the United States. According to Klein, a letter of intent to lease space had been sent to the GSA. On June 3 a meeting was held in the regional director's office, which requested that the commission prepare and submit a proposal for use of the space.

After his report, Klein introduced Charles Forberg, an architect, who presented "preliminary concepts" of the museum. Forberg used schematic charts and blown-up photographs of the old Custom House in an impressive pitch to "sell" the idea of the Custom House to the commission. He explained that the memorial museum's space requirements would include the second (rotunda) floor, the first floor, and the lower level, allowing the federal government to use the five upper floors. His concept had "one basic prerequisite," he pointed out, which was "to develop a plan whereby the Holocaust museum center space is a self-contained unit, that separate ingress and egress be provided for the federal facilities and for the Holocaust Memorial facilities." Klein, whose business depended on his ability to sell proposals for development, clearly knew how to present his proposal to the commission in a professional and persuasive manner.

The preliminary plan was unanimously approved, and co-chairs Klein and Morgenthau were authorized "to further develop a proposal and to enter into discussion with the General Services Administration and the New York City Department of Parks, in behalf of a corporation to be formed, to be known as the New York City Holocaust Memorial Commission, Inc., with a view towards obtaining a lease for such space in the Old Customs [sic] House and for use of Bowling Green Park as may be needed for the establishment of a Holocaust memorial and museum." Although this was basically a rubber-stamp commission meeting to approve a decision Klein had single-handedly set in motion, the commission members were assured that no decision on the site would be reached without the final approval of the full commission, and that other locations would also be considered "should the need arise." Klein ended the meeting by reminding commission members of "the urgency for financial support of the project."[10]

The certificate of incorporation announced at the meeting was signed by the State Attorney General's Office on June 8 and by Donald J. Sullivan, a justice of the state supreme court, on June 10, 1983, and then filed with the Secretary of State, under Section 402 of the Not-for-Profit Corporation Law. The purposes of the corporation included in this certificate were not exactly the same as those defined for the federal government six months later. According to the certificate, the commission became a not-for-profit corporation "(a) To perpetuate the memory of the six million Jews who died in the Holocaust; to commemorate the victims of the Holocaust not only as they died, but as they lived; to communicate the uniqueness of the Jewish experience in the Holocaust; to teach the history and lessons of the Holocaust to all people for generations to come. (b) To create a Holocaust memorial in New York City. (c) To conduct lectures, seminars and other educational programs and to publish articles, papers and research materials. (d) To raise funds. . . ."

Signatories, as initial directors of the corporation, were George Klein, Robert M. Morgenthau, Dr. Irving Greenberg (who headed Zachor/National Jewish Resource Center in New York and was the first director of the U.S. Holocaust Memorial Council), Judah Gribetz (an attorney active in Democratic politics and Jewish communal affairs), Benjamin Meed (survivor and head of WAGRO, the Warsaw Ghetto Resistance Organization), and Ernest Michel (a survivor and United Jewish Appeal executive). The firm of Weil, Gotshal & Manges, represented by Ira Millstein and other associates, provided free counsel for the incorporation and other legal matters.[11]

On December 6, 1983, when the Holocaust commission sent to the GSA Regional Office a memorandum regarding its "informal proposal" to lease space in the Custom House, the stated purposes were somewhat different from those listed in the certificate of incorporation. Now they were "(a) To perpetuate the memory of the 6,000,000 Jews who were murdered by Nazi Germany in the Holocaust. (b) To commemorate the lives of the victims of the Holocaust by creating a record of Jewish life, society and culture in Europe. (c) To portray the arrival of Jewish immigrants to New York City and to restore to memory the vigorous traditions and lifestyles which formed a trans-Atlantic bond between European Jewry and the Jewry of New York City. (d) To support and encourage the widest dissemination of educational materials and curriculum, so that future generations would gain knowledge of the history and lessons of the Holocaust. (e) To provide for appropriate commemorative ceremonies and remembrance programs honoring the memory of those who died in the Holocaust."[12]

Portrayal of Jewish immigration to New York City had not been mentioned in the incorporation document, and its inclusion for the GSA may have been an attempt to "Americanize" the image of the museum for the federal government. An intended use of space was appended, including square footage figures prepared by architect Forberg. The request was for 86,200 square feet for the commission's project, and referred to a November 18, 1983, letter from GSA to the commission, regarding the project and the square footage available.

On February 11, 1984, three months after the GSA's letter to the commission and nine months after Klein's (first-name-basis) letter to GSA administrator Carmen, the GSA officially and publicly announced the availability of space. In a display ad in the real estate section of the *New York Times*, the U.S. General Services Administration offered "to lease approximately 80,000 square feet of space on three floors of the building, including the Rotunda, to a non-profit cultural/educational institution." The space was offered "on an 'as is' basis," with the potential user "required to rehabilitate it for its intended use—subject to architectural control by the government." Proposals were to be received no later than May 9, 1984.[13] The commission had thus begun its "homework" of creating a federal iron triangle of support nine months before availability of the space was publicly announced.

Soon after the GSA's official announcement, Klein and Morgenthau (who at that stage cosigned Klein's letters, although he was not then as involved as Klein) took credit for this availability. They wrote to commission members on February 24, 1984: "After an arduous effort on the part of our Executive Committee, and with the superb help of government officials and friends [many of whom were on the commission], we are pleased to inform you that the GSA has finally consented to offer for lease approximately 80,000 square feet to a non-profit cultural/educational institution." But the battle was only beginning, since other "cultural/educational institutions" were also interested in the space and trying to align their own political allies.

One weapon in the commission's arsenal was a detailed twenty-four-page brochure describing the need for a memorial museum, the origins of the Jewish community in lower Manhattan (site of the Custom House), the suitability of the Custom House as a site, intended components of the memorial museum, architectural drawings of the museum in the Custom House, plans for reaching out to the community and networking with other Holocaust institutions, and, of course, the prestigious list of members and officers, headed by Founding Chairman Edward I. Koch. This was to serve as a public relations and fund-raising tool in the commission's effort to win the Custom House. The new brochure was announced in the February 24 letter, and described as the basis for the proposal to be submitted to the GSA by May 9, 1984.

"We had pretty much targeted the Custom House Building," Rickman told me, "and the mayor was in agreement with me that it was a suitable site. The Custom House became our target. We thought that would be the best site possible for the memorial. And what we did was, we pretty much put it on hold as far as the Feds were concerned. I reached out to Senator Moynihan's office and they were very supportive [as was Senator D'Amato's office]. The American Indian [museum] were trying to get hold of it then. It wasn't so much that we were stopping [the] American Indian [museum], but we had a strong commitment to keeping it in Washington Heights and to making sure it expanded its operations there and became an important vital part of the community." (A 1978 letter from Koch to the director of the Museum of the American Indian stresses the importance of this policy for the Koch administration.[14] However, the Custom House site was later given to the Museum of the American Indian, which opened there in fall 1994.)

Mayor Koch, Herb Rickman, George Klein, and others on the commission used their influence, which their affiliation with the commission had increased, to gain the support of a broad range of elected officials. Since many of these officials were already connected with the commission as associate chairpersons, it was easy to create a federal iron triangle of support and was not a difficult "sell." Senator D'Amato, who was close to the Republican Reagan administration, and George Klein, a high-level contributor to President Reagan, were influential in getting the federal government to agree to lease the space. "I am convinced that this much-needed and long-awaited memorial to six million people would find an appropriate home in this historic structure," Senator D'Amato told the JCRC at the time. "In New York City, we now have the leadership and the means to place before Christian and Jew, young and old, a living memorial to the people who were exterminated by the Third Reich."[15] (It is odd that D'Amato, who was addressing a Jewish organization, used the word "people" two times in two consecutive sentences to identify Hitler's victims, rather than the more specific and appropriate word, "Jews.")

In the next few months, the commission leadership continued to solicit support from elected officials, favorable press, and private funding from contributors in the Jewish community. A meeting of the commission was held in the Tent Room of the Regency Hotel on May 8, 1984, "to bring the Commission up to date on the progress being made regarding our site [Custom House] acquisition proposal." Klein asked for and received formal approval to make a proposal to the federal government to lease approximately 100,000 square feet at the Custom House, "for the creation, development and building of a memorial to the Holocaust."[16] Again, the full commission meeting was a rubber-stamp procedure, after Rickman, Morgenthau, a few others, and mostly Klein had already placed "all the ducks in a row."

One reason Herb Rickman had Mayor Koch create the

commission was to have a body of leaders from the Jewish establishment linked to the mayor, placing them in a position to
demonstrate their approval for decisions he had already made.
The commission was supposedly a structure of citizen participation, but it was deliberately created by the mayor to endorse his
proposals. The main function of Koch's (and later also Governor
Cuomo's) Holocaust Memorial Commission was to sell the project to the community and to assure acceptability—and funding.
As political scientist Robert Dahl has observed, in a pluralist
democracy the relationship between leaders and citizens is often
reciprocal: leaders influence decisions of constituents, but leaders' decisions are also influenced by what they think constituents
want.[17] In the case of Koch and the organized Jewish community,
a reciprocal relationship was relatively easy to maintain because
the mayor and the community often wanted the same things.
Like the community, Mayor Koch was outspokenly pro-Israel and
supportive of the parochial interests of Jewish New Yorkers.

In the case of the commission, one community leader—
George Klein—had as large a role in shaping policy as the mayor
and Rickman in this two way-street. Furthermore, as time went
by and the political coalition changed, the mayor was no longer
in control of the commission or the project. The many changes
in the alliance and the length of time that had passed since it
was formed led to a long impasse, rather than rapid implementation of the project it was created to develop.

In the beginning, Mayor Koch and Herb Rickman thought
the organized Jewish community wanted a Holocaust memorial
and, more specifically, that the Custom House site would please
the Jewish leadership. George Klein certainly wanted the memorial museum there and pushed hard for that location. At the
May 8 meeting, he "indicated that the commission is indeed for-
tunate that the Custom House, a quality, landmark building, is
being made available for public use." The cost of the museum
would be minimal, he pointed out, because the federal government had allocated $28 million for general renovation and many
supplies would be donated for the museum. The federal government could not grant use of the facility without the approval of the mayor of New York City, Klein added—the mayor
who coincidentally was the commission's creator and founding
chairman.[18]

Construction committee chairman Irving Fischer, a developer, reported that a team of architects and engineers led by James Stewart Polshek of Columbia University's School of Architecture had inspected the Custom House, with work donated by developers on the commission, including Klein. Klein announced that he and Leonard Stern had each agreed to make $500,000 contributions over the next five years, and he introduced a newly hired professional fund-raiser, Bernd Brecher. The goal was $40 million—$15 million for renovation and $25 million for an endowment fund to preclude yearly fund-raising. Klein asked that the executive committee be empowered to determine a realistic amount of rent for the GSA proposal before submitting it.

This "executive committee" was not defined on paper. Its membership changed over the years, but always consisted of George Klein, Robert Morgenthau, Herb Rickman, the official incorporators, and a few others. Generally, Klein and Rickman made the decisions and then rounded up enough members of the executive committee to make the decision official and "democratic." The names listed on the New York City Holocaust Memorial Museum's provisional charter, granted April 27, 1984, are George Klein, Robert Morgenthau, Irving Greenberg, Judah Gribetz, Benjamin Meed, and Ernest Michel—the same as those listed on the June 1, 1983, certificate of incorporation of the New York City Holocaust Memorial Commission.

Between July and October 1984, when the GSA made its decision about the Custom House, letters on file indicate there was a letter-writing campaign orchestrated by either the commission, the mayor's office, or both. William Diamond, GSA regional director, received letters of support for a Holocaust museum from Jewish organizations and elected officials that included the National Jewish Community Relations Advisory Council, the American Jewish Congress, Senator Moynihan, Senator D'Amato, Mayor Koch, and Governor Mario Cuomo. Executive Director Blumenfeld said the commission had sixty letters of endorsement from major Jewish organizations.[19] Ironically, while Governor Cuomo had sent a letter to William Diamond urging that the museum be situated in the Custom House, his political brokers were already beginning to think about locating the project in Battery Park City and making the governor Mayor Koch's equal partner.

Meanwhile, five other groups were also vying for the space, and one serious contender emerged to challenge the Holocaust commission in seeking support from the local Community Board, elected officials, and the press. At a Community Board 1 meeting on July 31, 1984, most of the six competing applicants made presentations, with Executive Director Blumenfeld appearing for the commission. The other proposal under serious consideration by the GSA was an arts consortium's plan to make the Custom House a cultural and educational center. The project included an ocean liner museum, seven theaters, restaurants, and a half-price theater ticket booth; the consortium included the Alliance of Resident Theatres/New York, the Byrd Hoffman Foundation, the Center for Arts Information, the Cultural Council Foundation, the Dance Theater Workshop, the Kitchen Center, the Ocean Liner Museum, and the Theatre Development Fund. The Community Board did not make a recommendation at the meeting, but complained they had learned of the GSA's plans to lease the space only one week earlier.[20]

The *New York Times* (in an editorial), Kitty Carlisle Hart, Governor Cuomo's head of the New York State Council on the Arts, chairman of the National Endowment for the Arts Frank Hodsoll, and others publicly supported the arts consortium. Hart had expressed her "support for the proposal which would bring together under one roof some of the most respected and productive arts organizations in New York."[21] This may have been a precursor of Governor Cuomo's later recommendation that the Holocaust project be housed elsewhere, in *his* Battery Park City. The *New York Times* had argued: "But is the Customs [sic] House, extravagantly decorated with statuary symbolizing civilization's triumphs, appropriate for a Holocaust memorial? In the midst of its celebratory art, somber revelations of depraved inhumanity may seem discordant, even trivialized."[22] Even the *Wall Street Journal* proposed its own concept: "Perhaps the mayor should consider putting the city behind a fresh and dramatic plan instead of encouraging the commission to pay rent in perpetuity to the federal government for a space that would never, legally or sentimentally or architecturally, be its own."[23] The article suggested that Klein use part of the property he would develop in Times Square (through the Urban Development Corporation) and build there as a Holocaust memorial a replica of a wooden Polish synagogue.

The GSA's decision, scheduled for August, was delayed until October. Meanwhile, David Blumenfeld spoke at a public session of Community Board 1 on September 12, 1984, to advocate the commission's project. Despite his oral and written arguments, the board voted eighteen to three in favor of a cultural center. The board's vote was only a recommendation. Endorsements for the commission, on the other hand, came from the elected officials who also sat on the advisory board of the GSA regional administrator, William Diamond, who was to make the final decision.

On October 17, after six months of lobbying and competition between the Holocaust commission and the arts consortium, the GSA announced that the commission would be awarded a lease in the Custom House. GSA administrator Diamond said the commission was chosen because its "proposal was the strongest and the best deal for the government, based upon the amount of money offered." The commission would provide $5 million toward the restoration of the building, but a twenty-year renewable lease had not yet been negotiated.[24] The commission had in its favor the facts that Mayor Koch, Governor Cuomo, senators Moynihan and D'Amato, and Congressman Ted Weiss sat on Diamond's advisory board, that all endorsed the commission's project, and that all but Weiss were on the commission. The commission's federal "iron triangle" had prevailed.

"We won the Customs [sic] House, despite local criticisms from people like Brendan Gill who felt it was ill-suited for our purpose and they wanted to use it for other purposes," Rickman said of the GSA decision.[25] The year 1984 thus ended on a high note for the commission. With $47,719 in the bank for operating expenses (as opposed to $23,741 a year earlier)[26] and the Custom House in its hands, it was going full steam ahead to complete the Holocaust memorial museum by the spring of 1986.

10
Governor Cuomo Intervenes

The Custom House, I believe, is a particularly fitting site for this significant endeavor.—Mario Cuomo, letter to William Diamond, GSA administrator, July 27, 1984
Objections have been raised that this building is an inappropriate place to house the museum.—Mario Cuomo, New York Times, front page, April 5, 1985

The early part of 1985 was an ambivalent and pivotal time for the Holocaust commission, influenced by the intervention of Governor Mario Cuomo in processes that since the spring of 1981 had been the province of the Koch administration. By the beginning of 1985, Governor Cuomo's political broker began negotiating with the commission for the site of the memorial museum to be changed from the Custom House to Battery Park City. The work of the Koch administration and New York City Holocaust Memorial Commission cochairman George Klein to win favor with the federal government and obtain the Custom House was about to be negated. Similarly, Koch's reciprocal two-way arrangement with New York City's organized Jewish community with regard to creating a Holocaust memorial was about to change drastically. The coalition backing the project was on the way to becoming a monstrous polygon of political forces, with two heads sometimes biting each other.

Governor Cuomo's public reason for intervening and "grabbing a piece of the pie" was his belief in the importance of memorializing the Holocaust. Sincere as this interest undoubtedly was,

Cuomo most likely had other motives for his public stance. He seems to have wished to take away some of the glory from his old rival Ed Koch, and he also must have seen the idea as a way to ingratiate himself with the organized Jewish community. In addition, it gave him the opportunity to find a suitable public museum for Battery Park City, in keeping with his plan to give the area "a soul." At the same time, he could seek a different use for the Custom House, more in keeping with his own purposes.

Cuomo's chief power broker for effecting the change was Meyer S. (Sandy) Frucher, who was his close friend and the president of the Battery Park City Authority (BPCA). Assisting Frucher were Ellen Conovitz, the governor's appointments secretary, who has close ties to the organized Jewish community, and Rabbi Israel Mowshowitz, then the governor's director of community affairs, whose unofficial title was liaison to the organized Jewish community. (As a former president of the New York Board of Rabbis, Mowshowitz had been named to Koch's task force and original commission in his own right. He later also served as Cuomo's representative on the commission.)

Perhaps Frucher (who also has close ties to the organized Jewish community) saw himself as a latter-day Stuart Eizenstat, performing for Cuomo the same act of ingratiation with the Jewish community that Eizenstat had organized for President Carter in 1978 (see chapter 7). Cuomo, however, already had good relations with the Jewish community in New York State. The idea of making him prominent in a major Holocaust memorial project— which was on a scale to compete with the national memorial— may have been intended to give him a more national connection with the Jewish community in the event he would decide to run for president.

Frucher could not give a specific date for his entrance into the project, but recalled that "at a point in time there was a lot of controversy associated with going to the Custom House. I saw a piece in the paper and it described the controversy. I read in the newspaper there was a lot of controversy associated with the Holocaust museum going to the Custom House." After reading the article, Frucher contacted two people whose opinions would influence him to pursue the project for the governor. First, he had lunch with Brendan Gill, chairman of the New York Landmarks Conservancy, to determine whether or not there was any great opposition to the notion of a Holocaust museum. After Gill explained that he was opposed to the location in the Custom House but thought the project appropriate, Frucher met with the head of the Municipal Art Society, Kent Barwick. When Barwick's reaction was the same as Gill's, Frucher decided it was time to call the governor.

"There might be a proposed compromise associated with all of this," Frucher told Governor Cuomo. "And that is to somehow move them to Battery Park City, and thereby save the Custom House." After the governor told him to pursue the idea, Frucher met with George Klein, and then Klein, Robert Morgenthau, and Judah Gribetz. "We walked around the site," Frucher recalled. "The initial proposal was to put them in a park that was to be in the southern tip of Battery Park. In the master plan there was an idea for a public institution in the park, like a museum."[1]

No doubt Frucher, who was one of Cuomo's top political advisors and closest friends and "plugged in" to the Jewish community, also discussed with the governor the political benefits of such a move. He insisted for the record, however, that his primary motive was not political. Asked whether his deal with Koch, Klein, and Morgenthau for the governor to become Koch's equal "founding cochairman" had political aims, Frucher told me: "I was not unmindful of the fact that making him a cofounder had some residual benefits. But it wasn't being driven by that. It was being driven by inequities and unfairnesses. If the state was going to be the principal player in securing the land and putting it together, at that point it became necessary and appropriate to have the governor do it. But I was not unmindful of the political benefits."[2] The state would have no other reason for becoming the "principal player" except for the purpose of giving the governor political benefits with the Jewish community; but Frucher would not say so.

Almost from the beginning of 1985, there were two simultaneous scripts being played out with regard to site selection. Publicly, the Custom House venture proceeded, with its federal "iron triangle" of forces in place. Quietly, meanwhile, Frucher was negotiating with commission cochairmen Klein and Morgenthau and Koch's political broker, Herbert Rickman, to make Cuomo and Koch "equal partners" and move the site of the Holocaust museum to Battery Park City. In mid-January 1985, there was already a public clue that negotiations with BPCA were under way. In the *New York* magazine "Intelligencer" column, philanthropist Brooke Astor was reported to be lobbying against placing the Holocaust museum in the Custom House. Astor told the magazine that she had expressed her opposition to both Koch and Morgenthau; according to Astor, the mayor agreed with her. Koch then told the magazine he "hadn't told Astor he was *against* the memorial—only that 'everyone has pointed out that there are problems with that site and there may be alternatives.'" *New York* then went on to report: "One of those is Battery Park City. The president of that state development, Sandy Frucher, said he is talking with Morgenthau and the commission's co-chairman, developer George Klein, about putting the museum on a three-acre site there. 'We proposed this before,' he said. 'Now that they have one bird in hand, they're looking at our offer.'"[3] (There is no evidence of any earlier offer by Frucher.)

Five weeks later, the *Jewish Week*, the Jewish Federation-linked establishment newspaper, reported that "the memorial commission is negotiating a lease with the U.S. General Services Administration for the Custom House after it was chosen last October to occupy the site over several other museum commissions and arts groups. Designs for a three-level 'living museum' include a chapel and meditation room, video and computer-based study centers and exhibit space devoted to the rise of Nazism, Jewish resistance and the birth of the State of Israel." The article said renovation of the Custom House was already under way, and that the museum was expected to open in about three years (almost two years after the original spring 1986 target). Commission director David Blumenfeld is quoted as defending the site as "very appropriate." He also noted that "a customs house fits in with the immigration theme. The beauty of the murals and the building in a way commemorate the beauty of European Jewish art and of the old world ambiance." BPCA was not mentioned in this story.[4] The two articles reflected the two-pronged negotiations then taking place: one between Koch's office and commission leaders and the governor's office, and the other between commission leaders and the General Services Administration (GSA). The appearance of the Custom House story in the Federation-linked *Jewish Week* at that time is an indication this was the negotiation the commission wanted publicized.

On March 1, 1985, the commission was still communicating with the GSA, providing information that had been requested. A proposed schedule of meetings between commission and GSA personnel was included, with dates running to May 21, 1985. That date was said to be the deadline for lease negotiations, extended from February 20.[5] (This extended deadline bought time for a decision regarding BPCA.) A March 3 story in the *Daily News* noted that "the memorial commission is still negotiating a home for the museum. Although use of the Customs [sic] House at Bowling Green was approved by the General Services Administration, the state is negotiating for a possible site in Battery Park City."[6]

In the midst of this wheeling and dealing, the New York City Holocaust Memorial Museum (which is different from the commission) became a legal entity. On February 15, 1985, the trustees of the New York City Holocaust Memorial Museum signed a "Statement of Organizational Action of Trustees in Lieu of Organization Meeting." Signatories were the same people who incorporated the commission: George Klein, Robert Morgenthau, Rabbi Irving Greenberg, Judah Gribetz, Benjamin Meed, and Ernest Michel. Officers (appointed by Koch) were Mayor Koch, Founding Chairman; Jacob K. Javits and Elie Wiesel, Honorary Chairmen; Robert Morgenthau and George Klein, Cochairmen of the Board; David Blumenfeld, Secretary and Executive Trustee; and Ira M. Millstein, Counsel. According to the bylaws, this board of trustees could not exceed twenty-five people.

Although the commission and the museum were officially two separate entities, the same men controlled both, and Koch was in command. Now, the governor wanted to step in and take away as much of that command as possible. The politics of site selection became crucial, because whoever controls the site of the museum has tremendous power over the commission and the museum's board of trustees. By accepting Battery Park City as the site, Koch, Klein, Morgenthau, and company would allow Cuomo to suddenly wield power over a project in which he formerly had virtually none.

Site selection has been a major component of creation of the Holocaust museum from the beginning. Consideration of how the site of the museum would affect elected officials was crucial, because the Custom House site was chosen by the Koch-affiliated commission leadership, and Battery Park City was chosen by the governor's political broker. As part of the deal for the land, Governor Cuomo was to (retroactively) become an equal "founding cochairman" with Koch. The choice of Battery Park City thus enhanced the governor's position and diminished Mayor Koch's. Experts first evaluated the Custom House as a site and deemed it highly suitable, a conclusion that was publicly seconded by all elected officials and commission leadership. This "scientific" or "expert" evaluation was used for public relations, to promote obtaining and public acceptance of the Custom House. Initiation of the project was then stalled while the experts determined that, in fact, Battery Park City would be a better location. A public relations campaign was then launched by the commission to convince the organized Jewish community that this second site was better.[7]

Meanwhile, encouraged by the leadership of the commission, on February 25, 1985, City Councilwoman Susan Alter's (D-Brooklyn) resolution, which placed the council's "moral support" behind the concept of establishing a Holocaust memorial, was approved by the City Council. The resolution (no. 1063-A) did not cite the Custom House, Alter stated, because it was not meant to focus on a specific project.[8] She did not say publicly that the commission's indecision between the Custom House and Battery Park City at that point precluded her from being specific. Most of those who testified at Alter's hearing were commission members, including Herb Rickman, George Klein, Ben Meed, Ernest Michel, former congressman Herbert Tenzer, Judge Simon Rifkind, Rabbi Judah Nadich, Henry Feingold, and Menachem Rosensaft.[9]

Because Alter's hearing was intended as a gesture of support for the commission, she did not invite testimony from representatives of groups that would be expected to be negative, such as emigré Polish or Ukrainian societies. The testimonies, in fact, were orchestrated by David Blumenfeld, who was then the commission director. Just as an "iron triangle" of support for the Custom House was built on a federal level with the GSA and members of Congress, in this instance the commission and the mayor's office were using the City Council to give the appearance of local unity and acceptance of the project. The Alter resolution was merely good public relations, as a resolution by the City Council then had no power to impact on the project.

The federal triangle and local support, however, had already been undermined by the governor's intervention. Exactly how Governor Cuomo got into the act with his Battery Park City offer is not clear, except that Frucher was his broker. Mayor Koch explained it this way: "We needed them [the governor]. The Holocaust is bigger than anybody I know of, and the more people you can bring in, and help, the better off you are. So the issue became where would it be—before a decision was made that the Custom House was not the best place. And we needed Battery Park City. You can't do Battery Park City without the governor, and the governor was very desirous of being involved. So it was a natural marriage made in heaven."[10]

This explanation makes it sound as if Mayor Koch and the commission decided that Battery Park City would be a good location, and then sought out the governor. However, according to Rickman and others, Sandy Frucher, on behalf of the governor, sought out the commission and "made them an offer they couldn't refuse." Rather than a "marriage made in heaven," it was more like a shotgun wedding. Frucher corroborated that he was the "marriage broker." He not only had the idea for moving the project to Battery Park City, but also was responsible for evolving the idea from the museum's standing alone in the park to its being part of an apartment building and thereby generating some revenue for the commission. Frucher went to Klein with his idea for a museum-apartment complex, and Klein liked the idea. "During the course of that, two things happened," Frucher told me. "One, if it was going to become a state project, it seemed appropriate to reconstitute the commission; and the mayor, who had originally been the founder, in this new construct would share the honorary founder role with the governor."[11]

Koch would not or could not tell me exactly how the governor got involved. "I can only tell you everyone agreed Battery Park City would be a better place than the Custom House," he said. "You'd start from scratch and build your building. In the Custom House, there was the problem of murals that are extraordinary, but don't fit in, and they'd have to stay there." Asked whether the governor came to him and the commission, or whether they approached the governor, Koch said: "I think this was probably all done through Klein and Morgenthau doing it, but I don't have a recollection of how we brought the governor in. I suspect it was they who initiated it."[12]

It was not, however, Klein and Morgenthau but Frucher who "brought the governor in." "I made the offer of Battery Park City to the Holocaust commission, but I did it with the knowledge of the [governor's] chamber," Frucher told me. "I personally spoke to the governor about it and to Michael Del Giudice, who was the secretary at the time. There was an effort to do it within the chamber. Del Giudice served as an intermediary and we were able to work it out so that the state was able to do it."[13]

Unlike Koch, Herbert Rickman, the mayor's special assistant responsible for the project, specifically stated that the initiative was the governor's. "The Reagan administration awarded us the Custom House, and no sooner did that happen than the governor interceded," he told me. "And the governor at the time, as we understood it, had strong interest in using the Custom House for his offices, or for offices that would be part of the state executive. The building would be shared by the governor's office and some other institution. The Indian Museum was again being mentioned. And we were given an offer that we could not refuse— and that was Battery Park City—which means a complete shift to a different kind of institution."[14]

Rickman, like Koch and Frucher, cited the problems with the incongruity of the architecture and decoration of the Custom House and the theme of the Holocaust. "The deal of the governor and the state was a brilliant one for us," he told me. "Not only did we get a site in a very attractive location, but we got a commitment to do the exterior shell of the building. The state was going to do nothing in the interior, but they would do the building as part of the deal. As I remember it, Battery Park [City] Authority had in its mandate the creation of a museum. And they had a lot of leeway here. So we were not just going to get a site. We were going to get either the entire exterior or help toward the entire exterior. It meant a great deal of production cost reduction."[15] However, there is no record of the state or BPCA offering to provide the exterior of the building. The promise was for air rights above the museum, where the commission could build an apartment house to offset the museum costs, and for token rent of one dollar per year.

The possibility of the new site was announced on April 5, 1985, in the *New York Times,* with Governor Cuomo prominent in the lead sentence, as he "announced plans yesterday to put a museum and memorial to Holocaust victims in a new apartment building at Battery Park City." The governor is mentioned four times in the article, before Mayor Koch is finally named in the sixth paragraph. At this point, in the print media, the governor had taken over as the prime player and Koch's position vis-à-vis the project had diminished.[16] The political coalition behind the project was evolving and changing shape.

Governor Cuomo had not always been opposed to the Custom House site. In a July 27, 1984, letter to GSA administrator William Diamond, Cuomo had expressed his "wholehearted support and endorsement of the proposal of the New York City Holocaust Memorial Commission to acquire leased space for the establishment of a 'living memorial' in the U.S. Custom House." He described the Custom House as "a particularly fitting site for this significant endeavor. Not only is the Custom House's grandeur and size ideally suited to a memorial of this importance, it is a building endowed with a feeling of tradition and Old World dignity which reflects the venerability of pre-war European Jewish civilization so brutally destroyed by the Nazis." He urged Diamond to approve the leasing of the Custom House to the Holocaust commission, "so that it can be put to the noble purpose for which it is preeminently suited."[17]

But by April 5, 1985, the governor was telling the press that "objections have been raised that this building [the Custom House] is an inappropriate place to house the museum."[18] Since nothing in the Custom House had changed in the nine months since Cuomo's letter to Diamond, the change must have occurred in the heads of Cuomo's political entrepreneurs who dealt with the Jewish community. They had determined that a connection with memorializing the Holocaust would be politically good for the governor because of the power of that subject for the Jewish community. They then found a way of linking him with the project under way: by making a generous offer of land and air rights to the commission, in exchange for Governor Cuomo's becoming founding cochairman.

As political scientist Edward C. Banfield observed regarding the structure of influence, government could not function without an informal centralized network of influence. Political leaders are willing to pay a price to people of influence such as newspaper publishers, civic leaders, and other elected officials in order to get their support. Banfield detailed how Chicago Mayor Daley and others "paid" to overcome the decentralization of government and how they "traded" with other people who had influence.[19] Governor Cuomo and his entrepreneurs did the same with regard to Mayor Koch and the commission. None of the players was willing to explain why Koch, who was getting full political credit for creation of the commission and the planned Holocaust museum, was suddenly so willing to share the limelight and the political benefits of the project with Cuomo. However, circumstances had placed George Klein in a prime position to wield considerable political influence with both the mayor and the governor. After a bitter Democratic primary battle for mayor in 1981 and another for governor in 1982, Koch and Cuomo were far from close political allies. Klein, who was Koch's friend and at the top of his list of contributors to both of those campaigns, surely must have had an important role in bringing him and the governor together for the Holocaust commission and museum.

In 1982 George Klein had been designated as the developer of the Times Square redevelopment project in Manhattan. He was strongly backed by Mayor Koch, and both the mayor and governor endorsed and praised the project, which was to be developed in connection with the state Urban Development Corporation (UDC). In 1984, the project came before the city Board of Estimate for approval, and both the governor and the mayor testified glowingly on its behalf. In 1984, Klein's agreement with UDC made him liable for all site acquisition costs up to the modest sum of $88 million. Anything beyond that would be reimbursed, with interest, by the city, although Klein had to pay about $25 million for subway improvements. The *Village Voice* noted that Klein, "the heir to the Barton's candy fortune, must see this as the sweetest deal of his life."[20] (It may be coincidental that BPCA, the state agency responsible for the new site for the Holocaust museum, was organized as a subsidiary of UDC.)

Klein's position as the designated developer for a huge and highly visible project that involved both the mayor and the governor gave him leverage to act as a middleman between them. They had both placed their bets on him to make a success of the Times Square project and thus to increase their own political positions. Therefore, although there is no concrete proof he did so, in early 1985 Klein was in a unique position to make a *shiddach* (betrothal agreement) between the mayor and the governor regarding the Holocaust museum.

The wheeling and dealing—in Banfield's term, political influence—that led to the commission's accepting Cuomo's proposed site change is reflected in an article in the *New York Times:* "Mr. Frucher has been negotiating aspects of the plan for months with the Holocaust Commission and developers. He said the Holocaust Commission would be renamed the New York City/New York State Holocaust Memorial Commission. Either directly or through a nonprofit subsidiary, the commission would sign a lease with the Battery Park City Authority for the site at the southern end of the complex." The article stated that an architect's rendering had been prepared by James Stewart Polshek, dean of Columbia University's School of Architecture, showing an apartment tower on top of the museum, with a separate entrance for residents. Frucher is quoted as expecting the ground breaking in the fall of 1986, making the site change a fait accompli before the commission voted.[21]

This vote formally took place on May 2, 1985, when a general meeting of the commission was held at the Regency Hotel on Park Avenue. The executive committee of the commission, which was empowered to make final decisions, had already approved the change of site during the week of April 8, "in principle, subject to further negotiations."[22] Once they had made their decision, they rounded up all of their heavy players in the luxurious setting of the Regency's Tent Room to get their decision rubber-stamped. Seated at the head table were Herb Rickman, Rabbi Mowshowitz (representing Governor Cuomo), Senator Jacob Javits, Comptroller Harrison J. Goldin, Robert Morgenthau, and George Klein. Former mayors Beame and Wagner were also present. (Neither Mayor Koch nor Governor Cuomo attended.)

J. Philip Rosen, an attorney from Weil, Gotshal & Manges, presented a legal report: BPCA would control the land until the year 2069, giving a developer group that included some members of the commission the right to build a 525,000-square-foot building; 400,000 square feet would be used for a residential building and 125,000 would be used as a memorial museum. The residential portion would either be sold as condominium units or rented, depending on market conditions. Profits would go first to the developer group to pay back costs, and the remainder would be used by the commission as a full-term endowment for the museum. BPCA would give the commission two separate leases, one for the apartment building's land and one for the museum. For Rosen, the advantages of "this scheme" were "terrific": the new building would be built according to the commission's plans, and once construction costs were repaid there would be an endowment forever. Rosen called the agreement "politically advisable," because the state and city governments wanted it and the federal government was amenable. BPCA had already approved a week earlier (with a letter of intent), he said, and the mayor, governor, and city legal department had given full approval. The consent of the Public Authority Control Board and zoning approval were also required. The commission wanted the BPCA deal legally approved by May 20, the day before the GSA deadline for the Custom House.

Klein announced that a group of developers, which he said represented 80 percent of the developers in New York City, had agreed to "join forces and oversee completion of the project." They included himself (Park Tower Realty), William Zeckendorf, Jr., Frederick Rose, Burton Resnick, Earl Mack, and Leonard Stern. There was some risk as to whether the apartments would sell, but if all went well the commission could build a major museum, have an endowment fund, and avoid the need to raise a great deal of money.

Polshek then gave an architect's report, pointing out that Site 14, the designated site at the southernmost tip of Battery Park City, was "forever protected by sea and land, with a view of Ellis Island and the Statue of Liberty." The museum would have its own identity and appear to be separate from the apartment tower, Polshek explained, making a strong pitch for the project by emphasizing that buildings in New York are "often wedded together invisibly" and that the thirty-four-story apartment complex would be a "background building." This explanation was always used by commission leaders whenever critics of the project pointed out the incongruity, or even the obscenity, of putting a luxury apartment tower above a Holocaust museum. It is a reflection of the impotence of the full commission that they read of Polshek's plan in the *New York Times* before they heard about it from commission leaders.

After Polshek spoke, George Klein presented another reason for moving the site. The Custom House rental would be $600,000 annually and BPCA was charging only one dollar per year. Although he did not enumerate how, he noted that the total savings to the commission would be $7 to $8 million a year if they chose Battery Park City. He proposed that the commission approve entering into a lease with BPCA, and then transforming the commission into a joint New York City–New York State Holocaust Memorial Commission. The mayor and governor were to become founding chairmen, and both were to have rights of appointment to the commission. In other words, there would be two heads of the commission instead of one, and a city-state-private coalition would be created.

During a question-and-answer session, Klein mentioned that the developer group, not the commission, would have legal responsibility for financing the apartment building. "No one will make any profit," he said. "This is not a gimmick. The developer group will assist in the development. The bank won't accept the signature of the commission—it has no money." When someone asked whether the commission could build a museum without an apartment house at Battery Park City, if enough money were raised, Klein replied no. The state was giving the commission the ability to build apartments—which is usually done with bidding—without bidding. An arbiter would determine the cost of building the apartment tower. The commission would then get the rights to build the museum free, and pay a fair price for the right to build the apartment house, for which it had the air rights.

The motion to move to Battery Park City was made by Senator Javits, and seconded by Governor Cuomo's representative, Rabbi Mowshowitz (which would seem to present a conflict of interests, on his part). "Resolved," it read, "that the commission continue its discussions with Battery Park City Authority and commence lease negotiations with the Authority for a ground lease of Site 14 at Battery Park City." The motion was accepted unanimously. Stating that the governor had initiated the idea, Mowshowitz then asked for a formal motion to thank him (which showed exactly where Mowshowitz's interest was). This was agreed to, only after it was decided to also thank Mayor Koch. Klein ended the meeting by stating the commission's determination to open the memorial museum in two-and-a-half to three years.[23] At the end of 1985, the commission had only $115,000 in assets, $50,000 of which came from a special grant from the New York State Legislature.[24]

After the May 1985 meeting of the full commission that voted to move the site to Battery Park City, there is no record of any action until 1986. On August 21, 1985, however, Eric Lane, then New York State Senate Democratic leader Manfred Ohrenstein's counsel and liaison to the governor's office, wrote to Michael Del Giudice, the governor's secretary, "to make some suggestions with respect to the planned proposal to reconstitute the New York City Holocaust Commission into a New York State and City Holocaust Commission." Lane pointed out Manfred Ohrenstein's role in creating a Holocaust exhibit and resource center in the New York State Museum, for which the senator had obtained $300,000 in state appropriations. He then suggested that Ohrenstein be appointed by the governor as one of the cochairs of the new board.

On February 24, 1986, the six directors of the commission gave their unanimous written consent for the name to be changed to the New York Holocaust Memorial Commission. This removed the word "City" from the title, and, in effect, also removed Mayor Koch as sole titular head of the project. It was no longer a "city" commission and the mayor was no longer in charge. The name change was officially approved by the office of the State Commissioner of Education, which had granted the commission's provisional charter, on March 7, 1986.

On April 21, 1986, a special meeting of the board of trustees of the museum and a concurrent meeting of the board of trustees of the commission were attended by trustees George Klein, Irving Greenberg, Ben Meed, and Ernest Michel. The following resolutions were adopted: State Senate Minority leader Ohrenstein, whose district was part of Manhattan, was elected a trustee and cochairman of the board of both corporations; Cuomo was elected a founding chairman of both corporations; the lease between BPCA and the corporation, dated January 16, 1986, was approved; any one of the cochairmen of the boards could execute the lease; and David Altshuler was elected project director of the corporation.

As we will see, the addition of Senator Ohrenstein, as well as Governor Cuomo, complicated the structure of the commission and the roles of the players. The project not only gained a new retroactive founding cochairman (Cuomo), but also a new cochairman. Frucher told me Ohrenstein was appointed by Cuomo because he "had been so intimately involved with sustaining the Holocaust commission through legislative action and because he had a strong personal feeling about it, felt strongly that he should be one of the three cochairs." He described Ohrenstein's appointment as "a combination of institutional as well as political realities." He then was more explicit, saying, "Fred went to the governor and insisted on it. I engineered that with Klein and

Morgenthau."[25] It must have been a difficult selling job, because Koch said he was not especially happy about it. "Manfred Ohrenstein imposed himself," he told me. "By that I mean he was not my choice."[26]

About a month after the new appointments, on May 23, 1986, the provisional charter of the New York City Holocaust Memorial Museum (granted April 27, 1984) was amended to change the name of the corporation to the Museum of Jewish Heritage. Then, in October 1986, a second petition for amendment to the provisional charter requested that the name become "The Museum of Jewish Heritage–A Living Memorial to the Holocaust." One reason for the name change was the concern of some of the commission's leaders about the potential to sell luxury apartments over a Holocaust museum.

At this June 16 meeting, the new names of the commission and museum were announced by George Klein. Governor Cuomo, now a "founding cochairman," had appointed fifty new commission members, many from outside New York City. David Altshuler was introduced as the new project director and Jeshajahu (Shaike) Weinberg, formerly of Beth Hatefutsoth Museum of the Diaspora in Tel Aviv, as consultant. (Weinberg later left the New York project and became the first director of the Washington, D.C., national museum project.) The goal was to complete the museum in three years, in the spring of 1989.

Klein announced that there was now a developers committee of "90 percent of the big developers in New York City," and that the museum would cost about $90 million, with about $10 million in materials donated by construction firms. The apartment tower would cost about $100 million, and income from sales of apartments would be about $160 million (assuming prices went up in the future). The shortfall to pay for completion of the museum was $20 to $25 million. The commission had embarked on an endowment fund campaign to pay for operating costs forever. They were trying to raise $40 million, and had already raised $8 million.[28]

At this time, after Governor Cuomo had rewarded "everyone and anyone" with appointments to the commission, the full commission became even more of a rubber stamp. Members appointed by the governor came from as far away as Buffalo and never attended meetings. Some of the newly appointed legitimate Holocaust experts were from out of state or even foreign countries. For the most part, Cuomo appointed people who came from New York State (but *not* New York City) and could fit into three categories: anyone who his aide Ellen Conovitz was convinced had credentials making him or her knowledgeable about the Holocaust (and some were "lightweights" at best); Jewish communal leaders from throughout the state to whom Cuomo owed political favors (in payment for campaign help); and a small number of Holocaust survivors.

The pivotal event of 1986 was the public lease-signing ceremony between the commission and BPCA, on September 4. Fundraising efforts were intensified, especially toward the end of the year. Meir Rosenne, Ambassador of Israel to the United States, was even brought to speak at a December 17 high-level fundraising dinner given by Erica and Ludwig Jesselson (who themselves pledged $500,000). This was the apex for the commission, which began showing signs of trouble by the end of the year. By December 31, 1986, the commission had $1,674,148 in contributions and $7,432,900 in pledged donations for a total of $9,107,048. In addition to George Klein, commission members S. Daniel Abraham, Leonard Stern, Peter Kalikow, and Howard Ronson each pledged $1 million.[29] Klein had previously pledged $500,000, and was now doubling his commitment. However, at about this time the project began to deteriorate.

11
The Holocaust Museum as a Real Estate Deal

*The profits from this [condominium] are being used—à la
MOMA—to pay for the construction of the museum. I find
something profoundly disquieting about this arrangement. . . .
Clearly some mixes are incompatible. One wouldn't add a
condo at a cemetery, at the Lincoln Memorial, at Treblinka
itself.—Michael Sorkin, Village Voice, June 23, 1987*

The deal that Governor Mario Cuomo and the Battery Park City
Authority (BPCA) offered the New York City Holocaust Memorial
Commission at first seemed like a dream come true. Yet this intervention by New York State, which changed the site of the
project and the structure and size of the political alliance, turned
into a nightmare after circumstances changed and the state reneged on its promises. The changing coalition of political forces
attempting to implement the Holocaust museum was becoming
embroiled in an impasse. Both the more complicated structure
of the political alliance and the extended time frame for the project's implementation contributed to a stalemate.

The plan to move to Battery Park City was probably difficult
for Mayor Koch to accept (although he did not admit this to me)
because he was forced to share the political glory associated with
the project with Governor Cuomo. However, George Klein and
the other leaders of the commission, who were trying to create
what they deemed the best possible museum at the least cost,
were overjoyed with the governor's offer. Battery Park City, the
biggest and most expensive real estate venture in New York City,

was real estate development at its apex, and this was where Klein wanted to be.

It was at this point that the plans for the museum took off in a new direction and became a real estate venture. The commission subsequently dropped the word "City" from its name as part of the arrangement with Governor Cuomo's office and became the New York Holocaust Memorial Commission. Not only did this newly constituted commission have two titular heads, Mayor Koch and Governor Cuomo, but the two heads were both playing dual roles. They were dealing with the commission as respective heads of New York City and New York State, but they were also part of the commission—its "founding cochairmen."

Once George Klein had been sold on BPCA president Meyer S. (Sandy) Frucher's idea of a luxury apartment tower on top of the Holocaust museum—following the example of the Museum of Modern Art's paying for the costs of its museum that way—there was no serious opposition from the executive committee. If such an arrangement seemed obscene, or at least inappropriate, any whispered questions were drowned out by Klein's enthusiasm and ability to promote the plan. From the very beginning, he had architect James Stewart Polshek's firm portray the project in two and three dimensions, and then emphasize how the entrances were different and the complex would seem like two different buildings. Megadeveloper Klein knew how to sell a new development project to his "clients," the commission.

In private discussions among cynics familiar with the commission's project—for example, support staff, Jewish journalists, and a few commission members who were not developers—there were sarcastic comments about naming the apartment complex "Treblinka Tower" and the surrounding streets "Auschwitz Avenue" and "Birkenau Boulevard." This reflected a gut feeling that the combination of luxury apartments and a Holocaust museum was hardly a fitting setting for memorializing Hitler's six million Jewish victims. However, ideological and philosophical discussions had no place in the meetings of the executive committee, presided over by developer Klein. The only serious discussion about this combined format, which afforded cost and construction advantages, concerned whether the market value of the apartments would be affected because of their location on top of a museum with an unpleasant theme. This was a real estate deal.

Since this deal was for a site in Battery Park City, some background on BPCA is in order. A public benefit corporation, BPCA was created by the New York State Legislature in 1968 to develop Battery Park City, a 92-acre landfill site at the southern tip of Manhattan, along the Hudson River. It is bounded by Pier A and Battery Park on the south and Chambers Street on the north. In 1979, following a hiatus caused by New York City's fiscal crisis, BPCA prepared a development Master Plan that zoned the property for different types of development: 42 percent residential, with 14,000 housing units; 9 percent commercial, with 6 million square feet of office space opposite the World Trade Center; 30 percent open space, including public parks, plazas, and an esplanade; and 19 percent streets and avenues.

The Master Plan and design guidelines were prepared by BPCA and Cooper, Eckstut Associates. The designs of private developers who responded to BPCA's Requests For Proposals (RFPs) had to follow these Master Plan guidelines. Battery Park City includes the $2.5 billion World Financial Center, a four-building office complex of 6 million square feet that has housed the headquarters of Merrill Lynch & Company, Dow Jones & Company, the Home Insurance Company, American Express Company, and Oppenheimer & Company.

In 1979 then governor Hugh Carey, Mayor Koch, and Richard Kahan, then president and chief executive officer of both the state Urban Development Corporation (UDC) and BPCA, signed a memorandum of understanding. This allowed the UDC to condemn the Battery Park City site, which was city-owned landfill. (UDC is a state agency that condemns city property to be used for redevelopment.) UDC then owned the land, which was released from the city's financial and planning control. In exchange the city received one dollar along with future profits and tax equivalents. Ownership was to revert to the city after BPCA bonds and funds advanced by the state had been paid off.[1]

Revenue collected by BPCA from the commercial and residential developments is the principal source for repayment of outstanding bonds in the amount of $200 million issued in 1972 and $185 million issued in 1986. The revenue will also support $400 million net in bonds issued to provide funds for low- and moderate-income housing, under the Housing New York Program. This program, passed into law in 1986 by the state legislature (section 1974 of the Public Authorities Law), created the Housing New York Corporation to develop low-income housing.

It also authorized BPCA to assign excess revenues to secure bonds and notes issued by the Housing New York Corporation for use by the City of New York to subsidize low-income housing. It projected that Battery Park City, when complete, would have a working population of about 31,000 in the offices and 20,000 to 30,000 residents in the apartments.[2]

Olympia & York Developments Ltd., a Canadian-based company owned by the Reichman family, developed and manages the four office towers of the World Financial Center. It is the tenant for three of the towers, with American Express occupying the fourth. Although the family was instrumental in rescue efforts during the Holocaust and is philanthropic to Jewish causes, Olympia & York is one of the Jewish-owned development companies in New York City that did not donate money to or become involved with the creation of a Holocaust museum in Battery Park City.[3]

The supposed implementation phase of the Holocaust memorial museum began in August 1986, when the Holocaust commission and BPCA began to plan jointly for a public lease-signing ceremony on September 4 at Site 14, the southernmost site. This was designed as a highly visible event, which would engender good press and stimulate fund-raising. Personal letters of invitation were sent to all past and potential contributors. In addition, two thousand invitations were mailed to commission members, elected officials, survivor organization leaders, leaders of major Jewish organizations, top contributors to United Jewish Appeal–Federation, clergy, the mayor's personal list, the Jewish Community Relations Council list, museum associates, BPCA invitees, Community Board 1, Holocaust organizations, financial sector leaders, university presidents, and union leaders. Phone calls were made to elected officials, the executive committee, the developers committee, major contributors, and other key people associated with the project.

At that time, the developers committee included most of New York's successful Jewish developers: Larry Fisher, Eugene Grant, Peter Kalikow, Earl Mack, Martin Raynes, Burton Resnick, Howard Ronson, Frederick Rose, Stephen Ross, Jack Rudin, Larry Silverstein, Sheldon Solow, Jerry Speyer, Leonard Stern, Robert Tishman, Fred Wilpon, William Zeckendorf Jr., and Morton Zuckerman. Howard Rubenstein's office sent out a press advisory and coordinated the press operation, working with press personnel from BPCA and new cochairman Senator Manfred Oh-renstein's office.[4]

A long agenda for the event was organized. Speakers included Sandy Frucher; "founding cochairmen" Governor Cuomo and Mayor Koch; cochairmen George Klein, Robert Morgenthau, and Manfred Ohrenstein; Senator Alfonse D'Amato; Elie Wiesel; Ernest Michel; and architect James Stewart Polshek. Rabbi Haskel Lookstein, president of the New York Board of Rabbis, gave the invocation, and Cantor Joseph Malovany chanted a concluding memorial prayer. The press release said ground breaking was "anticipated" in spring 1987, with an opening "projected" for 1989.[5]

Meanwhile, J. Philip Rosen of Weil, Gotshal & Manges, the commission's pro bono attorney, was examining the leases for the museum and for the apartment tower. He wrote to members of the executive committee on August 29, clarifying certain points in the leases and emphasizing that the base rent for the site of the museum was one dollar per year.[6] One paragraph discussed the right of the commission to assign completion of the apartment tower to a developer. The lease provided for this only with the consent of BPCA. The lease, however, specifically forbade assignment to Klein or his Park Tower Realty. "The Authority wanted this express prohibition in the Lease so that even the appearance of any sweetheart arrangement between Mr. Klein, as co-chairman of the Commission, and the Authority is avoided," Rosen wrote. The scheduled completion date of all buildings was to be December 15, 1989.[7]

The 165-page lease for the apartment tower at Site 14, which was signed with great fanfare on September 4, was a contract between BPCA and the New York Holocaust Memorial Commission, Inc. Construction was scheduled to start on April 15, 1988, and the lease would expire on June 17, 2069.[8] From commencement of the lease until "Rent Commencement Date," the base rent rate was to be one dollar per annum. For each lease year (or portion thereof) from the rent commencement date up to but not including the first appraisal date, the base rent was to be $1,234,800 per annum. For the lease year commencing on the first appraisal date and for each lease year until the end of the term, the rent was to be an amount per annum equal to 6 percent of the fair market value of the land—not less than $1,234,800.

For fifteen years thereafter, the base rent would not exceed $1,420,020 per annum.[9]

The second lease, for the museum (which was also signed at the ceremony), was between BPCA and "Museum of Jewish Heritage"—not the Holocaust commission. (These were two separate legal entities, although their boards of trustees were identical.) According to the terms of this lease, the commission was responsible for the completion of the apartment tower (either by building it or finding an outside developer to do so) and the museum board was responsible for building the museum. Under Article 3, Section 3.01 (a), the museum lease stipulates: "For each Lease Year beginning on the Rent Commencement Date and continuing thereafter throughout the Term, Tenant shall pay to Landlord, without notice or demand, the annual sum of $1.00 per annum (collectively, the '*Base Rent*')."[10] BPCA thus expected to collect a fair rental from the commission for the apartment tower, but only one dollar a year from the museum. Neither the commission nor the museum was paying any money for the lease of the land from BPCA. The museum and the air rights to build the apartment tower above it were to cost the museum only one dollar a year.

The purposes for use of the land for the museum were set out in Section 23.01 of the lease: "Subject to the provisions of law and this Lease, tenant shall use, occupy and operate the Premises on all Business days during Business Hours continuously and without interruption throughout the Term as a museum, conference center, exhibition area, library facilities, archives and facilities for exhibitions, scholarly research and other purposes consistent with the purposes specified in Tenant's Certificate of Incorporation, in accordance with the Certificate or Certificates of Occupancy for the Premises, the Master Development Plan and the Design Guidelines, and for no other use or purposes."[11] Under the terms of the lease, the state, through its entity, BPCA, imposed on the commission and the museum the regulations concomitant with choosing New York State land as a site.

In an earlier section, the lease had specified: "*Business Days*" as "any day which is not a Saturday, Sunday or a day observed as a holiday by either the State of New York or the federal government and, as long as New York Holocaust Memorial Commission, Inc. is the Tenant, the following Jewish holidays: Rosh Hashanah (both days), Yom Kippur, Succoth (first two [2] days), Shmini

Atzereth, Simchas Torah, Passover (first two [2] days and last two [2] days) and Shavuoth (both days)."[12] This definition of "business days" was to cause future friction between the governor's office and the commission.

As soon as the lease was signed, raising money and developing the site became the two most important topics in discussions about implementation. At a meeting of the executive committee immediately following the lease signing, Klein said he estimated that the museum would need $85 to $95 million to open. Since he anticipated $65 million from the sale of apartments, $30 million more was needed in donations. He also wanted additional donations of $30 million for an endowment fund that would take care of perpetual expenses and upkeep. He suggested setting an announced fund-raising goal of $75 million. The possibility of "flipping," or selling the air rights to another developer, was also discussed.[13]

At an October 6, 1986, meeting of the executive committee, professional staff, and "commission invitees" held in Klein's office, he announced that the proposed budget for the museum until May 31, 1987, was $7,795,000. This included $3 million for architects and consultants, $1,181,000 for a "design team," $1,750,000 for "exhibit fabrication," $869,000 for research, collections and administration, and about $1 million for construction and "soft costs." A list of "top prospects" for donations was handed out, and Klein, Morgenthau, and Michel took responsibility for a "Division of Top Prospects."[14]

By December 1986, the project's implementation phase was already in trouble. One significant clue to the commission's problems is found in a December 1 letter from architect James Stewart Polshek to George Klein. "I am concerned about the future of The Museum of Jewish Heritage and the Memorial to the Holocaust," Polshek wrote. "As we both agreed when we spoke last week, there is a general ennui—a sense of drift and lack of direction."[15] The architect pointed out that for the year and a half that he had been working with Klein, it was Klein's energy and leadership that had kept the project together. "But since the signing of the lease, you have become more and more isolated and the Executive Committee more fragmented," Polshek observed. "Obviously Fred Ohrenstein and Bob Morgenthau can put little time into this—this leaves you alone. The perception is that you have time, money, staff, and freedom from conflicts of interest—

all enabling you to be a one-man band, raise 30–40 million dollars, oversee the design of the building and exhibits and be the political and spiritual arbiter of its content. This is obviously absurd. You cannot be expected to do this and I do not believe any one person—even you—could do it under any circumstances."

Noting that this project was a once-in-a-lifetime opportunity that should not fail, Polshek suggested that Klein reorganize the executive committee, with only five or six committed people who would meet once a week, with an agenda that included progress reports on all phases of the project; hire an executive director; develop an immediate short-term fund-raising strategy; call in all pledges at once; and get the commission to commit itself to moving ahead to the point of actual construction. "It has always been my observation that nothing tests the reality of a project or moves it along better than the necessity to spend money," he concluded. "The aura of reality created by the forward movement of architectural, engineering and exhibition design documents will energize the entire effort."

Implementing a Holocaust memorial museum in New York City, the center of the organized Jewish community in the United States, would seem to be an easy job: The large Jewish population, concentration of Jewish wealth, largest Holocaust survivor population outside of Israel, and highly organized structure of the community should all contribute to the project's being politically beneficial to the governor, mayor, and other elected officials, and therefore easy to implement. By December 1986, however, the project had hit a number of snags.

Perhaps this was inevitable. As Jeffrey Pressman and Aaron Wildavsky observed in another situation, their analysis of the failure of the implementation phase of the Federal Economic Development Administration's employment project in Oakland, California, "People now appear to think that implementation should be easy; they are, therefore, upset when expected events do not occur or turn out badly. We would consider our effort a success if more people began with the understanding that implementation, under the best of circumstances, is exceedingly difficult."[16]

The implementation phase for the New York Holocaust museum project was difficult for some of the very reasons that would seem to make it easy. Because the Jewish population of more than 2 million is so vast, many Jews in the New York City metropolitan region are blasé about their affiliation with the organized community. In a small town with a small, isolated Jewish community, Jews often feel the need to "belong," but in New York City this need is often met simply by living in an ethnically Jewish "atmosphere" replete with synagogues, cultural events, ethnic food and restaurants, organizations, and many other Jews, easily and plentifully accessible. Thus a large Jewish population does not necessarily mean that most individuals in this population are active, affiliated Jews who would be financially or otherwise interested in supporting the project.

As the center of organized Judaism, New York City is a difficult locale in which to initiate a new, competing organization or major project—vying for both financial contributions and attention. Even the large concentration of Holocaust survivors does not necessarily contribute to success, because their number is great enough to have their own competing groups and space-seeking leaders. Polshek also alluded to another serious problem regarding implementation: George Klein had made the project too much his own personal effort, which some potential major contributors and other Jewish leaders resented.

Thus when the governor stepped into what Sandy Frucher and his other advisors thought was politically important for him in the organized Jewish community, he also stepped into a project that seemed easy to implement only on the surface. Delays and retrogression are part of the process of implementation, as Pressman and Wildavsky explain: "Our normal expectation should be that new programs will fail to get off the ground and that, at best, they will take considerable time to get started. The cards in this world are stacked against things happening, as so much effort is required to make them move. The remarkable thing is that new programs work at all."[17]

In the case of the Holocaust museum, the new program worked in accordance with Pressman and Wildavsky's "normal expectation": for more than five years after the first lease was signed, it did not get off the ground. The main reasons have already been enumerated. In addition, a vicious circle developed: no visible, concrete progress (such as a temporary exhibit or lecture series in another location, or a ground-breaking ceremony) because there was not enough money; and insufficient success in fund-raising because there was no concrete progress. This was compounded by the lack of a master plan for fund-raising. Architect Polshek had alluded to all of this in his letter.

At a December 4, 1986, meeting of the executive committee, there was a sense that the project was indeed drifting. Klein announced that the commission needed $3 to $4 million in the bank to move forward, that Polshek had been owed half a million dollars for many months, and that interior designers Chermayeff and Geismar (who had been hired for the project) would also need to be paid. He described the project as in a "crisis stage." When the need for a finance committee and chairperson was highlighted, Klein kept coming back to himself and to other developers, rather than expanding the fund-raising base. This, again, was a reflection of his personalizing the project too much for its successful implementation.

Government intervention was the subject of two informal discussions (non-agenda items) at the meeting. A week before, Governor Cuomo's office had conveyed his displeasure (or that of his attorneys) with the name of the museum, "The Museum of Jewish Heritage–A Living Memorial to the Holocaust." Now that Cuomo was, in effect, the landlord, his intervention regarding the name could not be ignored. Although the reasons for his complaint were not spelled out in detail, they were related to the emphasis on "Jewish Heritage" and a possible conflict between church and state. Eventually, pressure from the governor's office forced the commission to change the name of the museum to "A Living Memorial to the Holocaust–Museum of Jewish Heritage." The name was officially changed in November 1987 at a special meeting of the museum's board of trustees, and the next month a petition for an amendment to the provisional charter was filed with the Regents of the University of the State of New York. This was granted on April 22, 1988.

The second item of government intervention concerned Mayor Koch. George Klein, Robert Morgenthau, and Ernest Michel were to ask him to seek donations from potential big givers, principally the developers with whom he had close relations. They were also going to ask the mayor to host a fund-raising breakfast for developers on January 10, 1987, at Gracie Mansion. The possibility of a dinner at Gracie Mansion for big givers a little later, in March or April, was also discussed. (This event did take place on March 23, 1987, with Henry Kissinger as guest speaker.) Any fund-raising help from the governor was said to be contingent on compliance with his pressure for a name change.

At the meeting, Klein rattled off a lot of numbers about the lease for the apartment tower, pointing out the commission's lease at a rate of only $40 per square foot and current property value at $60 to $117. He reminded the commission that the lease allowed them to either build the apartment building themselves or "flip" a set of plans and a contract. At one point his numbers had the commission making $35 million for doing nothing, and at another, the commission could lose money. As he said, it all depended on the market. In other words, the project's financial success was not assured and was nothing but a speculative real estate deal.[18]

The next year, 1987, could be called the commission's year of "professionalization." Commission executive director David Blumenfeld, who had become superfluous, was eased out, and the commission no longer had a director. Instead, the museum director, David Altshuler, was in charge (with Klein still the unofficial ultimate authority). Altshuler's three-year contract was approved by the executive committee in November 1987. He came to the project from George Washington University, where he had been chairman of the Committee on Judaic Studies.

Jeshajahu Weinberg had been hired as a consultant for the New York project in the summer of 1985 and was a key member of the professional team in 1987. He came at the request of George Klein, who wanted him because of his experience and reputation in creating the Museum of the Diaspora (Bet Hatfutsot) in Tel Aviv. Weinberg had told Klein that Klein couldn't "run the shop" and create a museum without a person on staff who knew the Holocaust. Weinberg therefore brought in Altshuler (who had worked on the Washington Holocaust museum project) as the project manager. Earlier, Klein had played that role. With regard to Blumenfeld's departure, Weinberg told me: "He didn't know museums from a hole in the wall. Clearly he was not the guy to create a museum." Nevertheless Blumenfeld remained on staff until he ultimately resigned in 1988.

Like others who did not want to be quoted, Weinberg stated for the record that one of the major problems with professionalizing the project was Klein's personal stance. "George Klein is the moving spirit. With him, the project stands or falls," Weinberg said. He saw Klein as much too possessive about the project,

denying the director leeway. "He [still] acts as the project director very much and keeps David [Altshuler] as deputy," Weinberg
told me in 1990. "He shouldn't. David is talented and should
have the power of decision. Klein is very restrictive."[19] In October
1988, Jeshajahu Weinberg gave up his consultancy on the New
York project to become a consultant to the Washington museum,
of which he became the first director in April 1989.

Besides Altshuler and Weinberg, professionals working on the
New York museum project in 1987 included Ralph Schwarz,
Senior Advisor; Karl Katz (of the Metropolitan Museum of
Art), Museum Consultant; a grant secretary; a research team
with associated freelancers; a Hall of Learning coordinator and
computer specialist, with consultants; Polshek's architectural
firm; Chermayeff and Geismar's exhibit design firm; David Edell
and Linda Low, specialists in Jewish Federation "big gifts," as
fund-raising consultants; and Luisa Kreisberg, a specialist in museum publicity, as public relations consultant.

In addition to the expanded staff and consultants, a Survivors
Steering Committee and a Young Leadership Association were
created (both for fund-raising). An attractive new booklet was
created, primarily as a fund-raising tool, and a news brochure
was issued every other month. Fund-raising was the prime concern. The campaign was headed by Peter A. Cohen, who was then
chairman and CEO of Shearson Lehman Brothers, Inc.; Stephen
Robert, chairman and CEO of Oppenheimer and Company, Inc.;
and Rosa Strygler, a survivor. The announced goal was $100 mil-
lion, with $70 million for construction and $30 million for an
endowment fund. At a January 12 meeting, the Survivors Steering Committee agreed to raise $5 million among survivors.

At a September 15, 1987, meeting of the executive committee,
only a few members were present, along with many of the newly
appointed staff and consultants. Klein asked for approval to sell
the air rights for the apartment tower, and, since there were no
objections, he assumed that he had the approval of the executive
committee. Frucher had told him, he said, that BPCA was about
to seek an RFP (Request for Proposals) for a major hotel on the
southernmost parcel east of the museum, and that in the next
six to eight months there would be RFPs for the space between
the north and south sections of Battery Park City, which were
undeveloped. Klein said that based on this information, he
thought the timing was right for selling the air rights for the

apartment tower. He thought it was "impractical" for the commission to build the apartments, and that "flipping," or selling the right to the contract, would yield about $110 per square foot for property for which the commission was paying only $40 per square foot. In Klein's opinion, the commission would make about $28 to $30 million. The committee also discussed a November 9 symbolic ground-breaking ceremony, to coincide with the anniversary of *Kristallnacht*.[20]

Then an unexpected event occurred, which was to have a major negative impact on the project: Black Monday on October 19, 1987. After the stock market crash and subsequent loss of high-paying Wall Street jobs, luxury residential property in the Wall Street area, such as Battery Park City, dropped sharply in value. As a result, the bargain price that the commission had agreed to pay BPCA for the right to build the apartment tower was no longer a bargain. The November 9 ground breaking did not take place. But at a November 12, 1987, meeting of the executive committee, there was still some talk about "flipping" the air rights for the apartment tower. Before Black Monday the profit would have yielded $30 million, Klein said, but now there was no telling what the property value was or would become. An RFP was being prepared, but Klein now saw "no rush" to sell.[21] On December 31, 1987, the amount of contributions was $3,770,646, with $7,888,308 in receivables, for a total of $11,658,954—far short of the necessary amount, which continued to escalate as time went by.[22]

Klein's push to sell the air rights in September was followed by his being in "no rush," as a result of Black Monday, to do so in November. Besides prompting decisions not to sell the air rights and to cancel the November 9 ground breaking, the crash also seriously affected fund-raising activities, drying up or reducing some potential philanthropic sources. As Pressman and Wildavsky observed with regard to a different project, there had emerged in the "decision path . . . numerous diversions not intended by the program sponsors. The paths of required decisions, as we can see, were soon characterized by more unexpected elements than expected ones: they were anything but straight lines leading directly to goals."[23]

During 1988 more "diversions not intended by the program sponsors" would make the lines leading to their goals even more circuitous: the site would change, Sandy Frucher would leave the BPCA presidency, and the original deal of one dollar per year as rent for the museum would increase dramatically. Meanwhile, however, in January 1988, David Altshuler sent a memorandum to the staff, with copies to commission chairmen and others, recommending that ground be broken and construction begun in the spring. In the meantime, fund-raising efforts would be stepped up.[24]

At the March 15, 1988, meeting of the full commission, a resolution was passed to authorize ground breaking and the start of construction in June 1988. A second resolution authorized the launching of a capital campaign with a goal of $70 million, plus $30 million for an endowment fund; and a third, the establishment of links with related institutions.[25] The executive committee then met on March 29 to agree on how to implement these resolutions. A decision was reached to have the ground breaking take place on November 10, 1988—but this was not to be. The planned November 9, 1987, June 1988, and November 1988 ground-breaking ceremonies never took place, and the longer this implementation phase languished, the more both external and internal circumstances interfered.

12
New York State as a Fickle Landlord

*When a man you like switches from what he said a year ago,
or four years ago, he is a broad-minded person who has
courage enough to change his mind with changing
conditions. When a man you don't like does it, he is a liar
who has broken his promises.*—Franklin P. Adams, Nods and
Becks, *1944*

With plans progressing for a November 10, 1988, ground-
breaking ceremony at Site 14, both Mayor Koch and Governor
Cuomo, the New York City and New York State founding cochairmen of the Holocaust commission, intervened and delayed implementation plans once again. Commission cochairman George
Klein announced to the executive committee on June 27, 1988,
that they had been offered a new deal by the governor and the
Battery Park City Authority (BPCA), based on a connection made
by the mayor's office. NOGA, a Swiss firm, wanted to build a
luxury hotel in Manhattan. The company is owned by an internationally known philanthropic Jewish leader, the Swiss head of
the World Sephardi Federation, Nessim Gaon. Gaon had approached City Hall, and Koch deputy Robert Esnard had introduced him to BPCA, because such a project in Battery Park City
would provide New York City with funding for low- and middle-
income housing. BPCA president Meyer S. (Sandy) Frucher, who
was also a key member of the New York Holocaust Memorial
Commission's executive committee, then recommended Site 14,
the proposed site of the museum and apartment tower.

At this point in the new deal the two titular heads of the Holocaust memorial project, Mayor Koch and Governor Cuomo, were working in tandem: the deal seemed good for both of their images, as well as for the city, the state, and the commission. Sandy Frucher, representing Governor Cuomo and BPCA, suggested that the museum move to Site 13 (immediately to the north) and be freestanding, with the capability of selling the Site 14 air rights to NOGA. George Klein said the market for selling air rights for an apartment tower was "very soft," and recommended this as a good deal. There would also be savings in building the museum, because without the apartment tower, the foundation could be shallower.

Nessim Gaon was to enter into a letter of intent with BPCA for the purpose of building a hotel or apartment house. BPCA would then give a letter to the Holocaust commission, changing the site and granting a lease at one dollar per year for eighty-six years. The commission would then enter into an agreement with NOGA for transfer of the 400,000 square feet of air rights. NOGA would pay $30 million for the transfer as well as give a $2 million donation. BPCA would also make the same offer to other developers. A state Environmental Impact Study (EIS) was necessary, with a ULURP (Uniform Land Use Review Procedure) for the hotel but not the museum, according to the BPCA attorney. Both projects would need to be approved by the state Public Authorities Control Board, which oversees the issuing of bonds for Battery Park City.[1]

Based on this new arrangement, in September 1988 the commission was proceeding with plans for a November 10 ground breaking at Site 13, rather than Site 14. Newspapers reported on September 25 that the Koch administration had reached a preliminary agreement with NOGA, in which the Swiss company could build a hotel at Battery Park City in exchange for a $50 million payment to BPCA, most of which would be passed on to the city to build low- and middle-income housing, and an additional $30 million payment for the Holocaust museum.

However, Mario Cuomo, acting as governor rather than as one of the commission's leaders, suddenly decided to withhold his support from this deal (although *not* from the Holocaust museum project). Cuomo's press officer announced that the governor had not endorsed the agreement. This reflected a conflict between Governor Cuomo and the other founding cochairman of the project, Mayor Koch. The governor's office evidently felt that City Hall had intervened on his turf, by unilaterally releasing information on the deal to the press. Possibly there was also friction between Governor Cuomo and Sandy Frucher, although no one will admit it. At about the same time, Frucher, who had involved the governor in the Holocaust museum project in the first place and had encouraged the NOGA deal for BPCA, announced that he was leaving BPCA. He had accepted a high-level position with Olympia and York, developers of the World Financial Center in Battery Park City.[2]

Ultimately the ground breaking scheduled for November 10, 1988, did not take place because the governor, one of the leaders of the project, was at odds with the other founding cochairman, the mayor, and with the wishes of the commission's other leadership. Because Cuomo was the governor, he was able to take control as the central decision maker and block the deal. As governor, he could prevent those under his authority from acting; for example, the Department of Environmental Conservation did not act to approve an Environmental Impact Statement. This prevention of requisite action, in turn, stopped the Holocaust commission from carrying out the action of breaking ground. The governor had said the announcement of the ground breaking was "surprising and premature," and that substantive questions needed answers before the project could proceed.[3] By using his power as governor to block the NOGA deal, one head of the political coalition creating the Holocaust museum project was at least delaying the project, or possibly ultimately killing it. However, Cuomo did not sever himself from the coalition. He was simultaneously the hatchet man for this stage of implementation and the founding cochairman of the project.

By intervening in the NOGA deal, the governor established that he (and not the mayor or George Klein or anyone else) could act autonomously to take control of the Holocaust project. Cuomo was supposed to be an integral part of a political coalition created to carry out the project, but at this stage he became the obstacle. In any given situation there may be an actor who is autonomous and thus cannot be controlled, as Edward Banfield has written about the dynamics of political influence.[4] Mayor Koch, Governor Cuomo, and commission cochairmen developer George Klein, Manhattan district attorney Robert M. Morgenthau, and New York State Senate minority leader Manfred Ohrenstein were all linked with each other in varying ways and in positions of power aside from the museum project. They were also connected with each other to work for the benefit of the Holocaust museum, and each of them thought he had a certain amount of power to control the project. However, because Governor Cuomo controlled the site, he was able to act autonomously and create an impasse that superseded the other prime players' power to control the situation.

Frucher learned about the NOGA deal from Mayor Koch's office. "I got a phone call from City Hall that said there was someone in New York who was looking to do a five-star hotel, that was interested in doing it possibly at the tip of Battery Park [City]," he told me. "I met with this gentleman. His name is Nessim Gaon. He came in and said he wanted to build a five-star hotel. Initially we talked about doing it and having within it the Holocaust museum." One thing led to another, Frucher recalled, and then architect James Stewart Polshek came up with the idea of moving the museum to a second site. "Gaon would purchase the second site as part of the deal and would pay the Holocaust museum $30 million," Frucher said. "In exchange for that, he would get additional FAR [Floor/Area Ratio] on his site which would allow for him to recoup some of those dollars. We renegotiated the deal. The deal was probably one of the most lucrative deals that we had at Battery Park City. Unfortunately during my transition the deal was undone. That's the story." Frucher said in early 1991 that his leaving BPCA "killed" the Holocaust museum project.[5] It certainly threatened it seriously, since he had been the project's broker with the governor, wearing the hats of both government official and commission executive committee member.

Museum director David Altshuler agreed that Frucher's departure was detrimental to implementing the NOGA agreement. Other high-level members of Governor Cuomo's staff may have considered the NOGA–BPCA–Holocaust commission deal Frucher's "self aggrandizement," he noted. The fact that Frucher switched his allegiance from the government to a developer probably caused resentment among his former colleagues.[6]

Asked whether BPCA—or in reality, the governor—reneged on the deal with the commission, Frucher remained loyal to his old friend Cuomo. "Yes, BPCA and the state did renege on the deal with the commission," he told me. "I don't know if it was the governor. I don't know who drove that." There were many rumors, "people on the outside" questioning NOGA's integrity, Frucher said, adding that he had raised this issue with Morgenthau, "who checked [NOGA] out, and they checked out." Frucher also mentioned a rumor about other real estate people in the area (such as Peter Kalikow or Jerry Speyer) wanting to stop the hotel, but said he could not confirm it. Whether or not the governor himself "drove" the withdrawal, he must at least have approved of the move. One of Cuomo's high-level advisors such as Fabian Palomino, then chairman of the board of BPCA and a very close personal friend, may have been influential in the decision.

By November 1988, after the governor's stonewall, the situation had deteriorated rapidly and the implementation phase was not moving forward. On November 2, David Altshuler sent a memorandum to the executive committee members telling them a decision had been made the night before to postpone the ground breaking for the museum. The letter does not say who made the decision. Most likely it was George Klein, with the agreement of cochairman Robert Morgenthau, Koch operative Herbert Rickman, and Altshuler. Cochairman Manfred Ohrenstein was not consulted. A "Dear Friends" letter, which accompanied the memorandum, was signed by cochairmen Klein and Morgenthau and sent to a broader mailing list. "We are writing to inform you," the letter stated, "that our ground-breaking, scheduled for November 10, has been postponed. As you may know from having read the papers a few weeks ago, we are awaiting approval by the Battery Park City Authority and the Governor's office of a plan that will result in a site change for the Museum to a plot immediately adjacent to the one it was originally to occupy. To date, the review of the plan has not been completed, and it would be imprudent for us to break ground without those approvals. As you know, we had chosen November 10 as our groundbreaking date to coincide with the 50th anniversary of *Kristallnacht*, although actual construction was and still is scheduled to begin in the spring.

"We are very excited about the pending plan," the letter went on, "for its successful conclusion will provide us not only with a freestanding Museum adjacent to our original site but also with a major addition of $30 million to our capital campaign, permitting us to build and maintain the institution we have so long anticipated. We are confident that in the very near future, when we do break ground and begin construction, we will have reason to rejoice, for we will at long last be on our way to realizing our dream of honoring the six million who died by erecting a permanent structure of public education that will memorialize them by remembering how they lived. We know we can count on your continued good support in this important endeavor."[7]

Read between the lines, the letter implied that the governor's office had intervened and prevented the ground breaking from taking place. An integral member of the coalition of political forces had used his autonomous authority to cause detrimental delays for a project he was supporting, in fact nominally heading. The leaders of the commission were fearful that this intervention would not simply delay but possibly terminate their project, by disrupting momentum and drying up fund-raising. They were therefore trying to assure their contributors and potential contributors that they, too, had power to control the situation and that the implementation of the project was still a reality.

What Jeffrey L. Pressman and Aaron Wildavsky concluded about the failure to implement a federal employment project in California would seem to apply in particular to the fate of the New York Holocaust museum: "What seemed to be a simple program turned out to be a very complex one, involving numerous participants, a host of differing perspectives, and a long and tortuous path of decision points that had to be cleared. Given these characteristics, the chances of completing the program with the haste its designers had hoped for—and even the chances of completing it at all—were sharply reduced."[8] The structure of the Holocaust commission was so complex at this time that it was possible for one of its leaders to do damage at the same time that he remained an integral part of the coalition.

The delay in the ground breaking was clearly orchestrated by the Cuomo administration. Besides proving that the governor and not the mayor was the lead player for BPCA affairs, his advisors needed to carefully determine whether his close affiliation with the Holocaust museum project was, in fact, good for his political future. The resulting delay was very serious for the commission, however, because its credibility was at stake. It was not a delay the other members of the coalition had anticipated or wanted, although it was deliberately planned by the Cuomo administration. "Not all the delays were unplanned, accidental occurrences; some were caused intentionally by participants who wanted to stop an undesired action or to step back and reassess the development of the program," as Pressman and Wildavsky observed regarding the California project.[9] At this point, after Frucher's departure, Governor Cuomo (along with advisors such as Fabian Palomino) was apparently reassessing his affiliation with the commission and deciding whether to remain so closely connected with it.

At the end of September 1988 a new player had entered the scene, which undoubtedly was a factor in the governor's stonewalling on the NOGA deal and delaying the Holocaust museum. After Sandy Frucher resigned, Cuomo appointed as president of BPCA David Emil, a thirty-seven-year-old deputy commissioner in the state Social Services Department and the son of a prominent real estate developer. Although he is Jewish, unlike Frucher he is not an actively committed Jew. In addition to believing involvement in the Holocaust memorial project would help Governor Cuomo politically, Frucher genuinely believed there should be such a memorial in New York City. Emil acted as though it were just another real estate deal. Moreover, Frucher and Cuomo were close friends and political allies, and Frucher had played a major role behind the scenes in Cuomo's campaigns. Emil lacked these personal ties with the governor. As the *New York Times* said of Emil's appointment: "To political mavens, the main question is not what sort of leadership Mr. Emil will give Battery Park City, a complex of offices and apartments in lower Manhattan, but rather what sort of relationship he will have with the Governor."[10]

A November 21 story in a weekly serving lower Manhattan reported that David Emil had told the newspaper a new plan for use of sites 13, 14, and 1 would be announced in early December. (Sites 14 and 1 are the southernmost sites, with Site 1 east of Site 14; Site 13 is adjacent to and north of Site 14.) "We are still working with the principals at this point. There is no final resolution of the treatment of sites 1, 13 and 14 yet," Emil is quoted as saying in the article. While admitting that BPCA chairman (and Cuomo's special counsel and longtime friend) Fabian Palomino and other board members did vote to accept the NOGA proposal in August, Emil said they later shelved it because they had originally believed they were approving only a letter of intent, and not the transaction itself. "We're discussing conceptual ideas and some specifics. It's like any other real estate deal," Emil is quoted as saying. He expected to seek a zoning change for commercial use of one of the sites to allow for construction of a hotel, but he declined to say which site. He also pointed out that the museum had controlled Site 14 since 1985, and had been unable to develop it.[11]

The transaction between NOGA and the commission seems to have been a victim of the changing of the guard when Emil replaced Frucher, who had made the NOGA deal. Frucher had been a member of the executive committee and an active participant at its meetings, and also had represented BPCA and the governor. He thus was wearing three hats with regard to the project. In fact, housing the Holocaust museum in Battery Park City had been his idea. While he had a "paternal" interest in the project, Emil was an outsider and represented only BPCA. Although it cannot be proven, Emil was also probably acting as a "fall guy" for Governor Cuomo, whose interest in the project seems to have waned at this point. Palomino took over from Frucher as the governor's personal representative to negotiate with the commission. What Frucher had been willing to push through and implement as quickly and cooperatively as possible, Emil and Palomino wanted to obstruct. They did not want to be responsible for possible precedents engineered by Frucher that would make them, the governor, and BPCA vulnerable to criticism.

In comparison to Frucher's deep personal involvement with the Holocaust project, Emil's apparent interest was routine and his lack of knowledge remarkable. When I asked him in 1991 about the complicated and changing structure of the political coalition behind the project, he said: "Why are you asking me? I'm not involved in the Holocaust Memorial Commission." He told me that he did not know that the governor was a founding cochairman, or anything about the details of the commission. He also did not know that appointments to the commission had been made by the mayor and the governor.

"My experience of [the commission] is that it is a creature of a small group of people who are not politicians, and it happens to have politicians involved in it. It's really run by George Klein," Emil remarked. He considered the commission "indistinguishable from any not-for-profit entity in New York State. It has no greater or lesser governmental role—kind of like the Museum of Modern Art, in the sense that there are government officials who

are interested in its successful activities for various different reasons because—in the case of the Holocaust memorial because of
the commemoration of the event and so forth, in the case of the
Museum of Modern Art for other reasons—but it essentially func-
tions as a not-for-profit organization that has sort of ex officio
political figures at various levels who have different interests."
Emil had never heard of Herbert Rickman, Koch's political entrepreneur who had initiated the project and been heavily involved until Koch's departure at the end of 1989 (more than a
year after Emil's arrival on the scene).[12]

Besides Frucher's departure and his replacement by Emil,
another possible reason for Governor Cuomo's decreasing enthusiasm for the Holocaust museum project may have been his
interest in running for president. Although promoting a particularistic Jewish museum in New York City was politically good
for being reelected governor, it could appear somewhat parochial
in a presidential race. Fabian Palomino and another Cuomo
counsel, Evan Davis, repeatedly told the Holocaust commission
cochairmen and executive committee of their concern for First
Amendment issues. They did not want the governor to be accused
of supporting a project that could be questioned with regard to
separation of church and state (see Chapter 15).

While the *New York Post* is often too sensationalist to be a
reliable news source, on December 8, 1988, it broke a story on
the NOGA–Commission–BPCA situation that was to prove accurate in many respects. The article revealed that BPCA had announced for the first time that the Holocaust museum would have
to pay for its lease. Instead of the previously agreed upon one
dollar per year (in the lease for Site 14), the museum would have
to pay "market rent for cultural institutions," according to Emil.
The amount would be "in the millions" over the period of the
lease, Emil told the *Post*, running (as do all Battery Park City
leases) until the year 2069. The rent for private nonprofit arts
groups that signed leases in the two previous years in buildings
not owned by the city had averaged $10 to $12 per square foot
annually, according to the article. For the museum's 150,000
square feet on Site 13, this would make the annual rent between
$1.5 and $1.8 million a year.[13]

Regarding NOGA, the *Post* wrote that, under Frucher, BPCA
had passed a resolution on August 25 to take "all steps necessary

and appropriate related to the development of parcels 13 and 14 in accordance with" letters of intent between the parties. But Emil, who had not been present at the August meeting and succeeded Frucher by October, said that the vote "merely authorized me to investigate the NOGA deal." Palomino, Cuomo's special counsel and chairman of BPCA, told the *Post*, "We just authorized a letter of intent, talking about what we thought we intended to do. . . . We had certain reservations." He added that the legislation that created BPCA required that it be paid rent on all parcels, which the museum would not have done under the NOGA agreement. The original lease also did not require payment of rent, except for the symbolic dollar per year. This symbolic payment seems to have fulfilled the letter of the law under Frucher's leadership, but not under Emil's, which may have been a reflection of Cuomo's shrinking interest in the project and grander ambitions to run for national office at that time.

"There was a lease entered into in 1986 which allowed the Holocaust Memorial Commission and the Museum of Jewish Heritage to build a building on one of our sites—14, which would have contained the museum in the base and a residential building on top," Emil explained to me in 1991. "And the actual rent that was paid under that lease was much more than one dollar a year—[it was] $45 per square foot valuation of the property [for the residential portion of the complex]. But the thing you have to realize in order to understand the transaction from the economic point of view and from the authority's point of view is that the authority did not recognize the square footage of the museum for the purposes of our zoning calculations. In a nutshell we were allowing a bigger building to be built than might have otherwise been built. And we were getting paid for that portion of the building that would have been allowed on the site anyway. So we said to the Holocaust Memorial Commission, you can build a bigger building than the site currently allows and we won't charge you in excess of what's presently allowed. Now, what then happened is the Holocaust Memorial Commission was unable to find a builder that was interested in building a residential tower on top of the museum."[14] The Holocaust commission then looked for another transaction, in which they tried to sell the entire lease to NOGA. One critical problem for BPCA was the absence of a public bid process for the site. "Land here is for public bid, not through private deals," Emil said. "As regards the question of how rent came to be charged on Site 13, the position of the authority and the position of the governor in this particular regard was, 'Look, we gave you a lease on Site 14. You chose to sell the site and you're going to make a $30 million profit. That's what they got for the sale. Now you made a $30 million profit and you want us to give you another one.'"

When I pointed out to Emil that the commission didn't sell the lease to NOGA, he offered the following scenario: "It didn't go through, but if they did sell it . . . we weren't going to give them another one. This could go on forever. We could give them every piece and soon they would have hundreds of millions of dollars." Emil then admitted that this "seriously would never happen." If the transaction had gone forward, it would have been accomplished by means of "a negotiated understanding with the Holocaust Memorial [Commission], through which essentially the authority agreed to act as agent to sell the property for $32 million," he explained, "and the Memorial Commission agreed to rent the new site."[15] According to the terms of the NOGA deal, the commission would have ended up with about the same monetary compensation it had originally anticipated from its first lease with the state ($30 million, the value of the air rights before the October 1987 stock market crash). Since the NOGA deal essentially enabled them to build on a comparable adjacent site without air rights, Emil's explanation for the loss of free rent is not convincing.

At a December 14, 1988, meeting of the executive and development committees of the Holocaust commission, the information in the *Post* was confirmed and amplified. Because George Klein was out of the country, Robert Morgenthau conducted the meeting with Klein "attending" by speakerphone. Morgenthau and Klein had met with Emil and Palomino a week earlier, and BPCA had informed the commission that the NOGA deal was definitely off and would be given no further consideration. BPCA intended to find more than one developer to bid on a deal that would place a residential apartment building on Site 14, with the museum moving to Site 13 (as in the NOGA deal). The apartment developer would pay the museum $32 million for lease rights. BPCA had figured that the rent for the museum at Site 13 should be $10 million or more over the life of the ground lease, with the museum paying $5 million (or half of the rent) up front. Another

$5 million would be paid later, including a share of the proceeds from museum admissions. BPCA had told Klein and Morgenthau that it would be illegal to give anyone any site rent-free due to provisions in the 1972 bonding agreement. BPCA would know within two weeks whether they had developer interest or not for Site 14. If so, they would put out a challenge bid by mid-January 1989.

The loss of free (one dollar per year) rent was a major blow to the commission, and there were also other serious problems. The letter of agreement for the new lease was to expire at the end of December, 1988, and before that date the museum was required to submit schematics. Because the NOGA deal had not been firm, no plan had yet been developed. However, the commission expected to be able to work up a plan that would at least meet the legal requirements. But if the lease was renewed at the end of the year, BPCA would want the museum to begin paying rent of $100,000 per year.

Toward the end of the discussion of these problems at the December 1988 meeting, Sandy Frucher arrived. The governor was the commission's friend, Frucher told the executive and development committees, and "someone else" (unnamed) was causing the problems. Since this "someone else" would have to be subordinate to the governor, Frucher's explanation is implausible. So is his insistence that the governor called him almost daily out of genuine concern about the museum, since Frucher was no longer with BPCA and therefore not in a position to know the exact status of the project. Furthermore, this was not ever a project which Cuomo made a personal, day-to-day priority. The governor had more important things to discuss with Frucher on the telephone, such as campaign issues. Perhaps in this context the museum was occasionally a topic of conversation.

Although the governor had distanced himself from the commission and Frucher had left BPCA, Cuomo remained "founding cochairman" and the coalition remained in place, at least on paper. It was still agreed that there should be a Holocaust museum, but now there were negotiations *within* the coalition regarding the logistics of making it a reality. The executive committee authorized Klein and Morgenthau to go back to BPCA to obtain an extension of the lease and assurances that BPCA would put on the table by January 15, 1989, any names of potential developers for Site 14. They also wanted BPCA to agree to return to the

NOGA deal if no other developer emerged. As he had at earlier impasses, David Altshuler expressed fears about the project's loss of momentum and thus of funding.[16] Once again, there was the appearance in the "decision path of numerous diversions not intended by the program sponsors."[17]

13
More Steps Backward and Forward

There are always people who benefit, or think they do, from a widespread belief that a problem has been solved or that there has been substantial progress toward its solution.—Murray Edelman, Constructing the Political Spectacle, *1988*

The executive committee of the New York Holocaust Memorial Commission met on February 15, 1989, and decided to approve Battery Park City Authority's acceptance of an offer by a developer to build an apartment building on Site 14. The commission would thus relinquish the original site of the museum, and have the opportunity to build a freestanding museum on adjacent Site 13. Although BPCA said it would have in hand three offers for development of an apartment building by January 15, one month after that date there was only one such offer. The name of the developer was not revealed at the meeting: George Klein said he did not know who it was and did not want to know.

Klein and cochairman Robert Morgenthau had met with David Emil and Fabian Palomino of BPCA, who told them that the idea of a hotel had been turned down by BPCA because it would have been subject to a change of zoning, an Environmental Impact Study (EIS), and approval of the Public Authorities Control Board. The new deal, which still needed approvals from the city and BPCA, would, like the aborted arrangement with NOGA, give $32 million to the museum. Land would be rented from BPCA for about $4 million. On March 1, BPCA would send an RFP (Request For Proposals) for any offer that matched the one in hand. There would be a sixty-day waiting period, with a thirty-day extension. BPCA would accept only bids materially higher than the one in hand. There would then be thirty days for analysis, followed by two weeks for sealed and final bids between any parties that remained. Lease terms giving $32 million to the Holocaust museum would be attached to the RFP. For an apartment building, unlike a hotel, no EIS or rezoning was required.

Upon receipt of the $32 million, the Holocaust museum would give to BPCA $5 million for its required rental payment. This would leave $27 million for the museum. Payment would be due the next fall, when the apartment house developer would sign the lease with BPCA. The museum had to pay an additional $5.2 million to BPCA for an eighty-year lease (with no rent increases within the eighty years). Part of this payment was to come from 10 percent of any admissions contributions or fees that the museum would receive from the public after it opened, and BPCA agreed that this portion of the rent would not commence until the museum was operating. As the museum was in default of its lease with BPCA, and BPCA supposedly would not renew it unless the commission accepted this deal, BPCA had made "an offer one cannot refuse." The commission had boxed itself into a corner, dependent on the wishes of the state government. The governor was still part of the coalition, but on his terms. Approval of the new agreement by the board of BPCA was anticipated within ten days, possibly followed by a major press conference with the governor and the mayor.[1]

No press conference was held, but on February 23, 1989, there were press releases from BPCA, Mayor Koch, and the commission. BPCA announced that it had authorized that day "a series of steps that will provide for construction of a 38-floor residential tower, development of a luxury hotel, and construction of a memorial to the Holocaust and Museum of Jewish Heritage, and will provide $50 million of BPCA funding for New York City's housing program over the next three years." According to the press release, BPCA would issue an RFP for a 589,000-square-foot residential tower, 360 feet in height, for Site 14. There would be a minimum bid for rental payments of $121 per square foot of developable area, which included a $32 million payment to the Holocaust commission. The RFP also required annual rent payments from the developer to BPCA of about $3.8 million (to be adjusted over the eighty-year term of the lease). BPCA was also issuing an RFP for a luxury hotel or "mixed use hotel/ residential use" on Site 1, which was "consistent with previous plans for Battery Park City." In addition, BPCA was entering into an agreement with the Holocaust commission, in which the museum would relinquish its rights to Site 14 upon receipt of $32 million from the Site 14 developer and enter into a new lease with BPCA for Site 13. The commission had agreed to pay rent of $10.2 million, of which $5 million was to be paid immediately.

"Under these agreements everyone is a winner," Governor Cuomo is quoted as saying in the press release, which did not refer to the fact that one of the "winners," the Holocaust commission, was now losing $10.2 million—which it did not have to pay in the original agreement in 1986. For his part, BPCA board chairman Fabian Palomino referred to the "outstanding sites" and the "significant economic benefits from a first-class hotel and tourist attraction in Lower Manhattan."[2]

In his press release on the same date, Mayor Koch, who had taken a back seat to Governor Cuomo with regard to the project after the site changed to Battery Park City, stated that he had for many years "supported proposals for the creation in New York City of a museum and memorial to the victims of the Holocaust." He also praised the economic benefits from a new residential development, a first-class hotel, and a new tourist attraction in lower Manhattan, plus the generation of $50 million for affordable housing in New York City.[3] In a very brief statement the next day, George Klein and Robert Morgenthau said the museum would benefit greatly from being freestanding, and also from an infusion of $27 million in cash. They thanked Governor Cuomo, Mayor Koch, BPCA president David Emil, and BPCA chairman Fabian Palomino—their alleged colleagues in the coalition creating a Holocaust memorial museum.[4]

As Klein had announced at the February 15, 1989, executive committee meeting, the *New York Times* reported that one proposal meeting the condition of contributing $32 million to the Holocaust museum had already been received. The *Times* article named Property Resources Corporation (PRC), a developer that had already built a condominium project in Battery Park City, as the prospective developer. The letter of intent with NOGA had been terminated, the article went on, NOGA's good-faith deposit check was being returned, and NOGA was considering the possibility of suing BPCA.[5]

On April 4, 1989, David Emil for BPCA and George Klein and Robert Morgenthau for the commission and museum signed a letter of understanding that set forth the terms by which a free-standing museum could be built, with the project receiving $27 million ($32 million from the Site 14 developer, minus the $5 million rent to BPCA). Implementation could begin anew, after PRC or another developer was accepted by BPCA and signed a different letter of understanding with the commission and the museum (obtaining Site 14 in return for a payment to the commission of $32 million).

Meanwhile, on May 9, 1989, Stephen Robert, cochairman of the commission's development committee, announced that $17.2 million had been raised. Of this amount, only some $7 million was in cash. A financial statement on May 31, 1989, revealed there was a contribution income of $7,260,000, with $10,335,000 in pledges receivable. With $27 million anticipated from BPCA, the commission needed to raise an additional estimated $66 million. This would more than cover the projected $103,019,650 cost of the museum, repayment of a $2 million bank loan, and $300,000 owed for architectural fees.[6]

The commission decided at a June 8, 1989, meeting to go ahead with a massive fund-raising campaign to reach their goal of $103 million. (This did not include $30 million for an endowment fund.) After thirty-five years of prehistory, before the mayor convened his task force, plus more than seven years of this project, museum director David Altshuler announced, "We are now poised to succeed." The commission had to finish its work now, he said, because distortions and trivializations of the Holocaust were multiplying and survivors disappearing. David Edell, the fund-raising consultant, said it was possible to raise $100 million from the Jews of New York City.

Sandy Frucher, who was no longer working for the governor or for BPCA, believed the governor was committed to making the project work. "Make it a fait accompli, and then you'll get the $27 million," he said. George Klein hoped to have $38 million in hand by November, including the $27 million from BPCA. He then anticipated breaking ground in January 1990 and completing the museum by Yom Hashoah (Holocaust Remembrance Day) in April 1992. Those present voted to approve moving forward with the project as planned, without decreasing the size or scope of the exhibitions for the projected museum.[7]

The June 8, 1989, meeting was like a pep rally for a losing team. Everyone patted each other on the back and expressed confidence that the project would move forward. In reality, there were serious problems with finances, fund-raising, and closing a deal with PRC or any other developer. The commission was proceeding on the good faith of the governor and BPCA that the arrangement with PRC would go forward, but there were no guarantees. A commission leader later remarked off the record that Fabian Palomino had decided the NOGA deal was no good, but he did not want the governor to look bad by completely reneging on the Holocaust museum project. Palomino had therefore stopped the NOGA deal and found PRC as a developer for the site. I cannot verify or deny this, because Palomino would not talk with me. First he did not appear for a confirmed interview at his office in the World Trade Center. He then made an appointment for a telephone interview that he did not keep; and he did not answer questions that I sent him in writing.

At about the same time that the new PRC deal was in progress, the commission's fund-raising methods became diversified and intense, and some were in questionable taste. For example, proposals were prepared for foundations that included the Grace Foundation. In June 1981, Yeshiva University had canceled a major fund-raising dinner honoring J. Peter Grace, after the Jewish Telegraphic Agency revealed that Grace had aided a convicted Nazi war criminal.[8] In addition, there was a direct-mail campaign, using a personal appeal by popular television sexologist Dr. Ruth Westheimer. Although Westheimer is a refugee from Nazism (described as a survivor in the mailing), her role in fund-raising appears to trivialize the Holocaust by its association with a popular sex therapist.[9] An "Associates Division," created to attract younger donors, also held an event that seems inappropriate. On October 23, 1988, "The Associates Division of The New York Holocaust Memorial Commission invite[d] you to Rock and Roll the Night Away" at The Hot Rod, for a donation of $125 to the commission. Despite the fact that the event included an educational film, the location and the invitation did not dignify the commission's mission.

After June 1989, progress on the project barely crept forward for more than a year. In November, PRC was chosen as the developer of the apartment building at Site 14. The owners of PRC, Jerome Shatzky and Frank Lindy, then began searching for funding. PRC was supposed to put up the money for their project by April 5, 1990, the second extension BPCA had given them. Because of the soft real estate market for luxury apartments, especially in the Wall Street area, Citibank had withdrawn its financing. The museum therefore could not sign a lease with BPCA, because BPCA did not have the $27 million from the developer. Meanwhile, in March 1990 the Holocaust commission was trying to obtain money from such sources as Leonard Stern and was basically being told, "Don't call us, we'll call you." David Altshuler reportedly said in March that if there was "no hole in the ground by the end of June, we can all go home." But, he also said, a $27 million letter of credit from BPCA would help.[10]

An emergency meeting of the executive committee was held on April 19, 1990, in the office of George Klein. The main item on the agenda was money—or lack of it. The committee decided to appoint a five-member study group to explore how to scale back the day-to-day operations of the museum project. At that time there was a staff of thirty, with a $3 million annual budget. Almost $11 million had already been spent. Another subcommittee was to be appointed to scale back the museum costs from $100 million to $50 million. The committees were to report back in a month or less. Other suggestions included recommending that a state agency such as the Urban Development Corporation or the Education Department float tax-free bonds to cover the cost so a lease could be signed, and asking Governor Cuomo to tell BPCA that the commission wanted its dollar-a-year lease back. The possibility of Howard Rubenstein, Robert Morgenthau, George Klein, and maybe Sandy Frucher and cochairman Senator Manfred Ohrenstein meeting with Governor Cuomo was discussed. Mayor Koch, who had lost his reelection bid to David Dinkins in November 1989, was no longer actively in the picture, although he remained a founding cochairman. Nor was the new mayor, David Dinkins, showing signs of interest at this point.

The status of PRC's apartment project was also discussed at the meeting. After PRC had been selected, its source of financing, Citibank, had pulled out. Now Citibank was back in, but with unrealistic restrictions. Citibank had written a letter saying it would guarantee $150 million if the developer came up with $52 million (which would include a $12 million letter of credit and $40 million in cash). Citibank also wanted to be able to lay off $75 million to a third party co-lender so that it would not have to bear full responsibility for making the loan to PRC. Since virtually no one was doing this kind of residential financing at that time, it was an impossible condition for PRC to meet.

Klein admitted that accepting the governor's original Battery Park City deal was a mistake. It was a decision made by very intelligent, savvy people, he noted, but it was based on emotion—on the desire to be the best and have the best museum in the best location. In retrospect, he said they should have stuck to the Custom House. It was anticipated that PRC would default and lose its $250,000 deposit. Site 13 would still be set aside for the museum, with the commission selling the lease (with air rights) to Site 14. However, nothing could then be built. The site, with air rights, was worth about $30 million, but it seemed nothing was about to happen.[11]

By August 1990, there was still no progress. Harry W. Albright, Jr. replaced Fabian Palomino as the president of BPCA that month. Albright, CEO of Dime Savings Bank, was said to be close to the governor's son, Andrew Cuomo. (Andrew is also reportedly the governor's contact with Robert Morgenthau.) Museum director Altshuler thought that Palomino had caused some of the snags and that Albright, starting with a clean slate, was more likely to "undo the mess." According to Altshuler, Albright had told Morgenthau that his first assignment from the governor was to fix "our problem," which meant development of Site 14. There were a number of possibilities: to get a new developer for Site 14 (for which the museum owned the lease and air rights); to have the state give some concessions from its profit on a deal; to find a way for the commission to get money in some other way than development of Site 14; or to lower the commission's rent, or drop the $5 million up-front rental fee. "We are trying to be careful to stay out of how this is accomplished," Altshuler told me. "But they [the governor and BPCA] got us into this and should get us out. They signed up NOGA and then threw him out. They got us out of the Custom House and into Battery Park City."[12]

By the end of 1990, nothing had moved. Harry Albright, the new BPCA chairman, had promised progress by Labor Day, but then he became seriously ill. He then pledged to resolve the situation by the end of the year, but became ill again. PRC had been released from its pending agreement. The commission hoped to get some money from a deal including the sale of its lease and air rights when the market improved at a later date.[13] In February 1991, the commission was anticipating a new memo of understanding between the museum and BPCA. Altshuler expected the memo in weeks, and the lease in months. There would be a ground breaking before the end of 1991, but there was no rush, he told me, since the museum needed to be redesigned. The museum was to go back to Site 14 and use only half of the site— that closest to the water. BPCA would get back Site 13 and could build one or more apartment buildings both on it and the other half of Site 14—when the market got better.[14]

The expected memo from BPCA finally materialized on July 26, 1991. As Altshuler had anticipated, it called for a new museum lease on half of Site 14 and terminated the 1986 leases for a museum and a residential building on the site. According to this new arrangment, the commission would build a $50 million (rather than $100 million) museum on half of Site 14. BPCA would give the commission $10 million as a "construction draw," or a down payment for the air rights, which would later be recouped from the developer of the other half of Site 14. (BPCA would probably obtain the $10 million by floating commercial paper.) Later, when the other half of the site was leased to a developer for residential construction, BPCA would give the museum a minimum of another $10 million (depending on the agreement) and also recoup this amount from the developer. The museum claimed the half of the site facing the Hudson River and Statue of Liberty.

Although new external and internal designs for the museum would be necessary, the concept would remain the same. Of the $23 million the commission had raised, about $10 million was left. With this $10 million and the $10 million from BPCA, the commission would need to raise $30 million more to build the museum. The other $10 million from BPCA (from the sale of the second half of the site) would be used to begin the endowment fund. The new target date to begin construction was 1992, with the museum expected to open in 1994.[15]

Thus the project entered a new phase. Governor Cuomo and BPCA, which he controlled, had made a new deal with the Holocaust commission, one that even involved a $10 million investment. Former Mayor Koch was still officially a founding cochairman, but he was out of office and, in reality, out of the picture. The governor was thus the key elected official involved in the project. At that time, by coincidence or not, Cuomo seemed inclined not to run for president. "Of 13 current and former Cuomo aides surveyed in the last week, none said they believed that Mr. Cuomo would run for President," according to an article in the *New York Times* on the day before the memorandum was signed.[16]

Meanwhile, ten years had gone by since Ed Koch's initiation of the project, and time itself was an enemy. The first meeting of Koch's task force, the initial stage of the coalition behind the project, took place on July 22, 1981—almost ten years earlier to the day. Costs had escalated, unforeseen problems, such as the drop in real estate values, had developed, protagonists such as Koch had left the scene, and new players such as Cuomo, Palomino, and Emil had caused further complications and delays in implementation. Governor Cuomo and the BPCA had then come up with a plan to "save the day." As Jeffrey Pressman and Aaron Wildavsky observed about another implementation process, "The advantages of being new are exactly that: being new. They dissipate quickly over time."[17] In the case of the latest attempt to create a Holocaust memorial museum in New York City, there had been ten years of such dissipation.

According to the July 26, 1991, memorandum of understanding, the commission had an obligation to the state for funds in hand by July 1992, a deadline it did not meet. Meanwhile, on April 20, 1992, an agreement had been drafted but never carried out to locate the New York Holocaust memorial museum at 440 Lafayette Street in Greenwich Village, at least temporarily. The museum was to form a partnership with the YIVO Institute for Jewish Research and share facilities, while retaining autonomy. This plan may have been conceived in anticipation of the museum's failure to meet the state's July deadline for the Battery Park City site. However, the commission informed BPCA that it planned to occupy the Lafayette Street building as a temporary facility. At about the time in August 1992 that BPCA agreed to extend the July deadline for six more months, the Lafayette Street idea was dropped and the BPCA project moved forward.

On February 17, 1993, a new memorandum of understanding was signed between the Holocaust commission and BPCA. According to this document, the commission had 150 days from the initiation of the memo to raise some $12 million in hard cash or enforceable pledges for a scaled-down museum on part of Site

14 in Battery Park City. This building was to consist of 27,000 to 60,000 square feet, with BPCA contributing up to $10 million to cover 50 percent of the budget for such costs as design, construction, and the museum interior. Annual rent was to be 10 percent of the admission fees or contributions in lieu of fees paid by visitors to the museum.

As in the 1991 memorandum of agreement, the First Amendment of the Constitution of the United States is cited. The memorandum repeats the 1991 provisos forbidding religious worship, sectarian instruction, and the requirement that people observe any religious laws or customs. However, subject to these provisos, the museum could permit "other qualified nonprofit organizations, such as the Yeshiva University, to use a portion or portions of the building, not to exceed 12,000 square feet in the aggregate, for the public exhibition of materials related to the mission of the Museum."[18] This specific reference to Yeshiva University may have been in deference to Ludwig Jesselson, a survivor and philanthropist who had heavily endowed the university and had pledged $5 million toward the new museum. As though the project did not have enough problems, Jesselson died suddenly, soon after the new memorandum was signed.

According to the memorandum, the museum could not commence construction until it had sufficient cash in hand for completing construction and opening the museum. Furthermore, any debts incurred by the museum or the commission had to be covered by enforceable pledges or guarantees, and all debts had to be disclosed to BPCA. The memorandum was to expire in July 1993 if the commission did not have $10 million in hand and its current debts (about $2 million) paid. BPCA promised to make available another $10 million for construction, and any developer of the other half of the site was required pay to the commission the greater of $17.5 million or the appraised fair market value, less the amount of BPCA's $10 million construction payment. Before a new lease was signed, BPCA required that the commission and museum furnish them with an updated feasibility study, including debts, expenses, and projections for attendance and admission fees. The new memorandum nullified the 1989 letter of agreement and the 1991 memorandum of understanding.

The architect chosen for this new phase of the project was Kevin Roche, whose renovation of the Jewish Museum in New

York City was completed in June 1993. By July 20, 1993, the end of the 150-day deadline, the cochairmen of the commission wrote to BPCA asking for a 90-day extension. They said that they had raised more than $6 million, were in the midst of other solicitations, and Jesselson's untimely death had set them back. Once again BPCA granted an extension. This extension expired in November, at which time the commission had $8 million in hand, plus the promise of a $10 million advance from BPCA. Yet another extension was then granted, which expired at the end of February 1994. At that time, a new lease should have been signed, with money in hand and approvals for construction. However, the commission was still short $12 million to finish the project; and six more months of delays and extensions ensued. The total projected cost was about $30 million, for about 60,000 square feet of space. The 1993 memorandum of understanding was a tough one, requiring the commission to have 100 percent of its construction money committed "up front."

14
Internal Power Struggles and Conflicts

Dogs in a kennel snarl at each other; but when a wolf comes along they become allies.—Talmud: Sanhedrin 105a.

In an ideal political alliance, there is a genuine sense of harmony among the coalition members for the greater good of a common goal. In a less than ideal situation, the players at least try to project a public image of harmony. In the case of the New York Holocaust Commission, however, the relationships among Mayor Koch, Governor Cuomo, and other leaders have been unusually complex and subject to conflicts. In addition, the project has been so long in the making that the cast of characters, and their relationships, has changed over the years. The most obvious examples are that the commission's initiator, Mayor Koch, and the project's advocate in Governor Cuomo's office, Meyer S. (Sandy) Frucher, left their influential positions in government before any real implementation began. Their absences created gaps in the power structure of the commission that caused conflicts as others jockeyed to take their places. Furthermore, former governor Cuomo, former mayor Koch, former Battery Park City Authority president Frucher, and others were all part of the commission itself, but they were simultaneously the government officials with whom the commission was dealing. This situation created built-in conflicts of interest.

For four years (1986–89) the heads of the city and state governments shared the spotlight as "founding cochairmen." Koch and Cuomo had a say about the project both as commission officers and as elected representatives of government. In addition, two of the five cochairs, Manhattan district attorney Robert Morgenthau and New York State Senate minority leader Manfred Ohrenstein, were elected officials. The most active cochairman, George Klein, is a major real estate developer involved in multi-million-dollar deals with both the city and the state. The fifth and newest cochairman, powerful public relations broker Howard Rubenstein, has lucrative contracts with both elected officials and real estate developers, some of whom are connected to the commission. His firm also has been doing pro bono public relations for the commission. Because of the complicated structure and overlapping of roles, internal conflict has been inevitable.

In exploring the complex interrelation of politics, public position, and power in general, Harold Seidman offers a good example of the conflicts of interest that can occur when elected officials are also part of an interest group. "Intermingling of public and private duties places public officials in an ambiguous position," he writes. "There are many unanswered questions. Do the secretaries of housing and urban development and agriculture serve as directors of the National Home Ownership Foundation in their official capacity, or as private citizens? To whom are federal officials accountable for their actions as directors if the foundation is not an agency and instrumentality of the United States, what then are its responsibilities to the president, the Congress, and ultimately, through them, to the people?"[1] In this context, as founding cochairmen and members of the Holocaust museum commission, as well as elected officials, to whom were the governor and mayor responsible?

Although all of the commission leaders have remained faithful to the basic idea of a Holocaust memorial museum, they have expressed varying degrees of loyalty, involvement, and criteria for implementation. These differences have sometimes caused individuals to be at odds with one or more political forces in the coalition. (Governor Cuomo's midstream cooling down, detailed earlier, is the most obvious example.) In addition, the complex structure of the coalition, with its large cast of city, state, and private interest group players—and some people in more than one category at the same time—is subject to a number of conflicts between itself and various members. While some of these conflicts evolved from circumstances that had nothing to do with the project at hand, they nevertheless affected the coalition's unity.

The major players involved in the museum project have been Mayor Ed Koch, Koch political entrepreneur Herbert Rickman, developer George Klein, District Attorney Robert Morgenthau, Governor Mario Cuomo, Cuomo political entrepreneurs and BPCA officials Sandy Frucher and Fabian Palomino, Senator Manfred Ohrenstein, public relations man Howard Rubenstein, and, to a much lesser degree, Peter A. Cohen, who became inactive on the commission for an extended time after he lost his position as chairman and CEO at Shearson Lehman Hutton in 1987. By 1991, new BPCA officials David Emil and Harry W. Albright, Jr. were also involved in the coalition, but not as members of the commission. After David Dinkins became mayor in 1990, at a stage of impasse and stagnation in the project, he seemed to take little interest. If the July 1991 deal between BPCA and the commission had gone forward while he was still in office, most likely he would have publicly displayed great interest. This might have caused new friction with Governor Cuomo, who then had no competition in this endeavor from a mayor, as he formerly had from Koch. However, during Dinkins's four years as mayor there was little progress on the project that would have been politically useful to him, and little encouragement or input from him or his office. By the time the project looked viable in the summer of 1994, Mayor Rudolph Giuliani was on the scene to share the limelight, although he had taken no previous active role. His relationship with the rest of the coalition has been cooperative, as has that of George Pataki, who became the governor of New York State in January 1995.

Perhaps it would have been politically wise of former mayor David Dinkins to become an outspoken advocate of the Holocaust memorial museum project. Liberal Jewish voters supported Dinkins, who is black, more than other whites did in the 1989 New York City mayoral election. However, after an incident that took place on August 19, 1991, he lost a great deal of leverage in the Jewish community. On that day, a seven-year-old black child, Gavin Cato, was accidentally killed when hit by a car driven by a Lubavitch Hasidic Jew in the Crown Heights section of Brooklyn. The black community in Crown Heights and beyond was enraged, especially when the Jewish ambulance service attended to the relatively unharmed driver rather than the dying child.

In the ensuing riots and demonstrations a twenty-nine-year-old Australian Jewish student, Yankele Rosenbaum, was murdered by a black mob in Crown Heights. The next day, crowds of Hasidim and blacks had to be separated outside of the local police precinct, and the police commissioner met with leaders of both groups. Black leaders demanded the arrest of the driver who had killed the black child; Jewish stores were looted, cars burned, and homes stoned.

On August 21, radical black leader Al Sharpton called a press conference to demand the arrest of the driver, and that night 1,000 police were on duty in the area as the rioting continued. Eighteen civilians and forty-three policemen were wounded, and there were twenty-seven arrests. The next day Mayor Dinkins ordered the police commissioner to take stronger measures. The riots ended after sixty-two arrests by 2,000 policemen. On September 5, 1991, a grand jury cleared the driver of criminal charges. Finally, on September 9, Mayor Dinkins called the murder of Rosenbaum a "lynching." Since this term has historically been associated with racist murders of blacks by whites in the South in the United States, this seemed to be an acknowledgment by Dinkins of racism in Rosenbaum's murder. At the time of the rioting and afterward, some leaders of the organized Jewish community complained that Dinkins did not react swiftly enough.

On October 29, 1992, more than a year after the incident and about a year before the next mayoral election, the black teenager accused of murdering Rosenbaum was acquitted by a jury. This sparked new Jewish demonstrations against Mayor Dinkins, charging that he favored blacks over Jews. Five hundred Hasidim with signs reading "Wanted for murder: David Dinkins" protested in front of City Hall. On November 17, Governor Cuomo ordered an inquiry by New York State. Two days later, a new police commissioner admitted that the police in Crown Heights had been too slow in reacting to the riot. But he emphasized that this was not a result of orders from Dinkins, as some Jewish leaders had alleged. Mayor Dinkins tried to make peace with the Jewish community on November 25, 1992, when he went on television to offer a Thanksgiving message of "reconciliation and redemption." However, this effort did not recapture the confidence of enough liberal Jews to help him win the November 1993 race for reelection. (He never had been supported by the more conservative members of the Jewish community, including Re-

publican George Klein.) Perhaps a prominent role on the Holocaust commission would have helped David Dinkins politically
in the organized Jewish community. As the mayor of New York
City, he was automatically an official of the commission, but he
never gave it priority.

Unlike Dinkins, Ed Koch had always been close to New York
City's organized Jewish community, including the Hasidim.
Koch and George Klein were closely connected, and there were
no known conflicts between them regarding the Holocaust project. However, they had other business, including the
multimillion-dollar Times Square redevelopment project, which
caused friction from time to time. Koch recalled in his autobiog-
raphy, *Mayor*, how Klein came to see him in 1982 to complain
about the administration's limitation of tax abatements for some
of his other real estate developments, the skyscrapers he was
planning to build on the East Side. Klein complained that this
zoning change was "going to cost me millions of dollars," according to Koch. "We acquired property. I have forty-eight million dollars in this property. And now you are going to make it
impossible to build on it. We are going to sue!" Klein told Koch.
"Of course you should sue, George," Koch responded. "I am not
suggesting that you not protect yourself. I do what I have to do
and you do what you have to do. We can still be friends. Don't
be angry." According to Koch, Klein said, "I am angry," and the
mayor replied, "Well, I understand. But we are not going to
change on this." Klein then left Koch's office.[2]

Klein was also involved in one of the Koch administration's
scandals. Alex Liberman, who had been put in control of the
city's leasing bureaus soon after Koch took office in 1978, was
getting kickbacks from landlords to whom he issued leases for
use of their property by the city. In order to receive this money,
Liberman, a Holocaust survivor, used as a front (among others)
his synagogue. During the investigation of Liberman, it was discovered that Klein donated $5,000 to the synagogue after Liber-
man had leased three floors from him in an old Brooklyn building
that had been without a tenant for ten years. Klein insisted the
money was unconnected to the lease. He was never named as a
bribe payer in Liberman's indictment, so the question was left
unresolved.[3] However, this case, along with other connections
between Koch and Klein that involved material gains, would be
likely to affect their relationship regarding the Holocaust project.

While Koch and Klein were political friends with "one hand washing the other," Koch and Mario Cuomo had been political enemies more than once. They ran against each other in bitter Democratic primaries, for mayor of New York City in 1981 (which Koch won) and governor of New York State in 1982 (which Cuomo won). Klein backed Koch with large campaign contributions for both elections. As early as 1973, Koch and Cuomo were on opposing sides. Cuomo defended the development of a scaled-down public housing project in Forest Hills (which would bring blacks into the neighborhood), and Koch sided with the opponents (white, and mostly Jewish).[4] There was "no love lost" between them, and Koch must have let Cuomo become his equal founding cochairman of the Holocaust project only because he had no other choice. From Cuomo's perspective, he may have wanted to be Koch's equal on the project as a way of stealing some of Koch's popularity with the organized Jewish community of New York City and State. Since there is no written record of the steps leading to the inclusion of Cuomo, and since Cuomo's broker, Sandy Frucher, and Koch's broker, Herb Rickman, would say only what has already been detailed here, there is no way of further documenting how and why the merger took place. It is common knowledge, however, that these two founding cochairmen of the Holocaust commission were not political or personal friends. Although they are both Democrats, Koch is considered conservative, even "quasi-Republican," and Cuomo, a liberal. In the 1993 mayoral elections, Koch backed successful Republican candidate Rudolph Giuliani, rather than David Dinkins.

Koch-supporter Klein is very much a Republican, and was a high-level backer of presidents Ronald Reagan and George Bush. Klein's partisan feelings even temporarily barred from commission membership the congressman in whose district the current and former Holocaust museum sites are located. Although East Side Manhattan Congressman S. William Green (Republican) was a member, Congressman Ted Weiss (Democrat), whose district included both the Custom House and Battery Park City, was not originally invited to serve. Weiss, who died in the fall of 1992, was not only the congressman for the district, but also a Hungarian Holocaust refugee. Klein kept him off the commission because Weiss had introduced a resolution in Congress to impeach Klein's political ally President Reagan. Ironically, then commission director David Blumenfeld asked Weiss for his support in the quest for the Custom House in February 1984, and did not understand why Weiss was "neutral." At this point, Senator Manfred Ohrenstein and others strongly urged his appointment to the commission. Weiss was not named a member (and also associate chairperson because of his elected office) until June 1986, much later than other elected officials and after his absence became somewhat of an embarrassment for the commission.

When he was Manhattan borough president and Koch was mayor, Dinkins, by virtue of his office, was an associate chairperson and minor player in the Holocaust commission. In 1986 he had a disagreement with Koch, one of the founding cochairmen, regarding the activities of the commission. That year Dinkins went against a request of the Holocaust commission as a way of opposing Koch, whom he correctly considered his political rival for a future mayoral race. Dinkins favored a local community group, the former West Side Jewish Community Council, which was engaged in an activity to which Koch's special assistant Rickman was vehemently opposed.

The episode was trivial, but it was publicized in newspapers and is an example of how two members of the Holocaust commission were at odds about memorializing the Holocaust. The West Side group, then an umbrella for more than sixty-five Jewish organizations, decided to have a public ceremony on May 14, 1986, at the original Holocaust memorial site in Riverside Park at Eighty-third Street. Schoolchildren would enhance the site by planting flowers. Rickman, representing Koch, said this simple ceremony would hurt the Holocaust commission's fund-raising efforts and he begged the group not to follow through with a public ceremony. When Borough President Dinkins was approached by the group and learned about Rickman's opposition, he was eager to support the children's planting project (and thus make Koch look foolish).[5] One reason that Dinkins did not enthusiastically take a lead in the Holocaust commission after he was elected mayor was probably the project's close association with his longtime rival, Koch. He never became heavily involved, even when it would have been a politically expedient antidote to Crown Heights.

The exception, at least in public, to the internal conflict between players within the commission is the relationship between Klein and Robert Morgenthau. From their backgrounds, they seem like strange bedfellows. Morgenthau, a Democrat, is a rather assimilated Jew with roots in the German-Jewish elite families that have lived in the United States for many generations. His father was Treasury secretary in President Franklin D. Roosevelt's Cabinet, and his grandfather had served as U.S. Ambassador to Turkey during World War I. Following in their footsteps on the local level, he is a public servant as the elected Manhattan district attorney. Klein, a Republican, fled Nazi Europe with his parents and came to the United States as a child. He is an Orthodox Jew who inherited a fortune from his family's candy business and enhanced this wealth as a developer. Despite their different backgrounds, the two men's relationship as commission cochairmen since 1982 seems to have been smooth and cordial. In the beginning, Morgenthau let Klein take the lead and then signed what needed to be signed. Klein seemed to like being in charge, and Morgenthau seemed to like taking the back seat. However, Morgenthau became increasingly involved with the project, especially during the past five years. He has been particularly active in dealing with BPCA, and deserves major credit for the 1994 lease. He also committed himself to fund-raising efforts, and was instrumental in the museum's receiving gifts of $1 million each from Steven Spielberg's Righteous Persons Foundation and Time-Warner. Throughout the project's sometimes tense history, Klein and Morgenthau (both of whom were appointed by Koch) have had a harmonious partnership with no overt conflicts.

The third cochairman, Manfred Ohrenstein, was appointed by Governor Cuomo. Circumstances made his relationship the most conflicted and problematic in the commission. Like George Klein, Ohrenstein came to the United States from Nazi Europe with his parents, as a young refugee. By coincidence, his family, like Morgenthau's, came from Mannheim, Germany. He was elected to the New York Senate as a reform Democrat from the West Side of Manhattan in 1960 and became minority leader in 1975. Mayor Koch did not want Senator Ohrenstein to be cochairman, and emphatically told me so.[6] As Frucher observed, Governor Cuomo appointed Ohrenstein because the senator "insisted."[7] These sentiments by the two founding cochairmen of the commission (and the government officials with whom the commission was dealing) would in themselves indicate there were conflicts. However, political expediency could have overcome personal differences between Ohrenstein and the mayor or the governor. Unfortunately, another conflict arose that was unresolvable yet surprisingly did not do significant damage to the commission's image or implementation of its project.

On September 16, 1987, Senator Ohrenstein was accused of payroll abuses and indicted by his Holocaust commission co-chairman, District Attorney Morgenthau. By coincidence, he learned about the probability of the indictment on March 23, 1987. This was the very day of a high-level fund-raising dinner for the commission held at Gracie Mansion, with Henry Kissinger as guest speaker. Both Ohrenstein and Morgenthau were also on the program, and the senator was supposed to fly to Manhattan from Albany by helicopter, especially for this event. At the last moment he canceled his appearance and stayed in the state capital.

The 564-count indictment against Ohrenstein included grand larceny, conspiracy, and filing false documents. The *New York Post* headline on the day of the indictment was "Morgy Bags Ohrenstein." The next day the *Post* featured a photograph of Morgenthau thanking the paper for helping to expose Ohrenstein. It juxtaposed a photograph of the headline of the day before, which read "Ohrenstein Indicted."[8] The next week the *Daily News* specifically focused on the fact that the two were commission co-chairmen. With the catchy headline "The Morgy & Manny Show," the article pointed out that the indictment "could cause some awkward moments at the New York Holocaust Commission."[9] This was the only article that zeroed in on Ohrenstein's and Morgenthau's relationship as commission cochairs. For unknown reasons, this aspect of the case, which could have made "good ink" for the press, was never again picked up.

Although it was not reported in the press, the situation did cause some awkward moments. Since Morgenthau was "the man in the white hat" and Ohrenstein the one "in the black hat," the senator chose to stay away from commission meetings to avoid embarrassment. He made a conscious effort to keep the commission's project out of his legal battle with Morgenthau, to protect both the project and himself. Klein, who remained publicly neutral, suggested to Ohrenstein that he call and check to see if Morgenthau was attending each meeting before deciding whether to come. Ohrenstein, who was not pleased with this suggestion, decided it was better not to attend at all. He remained a cochairman, but the commission started having its communications signed only by Klein and Morgenthau.

In November 1990, 445 of the 564 counts in the original indictment were dismissed by the Court of Appeals, and in February 1991 Ohrenstein's trial was postponed indefinitely, although it still was pending. A Morgenthau spokesman said the delay was to await the outcome of efforts to first try another state senator, Howard Babbush.[10] In September 1991, Morgenthau dropped all remaining charges against Ohrenstein, and the senator was exonerated. (Both Morgenthau and Ohrenstein refused to be interviewed about the indictment and its effect on the commission and their cochairmanships.)

Meanwhile, by 1990 Ohrenstein had gradually begun participating in some commission activities. However, by then his two cochairmen and others on the commission were not happy with him for two other reasons. He was the governor's appointee as chairman, and the governor at that stage had become persona non grata for reneging on the Battery Park City Authority deal with the Swiss firm NOGA as well as the one-dollar annual rent. In addition, Ohrenstein had from the beginning obtained a legislative grant of $25,000 to $50,000 per year for the commission from his supplemental budget "member item" allowance in the state budget. The commission asked him in 1990 to allocate $100,000 from the 1991 state budget, but he allocated nothing. Ohrenstein blamed it on Majority Leader Ralph Marino, who had cut the Democrats' budget, but commission leaders blamed Senator Ohrenstein. By 1994, Ohrenstein was again an active member of the commission leadership, and he obtained a $250,000 legislative allowance for the project. Since then, he has continued to facilitate funding through the state legislature (from which he retired at the end of 1994). He has been especially involved with leadership discussions about the content of the museum.

The governor's reputation within the commission had gone from bad to worse once Sandy Frucher left BPCA and the NOGA deal fell apart (see Chapter 12). By October 1987 the name of the museum had been officially changed to please the governor's office. Its title "The Museum of Jewish Heritage–A Living Memorial to the Holocaust" had been deemed "too Jewish" or "too religion-related" by Cuomo's experts on the First Amendment, such as counsels Evan Davis and Fabian Palomino. The name therefore became "A Living Memorial to the Holocaust—Museum of Jewish Heritage." Then, during the summer of 1989, the governor again attempted to make the museum appear more secular and less Jewish.

On June 28, 1989, the commission met with Palomino, who represented BPCA and Governor Cuomo. The purpose of this meeting at George Klein's office was Palomino's attempt (on behalf of the governor) to put pressure on the commission to have the future museum open on Saturdays and Jewish holidays. Before the meeting Klein said that he had absolutely refused to agree to this. Palomino presented his case very poorly. As two precedents for the museum's remaining open on Saturdays and Jewish holidays, he named the Holocaust museums at Auschwitz and in Washington. The Washington museum was not yet open at all, because it had not yet been completed. As for Auschwitz, it seems unnecessary to comment on his comparing a Jewish Holocaust museum in New York City and the then Communist state museum at Auschwitz in traditionally anti-Semitic (and almost *Judenrein*) Poland.

The commission had the legal right, incorporated in its by-laws, to observe the Jewish Sabbath and holidays. On February 15, 1985, Klein, Morgenthau, Rabbi Irving Greenberg, Judah Gribetz, Benjamin Meed, and Ernest Michel, as officers of the corporation, had signed the following Statement of Policy of Organizational Action of Trustees in Lieu of Organization Meeting, adopted as part of the bylaws of the corporation: "The mandate of the New York City Holocaust Memorial Museum is to establish in New York City a perpetual living memorial to the 6,000,000 Jewish victims of the Holocaust. In upholding this solemn responsibility, the Corporation recognizes a sacred obligation on its part to respect the religious sensibilities of the Jewish community. Accordingly, all activities relating to the Corporation will conform with the religious laws, customs and traditions of the Jewish people."

The commission listened politely to Palomino, but held firm. Whether BPCA could later force them to comply and open on Saturdays and Jewish holidays would remain to be seen. With the subsequently defunct Property Resources Corporation (PRC) deal then up in the air (see Chapter 13), and the commission dependent on BPCA's bringing it to fruition, the governor and Palomino were in a good position to make demands. There were evidently two reasons why Palomino had urged that the museum remain open. Primarily, Cuomo's legal experts (of which Palomino was one) were concerned with the issue of separation of church and state. The commission was closely linked with the governor and BPCA, and therefore Palomino and others were worried about an appearance of a state-linked entity being a religious institution. This was especially true after the governor began having aspirations to run for president. In addition, the Catholic diocese had requested from BPCA land to build a church, with strong pressure coming from John Cardinal O'Connor.[11] The Temple of Understanding, which was housed at the Episcopal Cathedral of St. John the Divine and had as its president Reverend James Park Morton, had also requested free space from BPCA.[12] Possibly Palomino's insistence on having the museum open on Saturdays and holidays was to prove that the museum was not a religious institution. Governor Cuomo therefore would not have to give "equal time" (in this case, equal space) to Jews, Protestants, and Catholics.

A conflict between Fabian Palomino and David Emil within the Cuomo administration also indirectly affected the commission, because Palomino and Emil were both involved with the commission's project. Palomino, the governor's old friend, confidant, and counselor, apparently did not like Emil, Sandy Frucher's replacement in 1988 as BPCA president. Palomino, who at the time was chairman of BPCA's board of directors, in 1990 publicly called for an investigation of Emil's role in awarding a construction contract to a company that was not the lowest bidder. Soon afterward, Palomino resigned and his office was assumed by Harry Albright. Emil was subsequently cleared of the charges by the State Inspector General's Office.[13]

In addition to these conflicts among the principal members of the coalition behind the Holocaust memorial project, some of the less influential commission members also had various problems, possible conflicts of interest, and unrelated but potentially harmful affiliations that caused controversy in the commission. For example, survivor and executive committee member Ben Meed wore too many hats. As the president of the Warsaw Ghetto Resistance Organization (WAGRO), which runs the largest Yom Hashoah memorial commemoration in the city, he always wanted the new memorial museum to have a space for his ceremony. Furthermore, he was active on the U.S. Holocaust Memorial Council and head of its content committee. Since the New York and Washington museum projects were often seeking the same artifacts, this put him in a position of having a possible conflict of interest. By the spring of 1991, when the New York project was floundering and the Washington museum was rising on the Mall, his title for the national museum in Washington was "Chairman of the National Survivors Campaign." Since the U.S. Holocaust Memorial Council had in March 1991 opened a fund-raising office in New York City, competing for funds urgently needed by the New York commission, Meed's role in fund-raising for the Washington project was also a possible conflict of interest with his membership on the New York executive committee.

Commission member, Holocaust scholar, and survivor Yaffa Eliach also wore more than one hat. Not only was she a member of the commission's Academic Advisory Committee, but she also headed the Brooklyn Center for Holocaust Studies. For years the commission had tried to incorporate the Brooklyn institution (with its excellent archival material and oral histories), but Eliach resisted. Finally, in August 1990 A Living Memorial to the Holocaust–Museum of Jewish Heritage absorbed the Brooklyn Center for Holocaust Studies and its archives. The reason for the merger was the Brooklyn institution's own serious financial problems. Meanwhile, Eliach was also heavily involved with the Washington museum. Her magnificent collection of photographs of the prewar inhabitants of her hometown of Ejszyszki, Lithuania, is a highlight of that museum. Eliach was one of only twenty-nine survivors of the September 1941 massacre of the 3,000 Jews of Ejszyszki.

By December 1993, Eliach said she would ask her board to take back the archival material she had given the New York project and give it to another Holocaust center. "The material is sitting there in gray boxes, some of it is in storage, and this is to me one of the great pains," she said. "One of my guiding principles during the nineteen years I worked as director [of the Brooklyn Center] was to have the material accessible to everyone."[14] Although she did not say to which other Holocaust center she wanted to give her materials, her close connection with the Washington museum would have made it the likely recipient.

Another commission member, attorney Menachem Rosensaft, is founding chairman of the Network of Children of Jewish Holocaust Survivors. His family is very well connected to organized survivor activities. For example, his mother, Hadassah Rosensaft, was active on the Washington project, and his father-in-law, Sam Bloch, in the New York project and the National Gathering of Holocaust Survivors. Rosensaft himself became president of the national Labor Zionist organization. However, in December 1988, Rosensaft engaged in an activity that made him a pariah among many of the commission members, especially the survivors: well before it was acceptable to the organized American Jewish community, he met with Palestine Liberation Organization head Yassir Arafat to discuss a possible peace settlement with Israel. There was a general fear among most active commission members that this would somehow rub off on the commission's efforts and hamper them in the community.

Rosensaft told me that "some of the survivors who see things in stark terms weren't happy about it." However, he believes some people in the leadership of the survivor community "mellowed" after reading articles that he had written. "I've always refused to consider remembering the Holocaust, or children of Holocaust survivor activities, to be an all-consuming focus," he said. "Other things are equally important. I've been in the peace movement since the late seventies and have done what I believed had to be done."[15] Since most other commission members did not believe the things Rosensaft did (that is, meeting with Arafat) "had to be done" at that time, there was a temporary but sharp conflict between him and some commission members. By September 1993, when Arafat and Israel prime minister Yitzhak Rabin signed a peace agreement at the White House, Rosensaft's meeting, of course, was no longer an issue. However, by then he was no longer a supporter of the commission's project, although he remained a member. He said that the success of the Washington museum eliminated the need for a similar one in New York. "We don't have a Lincoln Memorial in New York; if you want to see the Lincoln Memorial, you go to Washington," he told the *New York Times* in December 1993.[16] Rosensaft's transference of loyalty from the New York to the Washington museum was rewarded in the summer of 1994. Upon his mother's retirement from the U.S. Holocaust Memorial Council, President Bill Clinton appointed him to the council.

The newest commission cochairman, Howard Rubenstein (who evaded many requests for an interview) has himself been a complex package of conflicting and overlapping interests. His highly political public relations firm has had as clients commission members that include both Ed Koch and George Klein's Park Tower Realty. Rubenstein himself was on the Holocaust commission from the beginning and his firm did some pro bono public relations work for the commission. Thus, at one point, one commission member had as his paying clients the founding cochairman and one cochairman, with the commission itself as his nonpaying client. In February 1993, Rubenstein became a fifth cochairman of the project, along with George Klein, Robert Morgenthau, Manfred Ohrenstein, and Peter Cohen. He was especially helpful in working and reworking the 1994 lease with BPCA, and in facilitating good relations between the museum project and the city and state governments. While both Rubenstein and Ohrenstein have devoted considerable time and energy to the project (complementing Klein's and Morgenthau's efforts), Cohen has been relatively inactive.

Another internal conflict emerged because of Academic Advisory Committee member and Israeli Holocaust historian Yehuda Bauer. Asked by museum director David Altshuler to evaluate a "Preliminary Concept Study" of the museum on June 24, 1987, Bauer sent back a letter that was nothing less than threatening. "I must say I am absolutely appalled at the program and its basic concepts," he wrote. "Let me explain why, but please be advised that unless this is immediately and radically changed I wish to have my name taken off any list associated with your Museum forthwith, and I must also warn you that I shall take every opportunity—starting with my forthcoming visits to New York and Los Angeles this fall—to attack this outrageous design from every public platform I have, not least of which will be a major public international conference on the Holocaust in Britain in 1988 at which most of the Holocaust scholars, some 250 of them, will participate."[17] Basically, Bauer considered the preliminary concept study too universal, although others (including the project's initiator, Mayor Koch) had argued that the museum was intended to have a particularistic Jewish bent. Bauer especially objected to the use of the term "Holocaust" for the murder of non-Jewish as well as Jewish victims. He indicated in his letter that he had sent copies to eight other Holocaust scholars, survivors, and academics, both members and nonmembers of the commission.

Altshuler responded with a placating letter, but added the following postscript: "I am sorry that as a member of the Museum's Academic Advisory Committee, you did not see fit to communicate with us directly *before* making a cause celebre by circulating your letter to others."[18] Thus the Holocaust commission was not without its academic, as well as governmental, politics. Just as prominent elected officials, such as Governor Cuomo, tried to control the activities of the commission at certain stages for political reasons, there were also internal academic disputes among Holocaust scholars for power and control of the museum's message. Finally, there was the "business as usual" maneuvering by heads of major Jewish organizations on the commission to protect their turf and to influence the commission to follow their particular agendas. For example, Bernice Tannenbaum, a past national president of Hadassah, the Women's Zionist Organization, said at a commission meeting that she thought the message of the museum should be more Zionist.

The political alliance that has endeavored to create a Holocaust memorial museum in New York City has been long-term and changing. Because of the time the project has languished, and because of changes in the cast of players and their roles over time, the members of the commission have not always worked in harmony. Interpersonal relations, political differences and agendas, conflicts between commission members that were unrelated to the activities of the commission, members' "wearing two hats," jockeying for position and influence, protection of "turf"— the complex and changing factors involved in an alliance of political forces working to create a Holocaust museum in New York City—have all been causes for friction.

15

Why Is This Holocaust Museum Different from All Others?

The mere choice of facts presented in an exhibition offers a definite point of view. When selecting historical data, one must consider what to exclude, what to emphasize and why. . . . A statement made by a museum carries great weight. It implies final authority and eternal remembrance."
—Martin Weyl, *Director, Israel Museum,* New York Times, *June 11, 1989*

The way the New York Holocaust Memorial Commission plans to present the history of the Holocaust in its projected museum, like the framework for commemorating any historical event, is affected by political and other considerations. While this account has been focusing on political influences, memorials and museums also shape memory according to different ideologies, interpretations of meaning, and artistic visions. These elements often overlap, and it is sometimes difficult to make clear distinctions between them. "When a particular definition of reality comes to be attached to a concrete power interest, it may be called an ideology," according to sociologists Peter Berger and Thomas Luckmann.[1] They argue that "the distinctiveness of ideology is . . . that the same overall universe is interpreted in different ways, depending upon concrete vested interests within the society in question." As in the case of the New York City Holocaust museum project, the ideology that prompts these "concrete vested interests" to interpret reality in different ways is usually politically motivated.

The composition of the coalition behind the project, as well as its location in New York City, give it a slant that is different from that of other American Holocaust museums, such as those in Washington, D.C., and Los Angeles. At the same time, the project's location in the United States gives it some commonality with other American Holocaust museums and a perspective different from, for example, that of Yad Vashem in Jerusalem. While the basic concept for the New York memorial museum has remained the same since its inception, the changing structure of its political coalition since 1981, fund-raising problems and consequent reduction in the size of the project, and other factors have caused some changes in plans.

The original conceptual design for A Living Memorial to the Holocaust–Museum of Jewish Heritage, as the museum is now called, had four central themes: (1) "The World Before," the European and North African Jewish civilization that thrived for two thousand years before it was destroyed by the Nazis; (2) "The Holocaust," particularly as it was experienced by the Jews, both those who perished and those who survived; (3) "The Aftermath" of survival, including the plight of refugees, the establishment of the State of Israel, and the pursuit of Nazi war criminals; and (4) "Renewal in America," Jewish immigration to the United States from 1654 to the present.[2]

The first two of these themes originated in a report entitled the "Mayor's Task Force on the Holocaust: Ideas for a NYC Holocaust Memorial Center," dated December 1981. Apparently a report of the original content committee headed by Rabbi Irving Greenberg, this document recommended that a Holocaust memorial center should address the culture of European Jewry that was destroyed, give a detailed factual account of the destruction of European Jewry (including resistance), and explain how this could have happened in "the supposedly civilized twentieth century." Components included an exhibition center, a scholarly archive, and a survivors' space with personal taped memoirs and memorabilia.[3]

The New York City Holocaust Memorial Commission's June 1983 certificate of incorporation also described the first two of the three current themes: "to perpetuate the memory of the six million Jews who died in the Holocaust," and "to commemorate the victims of the Holocaust not only as they died, but as they lived" (currently "The Modern Jewish World"). The proposed museum planned to "communicate the uniqueness of the Jewish experience in the Holocaust," and "to teach the history and lessons of the Holocaust to all people for generations to come." But when the Holocaust Commission sent the General Services Administration (GSA) regional office a memorandum asking to lease space in the Custom House on December 6, 1983, the stated purposes were somewhat different from those listed in the certificate of incorporation. Now they were to perpetuate the memory of the six million Jews who were murdered by Nazi Germany in the Holocaust; to commemorate the lives of the victims of the Holocaust by creating a record of Jewish life, society, and culture in Europe; to portray the arrival of Jewish immigrants to New York City; and to restore to memory the vigorous traditions and lifestyles which formed a bond between European Jewry and the Jewry of New York City. The idea of Jewish immigration to New York City was not mentioned in the earlier documents, and may have been an attempt to define reality in a way that would "Americanize" the image of the museum for the GSA and the federal government. This evolved into "Renewal in America," or Jewish immigration to the United States, a theme that became integrated into the other three (because of space limitations) in the present concept plan. The third current theme, "Jewish Renewal" (formerly "The Aftermath") emerged over time and, like the other two themes—"The Modern Jewish World" (formerly "The World Before") and "The War Against the Jews" (formerly "The Holocaust")—gives the museum a Jewish slant.

According to the literature on memorialization, the particular locale or ideological concept of a memorial or a museum affects its portrayal of history.[4] For example, Berger and Luckmann's theory of the "social construction of reality" explains how the historical reality created in a museum is a reflection of a museum's particular location. "Knowledge" differs in diverse societies, and "reality" is not the same everywhere, since it is redefined in response to different social, political, or cultural environments.[5] When an aspect of reality is highly charged with emotion and framed by an interest group's conscious effort to deliver a political message, the degree of its social construction is particularly striking. Not only is knowledge different in different societies, but it is purposely constructed differently, to defend a point of view.

Karl Deutsch's "feedback model of consciousness" is also concerned with social constructions of reality, but he specifically addresses the political forces that influence knowledge.[6] Deutsch focuses on the selective interests of the one who knows, concluding that knowledge is an activity in which subjective and objective perspectives meet. His behavioral theory identifies patterns of political knowledge, action, and value, including a system of symbols by which selected data are recorded and used for later application. As Deutsch puts it: "In government and politics, will is a pattern of relatively *consolidated preferences and inhibitions, derived from the past* experiences of a social group, *consciously labeled* for a relevant portion of its members, *and applied* to guide the actions, to restrict the subsequent experiences of that group and its members [emphasis in original]"[7]. Thus groups—such as those that create memorials—select certain aspects of experience and attach symbols to them, which may in the end distort the experience they intend to commemorate. The theories of Berger and Luckmann as well as those of Deutsch are useful because the influence of different locales as well as diverse ideals, ideologies, or political values needs to be considered to understand the different ways in which the New York project and other museums seek to memorialize and teach about the Holocaust.

A comparison of Yad Vashem, the official Israel government Holocaust memorial and museum, and the Buchenwald Concentration Camp Museum under the former German Democratic Republic offers a dramatic example of how memorializing the Holocaust serves different purposes in different places in support of different political agendas. At Yad Vashem in Israel, Holocaust memorialization conveys a Zionist message: the culmination of the Holocaust is the creation of the Zionist state of Israel; the exiles are ingathered from Holocaust to redemption. The Buchenwald Concentration Camp museum before German unification instead transmitted a Communist message: the culmination of the atrocities at Buchenwald was the creation of the Communist state, the German Democratic Republic. David Ben-Gurion, the Zionist founder, is the hero of Yad Vashem. When I visited Buchenwald in 1980, I saw how Ernst Thälmann, the German Communist leader murdered there by the Nazis, had been enshrined as the memorial's hero by the German Democratic Republic. The story told at Yad Vashem is a decidedly Zionist story, but in Buchenwald before the reunification of Germany the story was Communist. The only reference to Jewish victims was a small plaque in memory of those interned there after *Kristallnacht*. The Third Reich was the Third Reich, but its realities selected for remembrance—and the use of this memorialization for political purposes—have been very different at these two memorial sites. After unification, Germany began revising the exhibits at the three major concentration camp memorials that had formerly been part of the German Democratic Republic: Buchenwald, Sachsenhausen, and Ravensbrück women's concentration camp. The Thälmann memorial at Buchenwald has been dismantled, and in 1993 a formal competition was held for a Jewish memorial to be erected on the former site of Block 22 of the prisoners' barracks. The Communist interpretation of what had happened at these East German sites during the Nazi era was changed to conform to the new post–Soviet Union political reality, and new exhibits were prepared for the fiftieth anniversary of the liberation of the camps in 1995.[8]

There are less drastic but nevertheless dramatic contrasts between the United States Holocaust Memorial Museum in Washington, D.C., and Israel's Yad Vashem, and between the Washington museum and another American Holocaust museum that opened in 1993, the Simon Wiesenthal Center's Beit Ha-Shoah–Museum of Tolerance in Los Angeles. The two major American Holocaust museums are very different from each other, from Yad Vashem, and from the projected New York museum. The U.S. Holocaust Memorial Museum, the political genesis of which was described in detail in Chapter 7, opened on the Mall in Washington on April 26, 1993; the Simon Wiesenthal Center's Beit HaShoah–Museum of Tolerance opened in Los Angeles earlier the same year, on February 8. Although there are now hundreds of Holocaust museums, memorials, and mixed museum/memorials throughout the United States, only the new Washington and Los Angeles museums are imposing enough to be compared with the proposed New York memorial.

In the Washington museum, the "social construction of reality" or "feedback of consciousness"—the way the historical facts are presented—is related to its official government status and its location. This $147 million museum is on federal property adjacent to the Mall, which is designed to be a shrine that projects the political message of "America, the beautiful." The message here, although the museum clearly memorializes and teaches about the Holocaust, is a more specifically American and more universal message than that of the projected New York museum. As Michael Berenbaum, former project director and now head of research for the Washington museum, wrote: "The [Washington] Museum will take what could have been the painful and parochial memories of a bereaved ethnic community [the Jews] and apply them to the most basic of American values. Located adjacent to the National Mall—surrounded by the Smithsonian Institution and the monuments to Lincoln, Jefferson, and Washington—the building and its contents are being designed with the neighbors in mind so that the Holocaust Museum will emerge as an American institution and will speak to the national saga."[9]

As Berenbaum points out, the museum does tell the story of the Holocaust, and tells it powerfully. The striking architecture by James Ingo Freed, with its jarring angles, harsh brick and steel, narrow passages, blocked windows, dead ends, narrowing stairways, and sharp turns, gives the visitor a feeling of disorientation, malaise, even claustrophobia. In this way, the shell of the 300,000-square-foot museum works well to project the message of a world gone berserk, in which nothing is orderly or normal. Within this space, the museum presents a comprehensive history of the Holocaust, displaying artifacts such as Zyklon-B gas pellets, victims' shoes and tin bowls, an authentic railroad car used for deportations in Poland, and a barracks from Birkenau. There is powerful documentation through artifacts, photographs, survivor testimonies, models, and graphics. The museum is an impressive accomplishment, and, in the words of its project director, achieves what it set out to do: "[It] reminds each of us how fragile democracy is, and how vigilant we must all remain in defending the core American values—indeed the core human values—of individual dignity, social justice, and civil rights."[10]

What distinguishes the version of "reality" or "consciousness" conveyed by the Washington museum is the fact that it is filtered through a lens that enhances America's positive role during the Holocaust. Furthermore, the museum uses the example of the Holocaust to promote "core American values." A basic message is that the Holocaust is a negation of American democracy, a reminder that we must be alert in order to preserve our democratic society.[11] In keeping with its place of honor on the Mall, the museum emphasizes the role of American liberators of concentration camps. Even before arriving in the main exhibition area, visitors are confronted with films of liberators. The exhibition begins and ends with American liberators. Upon leaving the elevator and walking into the exhibit, one sees an enlarged photograph of generals Dwight D. Eisenhower and George Patton, taken at Dachau on April 15, 1945. Yet, while the museum is decidedly American, America's shoddy immigration policy during the war and its use of Nazi war criminals afterward—two decidedly American elements in the full picture of the Holocaust—are downplayed. A more balanced review of history would probably place as much emphasis on America's limiting Jewish immigration before and during the Holocaust as on the liberation of camps. In fact, it might even be argued that a more enlightened immigration policy could have reduced the need for liberators. The museum therefore presents a re-creation of history that accentuates America's positive role in the Holocaust and downplays its negative one. To the museum's credit, it does include a display that portrays the American role in the *St. Louis* incident, in which the government refused to accept or intervene on behalf of the 936 German-Jewish refugees who were denied entry to Cuba. It also addresses the issue of the refusal of the United States to bomb the railroad tracks to Auschwitz, and arrives at the conclusion: "Although bombing Auschwitz would have killed many persons, it would also have halted the operation of the gas chambers and, ultimately, saved the lives of many more."

The liberation of victims, which was not by any means an American priority, is featured as though it had been one of the prime reasons for America's involvement in World War II. As visitors leave the exhibit, they bump squarely into the seal of the United States. Above the eagle and "E Pluribus Unum" is the inscription "For the dead and the living we must bear witness." Thus the U.S. Holocaust Memorial Museum is a significant contribution to Holocaust memorialization, but it must be understood in the context of its locale and its sponsorship by the U.S. government.

From its inception, the President's Commission on the Holocaust, named by President Jimmy Carter to create a suitable memorial, deliberately did not consist entirely of Jews. The

Washington museum, unlike the New York project, has had as part of its political alliance representatives of groups such as Armenians, Poles, and Ukrainians. Its more universal and more American way of remembering reflects its locale in the nation's capital (as opposed to New York City, the center of organized Jewish life in the United States) and the federal government's involvement. In addition to representing other victims of the Nazis and other genocides, the Washington museum has always portrayed itself from an American, not a particularly Jewish, perspective.

A 1991 fund-raising letter for the U.S. Holocaust Memorial Museum previewed the American viewpoint of the museum: "Your visit begins in the elevator where you will be transported back to April 11, 1945—*the date American troops entered the Buchenwald concentration camp* [emphasis in original]. An American liberator will appear on a video monitor and tell how what he saw that April afternoon changed the rest of his life." This 1991 letter begins: "Eisenhower knew that what he and his men saw in 1945 would be the only testimony many Americans would believe." The museum will be "a museum of American values," the letter reads, "a museum of American experiences . . . a museum of American history," and "a museum of American people." It goes on: "It is a story of how 6,000,000 Jews and millions of other people were systematically and ruthlessly exterminated . . . a story of the evil that 400,000 American soldiers died fighting against 45 years ago. Though primarily a story about the extermination of the Jewish people, *it is also about the persecution of all people regarded as different or vulnerable* [emphasis in original]—of priests and patriots, Polish intellectuals and Soviet prisoners of war, homosexuals and the handicapped, and even innocent children."[12] Although the Washington museum gives full emphasis to "the persecution of all people regarded as different or vulnerable," the New York museum is planned as primarily a story about the extermination of the Jewish people and the richness of their life before and afterward and, to a much lesser degree, about the persecution of other different or vulnerable groups.

The Simon Wiesenthal Beit HaShoah–Museum of Tolerance in Los Angeles is also influenced by its locale and by the political agenda of its creator. The "reality" of this museum is different from that of either the Washington or the New York project. While the other two were initiated by elected officials seeking to bolster their Jewish constituencies, the Los Angeles museum was conceived by an ambitious Orthodox rabbi, Marvin Hier. Hier came to Los Angeles in 1977 to build a yeshiva for higher education, but instead created a religious secondary school and an internationally known Jewish defense agency, the Simon Wiesenthal Center. His museum has a split personality: half of it is devoted to prejudice, including anti-Semitism, as a universal problem, while the other half represents a particularistic Jewish approach to the Holocaust. Rabbi Hier has alienated many Jewish organizations, including the local Jewish Federation and the Anti-Defamation League of B'nai B'rith (ADL), because of his aggressive manner, usurpation of their programs (on anti-Semitism and the Holocaust), and successful use of sensationalistic scare tactics for fund-raising. He has won the financial backing of millionaires such as the Samuel Belzberg family and members of the film industry. Although the museum began as a private enterprise connected with a religious school, Hier managed to receive a $5 million grant from the California state legislature. In 1985 the ADL publicly opposed the grant on the grounds that it violates the separation of church and state. "Granting $5 million in public funds for a museum which would chronicle the Holocaust and the genocides which have befallen so many people during the twentieth century is an excellent idea," the ADL wrote to the grant's sponsor, state senate president pro tem David Roberti, a Los Angeles Democrat. The organization noted, however, that "the funds should be given to an appropriate public institution such as the University of California, or the California State University for this objective," adding that "we believe the museum should be located on public property under the direction of an appropriate public and academic governing body."[13] To discourage his critics and sidestep a legal battle, Hier then legally separated the museum from the school.

Despite criticism from the ADL, the local Jewish federation, the American Jewish Congress, and others (some of it, no doubt, because of Hier's distasteful tactics and some in envy of what these tactics accomplished), Hier opened his $50 million museum amid great fanfare in February 1993. The museum's Los Angeles site and high-tech, dramatized displays have led some critics to dismiss it as "too Hollywood." One journalist even described it as "Dachau-meets-Disneyland."[14] This museum is as up-to-date in museum technology as Washington's, and both use the contrivance of giving visitors computer-generated identity cards of Holocaust victims. However, the emphasis, the conception, and the message are different in Los Angeles, and the up-to-date interactive technology is much more geared to a slick media presentation. The 165,000-square-foot museum complex is divided into three parts: a "Tolerancenter," re-creation of certain events in the history of the Holocaust, and a smaller Global Situation Room. The Tolerancenter is an open "tolerance workshop" space that focuses on intolerance as part of daily life. Visitors must choose to enter a door marked "Prejudiced" or "Unprejudiced," and only the former opens. Upon entering, visitors are greeted by a man whose body is displayed on ten feet of stacked video monitors. Here one finds interactive computers that depict such situations as the 1992 Los Angeles riots. There are multiscreen videos dealing with civil rights in America and human responsibility. In a Whisper Tunnel, visitors are assaulted by racial, ethnic, and sexist slurs.

The historical re-creation includes scenes such as an outdoor cafe in 1930s Berlin, the Wannsee Conference, and walks through the Warsaw Ghetto and through the gates of a concentration camp. Visitors have the opportunity to eavesdrop on these scenes. Finally they arrive in the Hall of Testimony, a bunkerlike room where stories of Holocaust survivors are projected from eight wall-mounted television monitors. All of these scenic re-creations are high-tech stage sets rather than artifacts; the authentic artifacts and documents (of which the museum has collected an impressive number) are in archives or in display cases on another floor. The third portion of the museum, the Global Situation Room, displays daily updates of anti-Semitic attacks and human rights violations worldwide.

For the New York City project, the museum's viewpoint, or way of remembering, is influenced by the large, organized population of 1,844,000 Jews and the strong ethnic Jewish culture in New York City. With a Jewish population of nearly 2 million, New York State has the most concentrated population of Jews in America and the highest percentage in any state's total population, 10.3 percent. The largest concentration is in New York City and its environs.[15]

In addition to the size of the community, many of its members have high profiles in such fields as government, real estate development, finance, the arts, public relations, and higher education. The Holocaust project's initiator, Edward I. Koch, was himself an outspokenly Jewish mayor. His strong affiliation with the organized Jewish community, Israel, and Jewish ethnicity were part of New York City's uniquely Jewish ambience in the United States. Ed Koch himself described the New York project as follows: "This is the Jewish Holocaust. The Museum in Washington is not."[16] There were no pressures from other groups to be included, he said, and the project was all privately funded. (This is not completely accurate. There were some pressures, such as requests from gay, Polish, and Ukrainian groups, but the New York commission responded with minimal recognition, keeping the perspective essentially Jewish; also public land was offered for the project.)

Beginning with the name itself, "A Living Memorial to the Holocaust–Museum of Jewish Heritage," the New York project's way of remembering is more Jewish than Washington's. Rather than emphasizing American liberators of concentrations camps, promotional material has Jewish themes. The September 1991 news brochure, for example, focused on mementos of six Jewish-American families who migrated to America and "maintained their [Jewish] heritage and a sense of [Jewish] continuity in the midst of transition and change"; a traveling exhibit of Holocaust memorials; a gathering of hidden Jewish children during World War II; and rare film footage of prewar Jewish life in Poland. The Winter 1996 newsletter featured the Jewish ghetto in Shanghai. While the museum is secular, the subject matter is Jewish heritage and history. The New York project is consciously trying not to duplicate what is already available in other institutions.

Michael Berenbaum, the research director of the Washington museum, defends its pluralism and universalism: "A national council funded at taxpayers' expense to design a *national* memorial does not have the liberty to create an exclusively Jewish one in the restricted sense of the term, and most specifically with regard to audience. A purely Jewish museum is the task of the American Jewish community operating with private funding and without government subvention, as is the case with the New York Holocaust Memorial (appropriately titled 'The Museum of Jewish Heritage')."[17] However, the New York museum—the first half of whose name, "A Living Memorial to the Holocaust," he omitted—is not being created by the "American Jewish community," as Berenbaum stated. It is being created by a political alliance that includes a government-created interest group, or commission, made up of Jewish citizens of New York City and New York State. This alliance also consists of officials elected to the city and state governments, and always has had as its site government-owned land (as does the Washington project).

Despite this government involvement, the New York museum has a Jewish slant. This is because both the locale and the original political alliance are more Jewish than those of the Washington project. Koch, the Jewish mayor, initiator, and founding chairman of the commission, first shared power with, and then lost power to, a non-Jewish governor with sympathy for the project but potentially conflicting national political aspirations (because of concerns about separation of church and state). When the governor first became a retroactive founding cochairman, the purpose of his involvement, as seen by his political liaisons to the New York State Jewish community such as Sandy Frucher, was to ingratiate himself with the community. Therefore, Governor Cuomo's appointments to the commission, like Mayor Koch's, were from the Jewish community. Later in this process, however, the governor's office made an effort to minimize the particularist image of the project.

Although theories about the "social construction of reality" or a "feedback model of consciousness" are important tools for partially understanding the planned content of the New York Holocaust museum, they do not address the possibility of the imposition of a new "reality" or "consciousness" as a result of a changing political coalition over time. When Mayor Koch initiated the Holocaust memorial museum project in 1981, the Jewish leaders he chose to implement it expected to be able to make the content uniquely Jewish. Operating in ethnically Jewish New York City, with Koch's encouragement, they thought other elected officials would approve of a particularistic Jewish memorialization of the Holocaust.

When the proposed museum became a city-state venture and the political coalition changed, politics interfered and changed the "reality" or "consciousness" somewhat. Sandy Frucher, the governor's political entrepreneur who offered the commission the Battery Park City site, played three concurrent roles: governor's liaison to the commission, president of Battery Park City Authority (BPCA), and member of the commission's executive committee. Because of his deep personal commitment to such a project, his idea that it was politically good for the governor, and his close personal friendship with the governor, Frucher was able to smooth over any differences between the commission and the governor's office regarding the museum's particularistic Jewish way of remembering.

The first museum lease, signed by BPCA, the governor, and commission cochairmen on September 4, 1986, in itself proves the museum was to be decidedly Jewish. It defined "business days" to exclude Saturdays and all Jewish holidays.[18] As I have pointed out, such a definition should have warned them, but the governor and members of his staff seemed to become aware only later that the scope of the planned museum was parochially Jewish. Almost three years later, as we have seen, the governor's confidant and counselor Fabian Palomino tried to negotiate with the commission to change this definition. No subsequent leases or memorandums of agreement listed the Jewish holidays as days the museum would be closed, and they even cited the First Amendment provisions about separation of church and state.

In October 1986, the name of the museum (according to its provisional charter) officially became "The Museum of Jewish Heritage–A Living Memorial to the Holocaust." At the end of November, however, the governor's office conveyed his displeasure (or that of his attorneys) with the museum's name. The reasons for the complaint were not given in detail, but they were related to the emphasis on "Jewish Heritage." As with the issue of closing the museum on Jewish holidays and Saturdays, the governor's office was apparently worried about the appearance of a possible conflict between church and state. Eventually, pressure from the governor's office forced the commission to change the name of the museum to "A Living Memorial to the Holocaust– Museum of Jewish Heritage." The name was changed by the commission in November 1987, and made official in the provisional charter by the Regents of the University of the State of New York on April 22, 1988.

Governor Cuomo's staff feared not only criticism from advocates of separation of church and state, but also requests by other religious groups for parcels of land (see Chapter 14). They therefore tried to change the image of the museum and make it appear less Jewish, or religious, by having its name changed. At a time when Cuomo was seriously considering running for president, his advisers decided to please both his local and potential national electorates by keeping the name but reversing it to minimize the Jewish component. The commission, which knew it was now subject to the governor's wishes (because it had opted to build the museum in Battery Park City), accepted the change.

A new memorandum of understanding signed on July 26, 1991, between BPCA, the museum, and the commission, called for a scaled-down museum to be built on half of Site 14. Although new interior and exterior designs needed to be developed, museum director David Altshuler then stated that the original concept would remain the same, with these four main themes: "The World Before," "The Holocaust," "The Aftermath," and "Renewal in America." However, the 1991 memorandum brought other changes, with language that was quite different from that of the original 1986 lease. This, too, reflected the wishes of the governor's office and new BPCA president David Emil that the museum should not appear to be a religious, that is, Jewish, institution. At this time, the original founding cochairman, former mayor Koch, was completely out of the picture (although he retained his title). The new mayor, David Dinkins, had little or nothing to do with the project. The "social construction of reality" or "feedback of consciousness" had changed in response to the change in the structure of the political alliance: the governor and BPCA were now in command of the situation.

According to the 1991 memorandum, the museum to be established would be "an important cultural institution in the south residential neighborhood of Battery Park City, comprising a civic and cultural facility in furtherance of the public purposes the Authority was created to accomplish."[19] In case the term "civic and cultural facility" is not sufficient to clarify that the museum is not a religious, that is, Jewish, institution, the memorandum then spells it out in no uncertain terms: "The Building shall be operated at all times during the term of the New Museum Lease in accordance with the then current requirements of the First Amendment to the Constitution of the United States."[20] No longer are "no business days" defined as Jewish holidays and Saturdays, as they were in the 1986 lease. Instead, "The Museum shall be open to the general public for at least 240 days per year."[21] If the commission chooses to close the museum on Saturdays and Jewish holidays, it may still do so. However, this religious aspect of the museum is not now documented in the new memorandum, as it was in the old lease.

The following three new restrictions (repeated almost exactly in the 1993 memorandum and the 1994 lease) are even more telling, with respect to the governor's concern about separation of church and state: First, "The Building shall not be used for sectarian instruction or as a place of religious worship, or in connection with any part of the program of a school or department of divinity for any religious denomination." Second, "The Museum shall not organize, sponsor, coordinate or supervise public or private, group or individual prayer in the Building, and no portion of the Building shall be designated as a place for any such prayer." And third, "The Museum shall not require any person to observe or conform to the laws or customs of any religion or denomination as a condition to the use and enjoyment of the Building or any facilities located at the Building."[22]

These three provisos are extremely rigid, and indicate a forceful effort to prevent the museum from becoming a Jewish religious institution. From the inception of the current project in 1981, it had always been planned as a memorial project. A special space for remembering Hitler's victims was always included in the plan. If the museum provides such a special place for remembering those murdered in the Holocaust, is this considered a place for prayer? In Jewish tradition, remembering the dead is associated with prayer, and defining or separating the two is almost impossible.

Related to this is another question. The tradition of holding an annual Holocaust memorial ceremony in New York City began in 1944, even before World War II ended. On April 19, 1944, the first anniversary of the Warsaw Ghetto Uprising, more than 30,000 Jews gathered on the steps of City Hall to hear Mayor Fiorello LaGuardia and prominent Jewish leaders honor the memory of those who had died in the uprising.[23] After the war, this evolved into an annual ceremony on Yom Hashoah, Holocaust Remembrance Day (the twenty-seventh day of the Hebrew month of Nissan), sponsored by the Warsaw Ghetto Resistance Organization (WAGRO). Benjamin Meed, head of WAGRO and a member of the commission's executive committee, stressed for years that New York City needed an appropriate site for such a ceremony—which has been held in various locations such as Temple Emanu-El, the Felt Forum of Madison Square Garden, and the Javits Convention Center. From the inception of the New York City (later New York) Holocaust Memorial Commission, members of its executive committee assumed and informally discussed the idea that the annual ceremony would be held in or at the anticipated Holocaust memorial museum. Yom Hashoah commemorations always include prayers, such as Kaddish for the dead and the *El Maleh Rahamim*, the Jewish memorial prayer said at funerals. According to "the letter of the law" of the memoranda and newest lease, it appears that Yom Hashoah commemorations and other memorial observances will be prohibited. (The reduced size of the project may make it impossible to hold the annual WAGRO event at the museum, but there are other occasions when it is appropriate to hold memorial ceremonies for the victims of the Holocaust.)

The particular way in which a museum represents history is a reflection both of who is doing the remembering and where the remembering is taking place. The diverse representations of the Holocaust in Washington, Los Angeles, and New York, as well as other locales within and outside of the United States, attest to the different ways in which ideology, politics, and memory may be linked and interpreted.

16

A Holocaust Memorial for New York City—Fifty Years and Counting

Once the Holocaust expanded beyond the private realm of Jewish memory and entered the public domain, it became subject to all of those forces that shape and reshape images in the public's consciousness and, by so doing, shape public memory itself.—Alvin H. Rosenfeld, 1986

On August 18, 1994—the "Bar Mitzvah" of the July 1981 initial meeting of Mayor Koch's task force, as he quipped—the New York Holocaust Memorial Commission and Battery Park City Authority (BPCA) signed a lease that is finally resulting in the construction of a Holocaust memorial museum in Battery Park City. The new lease for part of Site 14 provides for a two-story 30,000-square-foot museum and memorial designed by Kevin Roche of Kevin Roche John Dinkeloo Associates, with the interior adapted by the Douglas|Gallagher exhibit design firm. The cost is estimated at about $18 million, with BPCA providing $7.5 million. The design is a simple, austere form, with six sides representing the 6 million victims of the Holocaust. The new structure will consist almost completely of public space, with a central 85-foot memorial shaft rising from a pool of still water. Sculptured bronze doors will lead visitors from the memorial to three floors of exhibition space. The granite building will have a steeped louvre roof, designed to receive filtered daylight or artificial illumination at night. The new lease also allows for architectural expansion at a later date. The original 1986 lease was for all of Site 14, for construction of a 525,000-square-foot building that included a 400,000-square-foot apartment building and a 125,000-square-foot memorial museum; the cost of the museum portion was estimated at $90 million.

At the time of the 1994 lease signing, the museum had $10.3 million in cash or pledges, plus the promise of $7.5 million from BPCA. The commission "gave up something of great value" when it scaled back its project and returned some 42,000 square feet of its original 64,000-square-foot Site 14 parcel, according to then BPCA president David Emil.[1] In exchange, BPCA agreed to pay half of the construction costs, matching private contributions up to $10 million. This is an advance against revenue BPCA expects to recoup from the property that the commission returned. Two days before the October 16, 1994, ground breaking, Steven Spielberg's Righteous Persons Foundation promised the project a million-dollar contribution.

The new memorial museum "will teach people of all ages and backgrounds about the unique tragedy of the Holocaust," director David Altshuler said at the lease-signing ceremony. "It will also convey the rich diversity of Jewish life in Europe and North Africa prior to the devastation of that community a generation ago, and it will depict the renewal of Jewish civilization in Israel, the United States, and throughout the world during the decades since the liberation of the survivors of the death camps." Thus the general themes of the new, smaller version of the project will not deviate from the original conceptual plans.

My account of the political history leading to completion of a Holocaust memorial museum in New York City ends in the spring of 1996, with construction under way and the museum beginning to rise. Following the October 16, 1994, symbolic ground-breaking ceremony, piles were driven for the proposed memorial museum in February 1995. The general contractor, Turner Construction Company, is obligated to complete the building by the end of 1996, with the opening planned for 1997. This book is not about the museum itself, but recounts the prehistory and history of the project, the fifty years between the first concept for a major memorial in New York City in Riverside Park in 1946 and the ongoing construction of a Holocaust memorial museum at the southern end of Battery Park City in 1996. The new museum is not the same project as the original effort, and there have been a good number of attempts in between. Although New York was the first city in the United States to attempt to create a major Holocaust memorial after World War II, no such memorial in the city was completed by the fiftieth anniversary of the end of the war. However, after the long struggle detailed here, a Holocaust memorial for New York was finally under construction by that date, and one year later it is becoming a reality.

The year 1994 was pivotal for the New York Holocaust Memorial Commission. As the year began, the commission was facing prolonged extensions for state-imposed fund-raising deadlines, the repercussions of a damaging front-page story in a Jewish newspaper, the successful 1993 openings of major Holocaust memorial museums in Washington, D.C., and Los Angeles, and a new mayor (again) in City Hall. Meanwhile, there had been little visible progress on a Holocaust museum for New York City. By the end of the year, there had been a ceremonial ground-breaking ceremony, but Founding Cochairman Mario Cuomo had been defeated in the gubernatorial election.

In November 1993, with $8 million in hand and some $12 million more needed to finish the scaled-down project, a big fund-raising push was to culminate in a $300-a-seat dinner at the luxurious Hotel Pierre. In the midst of that fund-raising effort, the *Forward*, a New York English-language weekly newspaper— descended from the popular Yiddish immigrant daily published by the Workmen's Circle—published a front-page article that could be described as a smear job.[2] Entitled "The Harrowing Tale of 'Holocaust Heights,'" the article contained inaccuracies and seemed to go out of its way to quote detractors. The November 19 article generated a storm of letters to the editor protesting the inaccuracies, misquotes, and generally questionable judgment of publishing an article that could contribute to sabotaging the project. According to the article, Holocaust scholars at a Yad Vashem conference "several years ago" had criticized the idea of a luxury apartment complex above a Holocaust museum, calling the planned project "Treblinka Towers" and "Holocaust Heights." Ignoring the fact that the idea of constructing an apartment tower had been abandoned after the "Black Monday" stock market crash of October 19, 1987—six years earlier—the article went on to state that $15 million had been raised and spent, "yet all that can be shown so far are architectural drawings, a collection of artifacts tucked away in storage, overdue architects' bills, bank debts, and a bevy of angry voices disputing whether the museum should be built at all." It questioned whether the museum was "redundant in the wake of the gala openings this year of major Holocaust museums in Washington D.C. and Los Angeles and of the $50 million renovation of the Jewish museum," and whether it was "the best use for limited community resources."

The reporter seems to have sought out critics of the project, without presenting a positive counterbalance. For example, Richard Ravitch, the founding president of the Jewish Community Relations Council and a proponent of a New York memorial project in the 1970s, told the *Forward:* "Why should the Jewish community support multiple institutions? We have the Jewish Museum, we have YIVO, we have Leo Baeck, we have the Tenement Museum, the oldest synagogue in the Lower East Side is trying to restore itself and there's not unlimited financial capacity." Rabbi Irving Greenberg, a member of the executive committee who later protested that his remarks were used out of context, is quoted as saying that the project "became much too ambitious and broad and it didn't have the kind of glamorous national support of the president that Washington had." He also reportedly said that "there was no realistic or effective leadership" and that "George Klein and David Altshuler have to take some of the leadership blame." According to the article, "A growing number of Jewish organizational leaders, academics and Orthodox leaders are calling for an end to the disproportionate millions spent on the business of Holocaust memorialization." This broadly inclusive statement is then followed by quotes from only three people: historian Henry Feingold (a member of the commission's academic committee who was simply criticizing the general idea of presenting Jews as victims), Jewish Museum director Joan Rosenbaum (whose museum had just opened a permanent exhibit that includes some of the concepts planned for the Holocaust museum), and Menachem Rosensaft (a commission member but an outspoken critic who had switched his allegiance to the Washington museum). The only positive comments came from cochairmen George Klein and Robert Morgenthau, and they were minimal in the context of the story.

In addition to an extensive reply by museum director David Altshuler and an editorial column, the newspaper published seven letters, including mine, on December 2. Altshuler wrote to point out the accomplishments ignored by the article, such as more than 550 video testimonies, a film and discussion series, a speakers bureau, and a collection of some 13,000 objects. More than 35,000 photographic images had been catalogued for exhibitions, and a 6,000-volume reference library had been amassed. In addition, cooperative agreements for research had been reached with other museums and research institutions in Israel, Europe, and the United States. The article ignored all of this work, Altshuler added, and "on the basis of a handful of quotes, the article judges that the museum has little to show for the efforts and monies expended to date." Claiming that the museum had been created as an *institution* and needed only a permanent home, Altshuler ended his letter to the editor, "In response to economic realities, our leadership limited the size of the museum's home, curtailed its budget and drastically reduced ongoing planning and research expenses. From hindsight, any of us could find times we might have pushed harder, avenues we might have explored more carefully. Today, however, one thing is clear. There never was a moment when the realization of this museum facility was closer. We call upon every member and friend of the largest Jewish community in the world to help complete the task."[3]

Museum professionals such as the director of the Smithsonian Institution's traveling exhibition service, the director of the Judah L. Magnes Museum in California, and the chairperson of the Council of American Jewish Museums sent supportive letters. Commission member Rabbi Irving Greenberg wrote to say he strongly supported the need for a memorial and that he had been quoted out of context. My own letter took exception to the sarcastic (and inaccurate) slur at the beginning of the article, the unbalanced use of negative quotes, and the omission of the project's accomplishments to date.

One letter that was not published came from Ernest Michel, a loyal member of the commission who is an Auschwitz-Birkenau survivor and retired fund-raising executive for the United Jewish Appeal. He wrote that he was "disappointed, saddened, and incensed over the sarcastic and derogatory tone" of the article: "Instead of helping to support these efforts [to build a Holocaust museum], which one should have expected from a responsible newspaper, you heap scorn and ridicule. Instead of reporting— as you have been told by a number of individuals, including myself—that we are on the verge of completing our fund-raising efforts, you are contributing to put these plans in jeopardy. Instead of supporting our efforts you use a cheap and insulting headline, as well as negative reporting, thus making our already difficult task even more difficult. What is your motive?"[4]

On December 12, 1993, a more balanced article that referred to the controversy generated by the *Forward* appeared in the *New York Times*. But even though it was more balanced, it clearly did not improve the situation for the commission. While stating that $14.6 million of donors' money had been spent in ten years, the article acknowledged the "impressive collection of documents, artifacts and videotaped interviews with Holocaust survivors." It also pointed to "the many changes in the museum's proposed size and location" as the reason that much of the $5 million already spent on architectural and exhibit designs "will end up in the wastebasket." Like the *Forward*, the *Times* attributed difficulties to the collapse of the real estate market, which was certainly one contributing factor. Black Monday had resulted in unemployment on Wall Street, and consequent sharp drops in property value at Battery Park City and in the private fortunes of many of the developers who had been the project's foremost financial backers. For example, by March 1991, Peter Kalikow, a prime early backer, had been sued by three banks to which he owed $60 million.[5]

The article in the *Times* gave a brief review of the various stages of the project and interviewed both supporters and critics. Ernest Michel, who was not quoted and did not have his letter printed in the *Forward*, told the *Times* that the project had lost momentum and goodwill, and he could understand the frustration. "But we're so close," he said. "We're just a few million dollars from our goal." Robert Morgenthau, probably bitter about the bad press the project had received in the *Forward*, said the project's "only real problems would result from critical press reports as it tried to raise money." Menachem Rosensaft and Yaffa Eliach, two commission members closely involved with the Washington museum, were negative about the New York museum. Commission member Benjamin Meed, an early advocate of a memorial in New York and also a prominent member of the coalition that created the Washington museum, managed to make a somewhat more neutral statement. "I feel sorry for what is happening here," he said. "But I never give up."[6]

As the stories in the *New York Times* and the *Forward* indicated, the successful 1993 openings of major Holocaust memorial museums in Washington and Los Angeles probably did not help the New York project. Neither newspaper reported the fact that both the U.S. Holocaust Memorial Museum and the Simon Wiesenthal Center had fund-raising operations in New York City. Morgenthau told the *Times* and Altshuler told me that the success of the Washington museum, fifteen years after its conception, demonstrated that the New York project could also be successfully implemented. Nevertheless, some Holocaust survivors and others, even some people who are or were actively involved in the commission, seemed to believe that the existence of two other major Holocaust museums negated the need for one in New York. Those who arrived in the United States as survivors or refugees appear to be especially proud of the way the Holocaust has been "Americanized" in Washington. Perhaps it gives them the sense that they, too, have now been completely Americanized. It is not easy to explain that the New York museum is important in its own right, because it will present the story of the Holocaust from a different, more Jewish and less American, viewpoint.

Most Americans, even most American Jews, are not concerned that representing the history of the Holocaust depends on who is shaping the memory and where it will be memorialized. For most people, the Holocaust is an absolute, and a Holocaust museum is a Holocaust museum. For this reason, the existence of the other two new major museums could easily act as a deterrent to the creation of the museum in New York. However, with the Washington museum emphasizing America's positive role and "core values" of democracy and the Los Angeles museum divided between universal tolerance lessons and slick high-tech dramatizations of the Holocaust, perhaps the American Jewish community should realize the importance for future generations of the New York City project. Based in the most ethnically Jewish city in the United States, it will present the history of the pre-Holocaust Jewish world in Europe, the destruction of that world, and its aftermath. Its location near the embarkation point to the Statue of Liberty should attract not only Jewish and non-Jewish New Yorkers but hundreds of thousands of tourists. Museum director David Altshuler expects the museum to draw 300,000–400,000 visitors a year.

On October 16, 1994, the some thousand Holocaust survivors and their families, community leaders, and elected officials at the ground breaking were euphoric that the memorial museum finally seemed to be coming to fruition. However, at the beginning of 1994 the future of the project was still up in the air. In addition to overextended deadlines, unfavorable press, and competition from two new museums, the New York Holocaust commission also had to contend yet again with a new mayor. Former mayor Koch had used the idea of a memorial museum to gain approval from Jewish constituents, but he genuinely believed in the idea. As the elected official who conceived of it and as a committed Jew, he had a proprietory and personal interest. Governor Cuomo joined the commission as a retroactive founding cochairman at the request of another committed Jew, his close friend and political advisor, then BPCA president Meyer S. (Sandy) Frucher. After Koch lost the 1989 election the power shifted to the governor, who also believed in the project. However, Frucher had left BPCA in the fall of 1988, a year before Koch's defeat. Therefore, the project no longer had a proponent with "paternal" interest and a sense of personal involvement either in City Hall or in the governor's office.

Koch's replacement, Mayor David Dinkins, showed little interest in the powerful political symbolism of the Holocaust or the project. Just when the commission was hoping to gain more support from him, he lost his 1993 reelection bid. Then the commission had to begin all over again in January 1994, courting Republican mayor Rudolph Giuliani. Giuliani did not seem likely to be interested in a project that would give more glory to a Democratic governor than to himself. However, unlike Dinkins, he was close to George Klein, and he seemed more than pleased to share the spotlight with Klein, the governor, and others at the lease-signing and ground-breaking ceremonies. In fact, shortly after the ceremonies, Giuliani announced he was endorsing Cuomo for the 1994 gubernatorial race, rather than Republican candidate George Pataki.

Despite this backing and strong support from Jewish voters, Governor Cuomo lost the election. The Holocaust commission then had to contend with yet another political upheaval at the beginning of 1995. Rather than Founding Cochairman Mario Cuomo, the commission's new "landlord" was virtually unknown to them—Republican governor George Pataki, a former state senator from Peekskill. However, this latest change of sponsors has not caused further delays in implementation of the Holocaust

memorial museum, and Governnor Pataki has cooperated to
keep the project moving forward. Although Pataki did not receive
the support of most Jewish voters, his principal political patron,
Senator Alfonse D'Amato, has traditionally received strong backing from the Jewish community.[7] Pataki has followed the lead of
D'Amato, a staunch supporter of the Holocaust commission and
George Klein's close political ally. His wife, Libby Pataki, was
honorary cochairwoman of the museum's spring women's lunch-
eon in June 1995. Mayor Giuliani campaigned bitterly against
the new governor, and their evolving relationship as they learn
to cooperate could have some residual effect on the commission.
However, the project is probably too far along to be influenced
by any potential conflict between the mayor and the governor.
Former governor Cuomo, like former mayor Koch, will remain a
founding cochairman.

But these latest changings of the guard are just one aspect of
how the passing of time has affected the project. Long before
Mayor Giuliani and then Governor Pataki took office, a series of
delays, new sites, and restructured plans had resulted in a vicious circle: the need to show concrete progress in order to raise
money, and the inability to raise money with no concrete progress to show. Although working for implementation, the coalition
instead reached an impasse. So much time has gone by since
the inception of the project that many commission members are
either out of office, disenchanted, bankrupt, dishonored, or dead.

Furthermore, the changing political coalition working on the
New York City Holocaust museum project has been extremely
complicated. Not only are there newly elected officials as new
members, but many of the participants also have worn more
than one hat. This has produced yet another vicious circle: the
changes in the complex coalition over time are one reason the
project has taken so long, but the prolonged process has contributed to the fact that the coalition has changed. During the thirteen years between the initiation of this Holocaust memorial
project and the ground breaking, the power of various members
and components of the coalition has increased or diminished. In
addition, new partners have joined the coalition and others have
drifted away. The bylaws of the New York Holocaust Memorial
Commission are flawed, because there is no provision for removing anyone. While no one was ever officially dismissed from office

or membership, a few people, such as Ivan Boesky, have officially resigned and others have merely lost interest.

Perhaps one reason the project floundered was because it was a creation of the Koch era, the years when Mayor Koch's close symbiotic relationship with the developers in New York City, most of them Jewish, created an empire of "masters of the universe" with seemingly endless power and wealth. The project was conceived in this heady atmosphere, and probably would have succeeded if it had been implemented under those circumstances. However, before it got off the ground, the real estate market became depressed and then Koch was no longer in office. The influential alliance between the developers and the mayor was no longer in place, yet for some time the commission continued to act as though it was. Meanwhile, the reality was that times had changed; Governor Cuomo held the cards after the project moved to Battery Park City, and he was playing by new rules. (Under Republican governor Pataki, there could be more changes, but the project is in its final stages and therefore less in the hands of the governor.)

Despite all of the delays, financial disasters, reshuffling of supporters, and changes in elected and appointed officials, and after several BPCA-imposed deadlines were postponed, an agreement was finally reached in the summer of 1994. I learned from cochairman Manfred Ohrenstein in a May conversation that a new deal with BPCA seemed likely. Then, toward the end of July, David Altshuler told me that he expected to have good news for me by August 18. His "good news" actually occurred on that date, when the new lease was signed. At the lease-signing ceremony, many old conflicts and animosities seemed to be resolved with the promise of success. Governor Cuomo was a hero, now that $7.5 million was forthcoming. His remarks at the lease signing must have pleased the commission more than they did his First Amendment experts. "This museum will tell New Yorkers and visitors from around the world the story of the Jewish people, before, during and after the Holocaust, and document the long and proud history of the Jews who helped to build America," he stated. "This is a story that all of us—not just Jews—need to learn. Just as we must never forget the lessons of hatred gone mad taught by the Holocaust, we must never forget the lessons of Jewish survival and achievement over the centuries."[8]

It may be coincidental that Governor Cuomo was running

for reelection that fall in a very tight race, and desperately seeking the support of Jewish voters. He also seemed to have a genuine belief in the significance of the memorial museum. If he were to lose the election, at least he would go down in history as the governor who initiated the project and brought it to its construction stage before leaving office. If he were to win, his man at BPCA, Harry Albright, would see that the project was finalized during his forthcoming term. The ground-breaking ceremony in October took place right before elections. Thus, Mayor Koch launched the idea of a New York City Holocaust memorial in 1981, the year he was running for reelection, and Governor Cuomo was the feature speaker at the ground-breaking ceremony for the same project thirteen years later, during *his* reelection campaign.[9]

At the October 16 ground-breaking ceremony on a crisp and sunny fall day, Governor Cuomo jokingly acknowledged the political implications of the event. Pointing out that he "resisted" the idea that the audience of Jewish leaders and survivors "owed him a debt of gratitude" for the museum, he kidded that "if you feel you do, I could suggest how you can repay it." Mayor Giuliani made it clear that he was now part of the political coalition heading the effort. Acknowledging that he had "inherited" a project that others had worked on for years, he said that he was committed to building the memorial museum and expected to officiate as mayor at the opening in 1996. BPCA Chairman Harry Albright acted as master of ceremonies for the ground breaking, and speakers included four of the five cochairmen: George Klein, Robert Morgenthau, Manfred Ohrenstein, and Howard Rubenstein.

Albright deserved to preside at the ground breaking, because he was instrumental in BPCA's recommencing lease negotiations with the Holocaust commission leaders immediately after he took office in 1990. As soon as he recovered from a serious illness, he began to play an active role in planning, and then during the actual construction of the museum. Identifying himself as a Catholic, he has spoken publicly and privately about the importance of the museum for New Yorkers and visitors. (He remained in his post under Governor Pataki.)

Ed Koch was recognized at the ground breaking for his role in initiating the project, and he eloquently connected the uniqueness of the Holocaust with other current attempts at genocide in Bosnia and Rwanda. Former mayors Abraham Beame and David Dinkins were also present. In addition to Governor Cuomo and

Mayor Giuliani, many other elected officials and candidates for the November elections were in the audience. Senators Alfonse D'Amato and Daniel Patrick Moynihan and Speaker of the Assembly Sheldon Silver (all of whom spoke briefly), congressmen Charles Rangel and Jerrold Nadler, New York State Comptroller Carl McCall, Manhattan Borough President Ruth Messinger, state senators Franz Leichter and Roy Goodman, and City Comptroller Alan Hevesi were all present for at least part of the three-hour ceremony. Previous actors in the process who attended included former BPCA officials Sandy Frucher and Fabian Palomino and former commission director David Blumenfeld. Senator D'Amato made a hasty retreat after speaking, annoyed that his gubernatorial candidate, George Pataki, did not receive more recognition during the ceremony.

Ernest Michel, who opened his speech by remarking, "I'm Auschwitz number 104995," inadvertently brought up the issue of separation of church and state that Governor Cuomo's office had so zealously guarded in the new lease. Michel spoke of witnessing the public hanging of three good friends at Auschwitz, and of his vow never to forget them or his family members who were murdered by the Nazis. "Why, after the success in Washington, should we have a memorial in New York?" he asked. "I would like to be able to come to this place and say Kaddish [the memorial prayer] for my parents who have no grave," he then answered. Since Kaddish is a public prayer that requires a quorum of ten, the lease, in theory, could prohibit this activity, or possibly even a private prayer. According to Section 26.2 of the lease signed on August 18, 1994, the museum cannot permit "any public or private, group or individual, prayer" that is "organized, sponsored, coordinated or supervised by or on behalf of the tenant," and no part of the building can "at any time be designated as a place for any such prayer."

While the intent of the lease is to prohibit construction of a synagogue or sponsorship of a formal prayer service, the wording of this section is absurdly stringent. This clause, taken literally, seems to be at odds with Michel's remarks as well as with the presentation of a rescued Torah scroll that museum director David Altshuler described as "a quintessential symbol of our museum's message and mission." Since people routinely offer public prayers in the White House, the Congress, the New York State Capitol, and other government buildings, specific prohibition of public and private prayers even "supervised" by the museum is inconsistent with accepted practice. As it is inconceivable that the state would object if a Christian recited the Lord's Prayer or a Jewish group recited Kaddish at the memorial, this section of the lease should have been reworded.

In addition to the local political implications, complications, and inconsistencies of the New York City Holocaust memorial project, and the political machinations that have delayed it during the nearly half century since the first attempt to create a memorial, the project is coming to fruition at a time of global political changes regarding Holocaust memorialization in museums. Before ground was finally broken for the New York City museum in October 1994, three unrelated events in the early 1990s dramatically changed the way the Holocaust will be publicly remembered in the future. The first event, the fall of the Berlin Wall on November 9, 1989, and the subsequent reunification of Germany, removed three major concentration camp memorial sites in eastern Germany from Communist control. The memorial museums at Buchenwald, Sachsenhausen, and Ravensbrück women's concentration camp, all of which had been designed to glorify Communism and denigrate capitalism, were suddenly part of the Western world.[10] Exhibits and monuments that had followed Communist ideology and barely acknowledged that Jews had been among the prisoners in the camps began to be revamped to acknowledge that the Nazis were not only "fascists" but also genocidal murderers who had tried to wipe out Europe's Jewish population.

For example, when I visited Ravensbrück in 1980, I was shown a 1968 informational film about the camp. This film singled out and told the history of the Communist heroines who had been incarcerated there, and used such terms as "class rule," "bourgeoisie rule," and "social disadvantages." Only Communist survivors told their stories. Hitler's Third Reich was described as a consequence of the Weimar Republic, which denied the interests of the working people and then reaped the harvest. In the museum exhibit there was no evidence that any Jewish prisoners had suffered and been murdered at the camp, although an estimated 10 to 20 percent of the 132,000 women in Ravensbrück were Jewish (and only about 15,000 women survived).[11] When I went to Ravensbrück again in March 1994, there had already been some changes and more were under way. A small new memorial exhibit about Jewish women had been inaugurated in 1992, and a documentary videotape made in 1989 was shown.[12] As the videotape had been produced by the German Democratic Republic during a transitional period, it was no longer dominated by the Communist survivors. Rather than singling out specific women, it told a generalized story. It was no longer available for sale, because it was soon to be replaced by a post-unification version. Similarly, the small Jewish exhibit was to be replaced by a larger one, to be ready for ceremonies marking the fiftieth anniversary of liberation in April 1995. At these April 22–24, 1995 ceremonies, I was present to witness the inauguration of new museum exhibits, which indeed now include Jewish women in the official commemoration at the camp. The assistant director of the museum said the new, larger exhibit was the result of criticism from the Jewish community that the 1992 exhibit was too small and insignificant. Thus, political considerations have clearly affected the way the Holocaust has been and will be memorialized at Ravensbrück. As a Communist memorial museum, it ignored the Jewish women who suffered and died there as Jews, and as a Western memorial it records their experience. The memorial staff even met with Israeli suvivors of the camp who attended the fiftieth anniversary ceremonies to ask for suggestions about future memorialization plans.

Changes are also taking place in the other concentration camp memorials that were formerly in the German Democratic Republic. The shrine to Ernest Thälmann, the German Communist leader murdered by the Nazis at Buchenwald, dominated that memorial exhibit when I visited in 1980. After reunification, the memorial was removed. Along with more recognition of Jewish victims of the Holocaust and less homage to Communist heroes and heroines, the new Western dominance over the former German Democratic Republic has brought a potential new problem for the future of memorialization in Germany. Some leaders of the Christian Democratic government are beginning to equate Soviet atrocities during and after World War II with Nazi policies of genocide. For example, there is a movement in Germany to memorialize at the Buchenwald and Sachsenhausen concentration camp sites the Nazi prisoners of war who were murdered there by Soviet troops after the war. If this movement succeeds, it will help today's Germany to make the case that *it* was a victim, as well as, or perhaps, rather than, a victimizer.[13]

In addition to the reunification of Germany, the opening of the U.S. Holocaust Memorial Museum in Washington, D.C., is beginning to have great impact on how the Holocaust will be remembered in the future. While the opening to the West is resulting in the transformation of the sites in the former German Democratic Republic, the Washington museum is even beginning to overshadow Yad Vashem, Israel's shrine to the Holocaust and Zionism. When it was established by Israeli law in 1953, Yad Vashem was intended to be *the* world Holocaust museum that would commemorate not only the Holocaust but Israel's very existence. As an institution that publicly remembers not only the Holocaust but its survivors' redemption in the new state of Israel, Yad Vashem reflects the central role of the Holocaust in Israel's political culture and collective memory. Yad Vashem has been described as "second only to the Western Wall in its sacredness as a shrine of the Israeli civil religion. It is the place to which foreign dignitaries are taken to celebrate and solemnize their relationship to Israel by sharing its identification with the victims of the Holocaust. Yad Vashem is the major memorial to the Jews and Jewish communities destroyed in the Holocaust. It is maintained as a religious institution. Visitors are expected to cover their heads. . . ."[14] The centrality of the Holocaust in Israel has affected the country's image of itself, its commemoration of that time, and its relations with other nations. Israel's political culture is permeated by the Holocaust to such an extent that it has developed a sense of "ownership." "One cannot understand Israel without understanding the Holocaust," according to Yitzchak Mais, the director of the Yad Vashem museum, in a 1987 interview. He associated with the Holocaust the fact that Israel is the "only one country in the world that puts Jewish survival as its number-one priority."[15] (In July 1995 Mais became the new Chief Curator of the Core Exhibition for the completion of the New York Holocaust museum project.)

Suddenly, after April 1993, Yad Vashem had a rival as *the* Holocaust museum. The Israeli memorial was in the process of modernizing its history museum, but the new Washington museum seemed to surpass it in architectural design, state-of-the-art technology, artifacts and exhibits, access to archival material, research facilities, and fund-raising and public relations capabilities. Concern in Israel was aptly summarized by the title of a *Jerusalem Report* cover story just before the Washington museum opened: "Who Owns the Memory?" According to the article, "American Jewry is implicitly declaring its independence from Israeli hegemony on Holocaust commemoration," and "Yad Vashem's leadership is understandably wary. Until now, Yad Vashem had been the undisputed world center for Holocaust education...."[16]

Along with this "independence"on the question of Holocaust commemoration, the organized American Jewish community has not yet come to terms with a third change: the possibility of Israel's ability to live in peace with its neighbors. Just two days before the ground breaking in New York City, Israel's Prime Minister Yitzhak Rabin and Foreign Minister Shimon Peres, along with PLO leader Yassir Arafat, received the Nobel Peace Prize for their efforts to bring peace to the Middle East. The night before the ground breaking, Israel signed a new agreement with Jordan. Perhaps in the future, if Israel becomes an integral part of the Middle East and thus less dependent on American Jewish funding and lobbying, its importance for the American Jewish community will diminish and the Holocaust will become even stronger as a reference point for the community's interest in Judaism. Meanwhile, the community's approval of the U.S. Holocaust Memorial Museum in Washington implies its acceptance of a new form of American, rather than Israeli, Holocaust memorialization. Whereas Yad Vashem emphasizes the need for a Jewish state, the Washington museum glorifies the United States as the liberator of concentration camps, "the land of the free and the home of the brave." Perhaps the point can best be expressed figuratively: the anthem of Yad Vashem is *Hatikvah*, the anthem of the U. S. Holocaust Memorial Museum is *The Star-spangled Banner*, and that of Ravensbrück, Buchenwald, and Sachsenhausen was until recently *The Internationale*.

The new Holocaust memorial museum in New York City, A Living Memorial to the Holocaust–Museum of Jewish Heritage, is coming on the scene at a time of change in the future of Holocaust memorialization. It will be influenced not only by its own tortuous political history, but by major changes in how the history of the Holocaust is being presented in such diverse locations as Washington, Jerusalem, and Germany. Like all other Holocaust memorial museums, the New York museum will influence the political message that future generations of Jews and non-Jews will receive about the history of the Holocaust.

This book comes to a close with steel construction beams rising into the air in Battery Park City in the summer of 1996. After years of impasse, the New York Holocaust Memorial Commission is finally going forward and creating a memorial museum. While the project is not yet fully implemented, it is well underway, and I will end with the optimistic assumption that I have chronicled the political prehistory and history behind an ultimately successful project, scheduled to open in 1997. This new memorial museum, like all Holocaust museums and memorials already in place in Israel, Europe, the United States, and elsewhere, will become part of the way the memory of the Holocaust is transmitted to future generations. Its final form is being influenced not only by the interpretation of the experience it remembers, but by local politics, global events, new technology, and new inroads in the art and science of memorialization.

Notes

Chapter 1. The American Jewish Community's Emergence as an Interest Group

1. There is a considerable literature on the organized American Jewish community's rescue efforts (or lack of them) during World War II. See, for example: Yehuda Bauer, *American Jewry and the Holocaust: The American Jewish Joint Distribution Committee, 1939–1945* (Detroit: Wayne State University Press, 1981); Henry L. Feingold, *The Politics of Rescue* (New York: Holocaust Library, 1970) and *Bearing Witness: How America and Its Jews Responded to the Holocaust* (Syracuse: Syracuse University Press, 1995); Saul S. Friedman, *No Haven for the Oppressed* (Indiana: Wayne State University Press, 1973); Nahum Goldmann, *The Jewish Paradox* (New York: Grosset & Dunlap, 1978); Raul Hilberg, *Perpetrators, Victims, Bystanders* (New York, HarperCollins, 1992), pp. 225–48; Walter Laqueur, *The Terrible Secret: The Suppression of the Truth About Hitler's "Final Solution"* (Boston: Little, Brown, 1980); chapters by Herbert Hochhauser, Frederick A. Lazin, and Robert W. Ross in *In Answer. . . . Is the Story True? Why Did the World Community Not Respond? What Are the Lessons?* edited by Franklin H. Littell, Irene Shur, and Claude R. Foster, Jr. (West Chester, Pa.: Sylvan, 1988); Haskel Lookstein, *Were We Our Brothers' Keepers? The Public Response of American Jews to the Holocaust, 1938–44* (New York: Hartmore House, 1985); Rafael Medoff, *The Deafening Silence: American Jewish Leaders and the Holocaust* (New York: Shapolsky, 1987); Arthur D. Morse, *While Six Million Died: A Chronicle of American Apathy* (New York: Overlook, 1983); and David Wyman, *The Abandonment of the Jews: America and the Holocaust, 1941–1945* (New York: Pantheon, 1984).

2. Melvin I. Urofsky, *We Are One* (Garden City, N.Y.: Anchor, 1978), pp. 21–33.

3. Naomi W. Cohen, *Not Free to Desist* (Philadelphia: Jewish Publication Society, 1972), p. 311.

4. Peter Grose, *Israel in the Mind of America* (New York: Schocken, 1984), p. 226.
5. Urofsky, *We are One*, pp. 33–34.
6. Arthur Hertzberg, *The Jews in America* (New York: Simon & Schuster, 1989), p. 300.
7. Urofsky, *We are One*, pp. 94, 126.
8. Daniel J. Elazar, *Community and Polity: The Organizational Dynamics of American Jewry* (Philadelphia: Jewish Publication Society, 1976), p. 166.
9. Leonard Fein, *Where Are We? The Inner Life of America's Jews* (New York: Harper & Row, 1988), pp. 222–23.
10. Grose, *Israel in the Mind of America*, p. 218.
11. Urofsky, *We Are One*, p. 147.
12. Adolph R. Lerner, "The Case of the Memorial," Archives of YIVO Institute for Jewish Research, New York, n.d., p. 4.
13. On March 5–6, 1955, representatives of the following 20 national Jewish organizations met at the Shoreham Hotel in Washington: American Jewish Congress, American Trade Union Council for Labor Israel, American Zionist Committee for Public Affairs, American Zionist Council, B'nai B'rith, Hadassah, Hapoel Hamizrachi, Jewish Agency, Jewish Labor Committee, Jewish War Veterans, Labor Zionist Organization of America, Mizrachi Organization of America, National Community Relations Advisory Council, Progressive Zionist League, Union of American Hebrew Congregations, Union of Orthodox Jewish Organizations, United Synagogue of America, United Zionist Labor Party, Zionist Organization of America, and Zionists-Revisionists of America ("Conference of Presidents" file, Library of the American Jewish Committee, New York).
14. According to the 1990 National Jewish Population Survey of the Council of Jewish Federations, the "Jewishly identified" population of the United States was 6,840,000. Including "gentile adults living with this total" (excluding institutionalized persons), the total population is given as 8,100,000. See *Highlights of the CJF 1990 National Jewish Population Survey*, edited by Barry A. Kosmin et al. (New York: Council of Jewish Federations, 1992), pp. 1–7.
15. Elazar, *Community and Polity*, p. 216.
16. Ibid., pp. 320–22.
17. Brochure of the Conference of Presidents of Major American Jewish Organizations, New York, 1993. A review of the early history of AIPAC and its relationship to the Conference of Presidents can be found in I. L. Kenen, *Israel's Defense Line* (New York: Prometheus, 1981), pp. 106–13.
18. Affiliated organizations in 1996 were: AIPAC, American Friends of Likud, American Gathering/Federation Jewish Holocaust Survivors, America-Israel Friendship League, American Jewish Committee, American Jewish Congress, American ORT Federation, American Sephardi Federation, American Zionist Movement, Americans for Peace Now, AMIT, Anti-Defamation League of B'nai B'rith, Association of Reform Zionists of America, B'nai

B'rith, Bnai Zion, Central Conference of American Rabbis, Council of Jewish Federations, Development Corporation for Israel, Emunah of America, Jewish Reconstructionist Federation, Hadassah–Women's Zionist Organization of America, Hebrew Immigrant Aid Society, Jewish Community Centers Associations, Jewish Institute for National Security Affairs, Jewish Labor Committee, Jewish National Fund, Jewish War Veterans, Jewish Women International, Joint Distribution Committee, Labor Zionist Alliance, Mercaz USA, NA'AMAT USA, National Committee for Labor Israel, National Conference on Soviet Jewry, National Council of Jewish Women, National Council of Young Israel, NJCRAC, Poale Agudath Israel, Rabbinical Assembly, Rabbinical Council of America, Religious Zionists of America, Union of American Hebrew Congregations, Union of Orthodox Jewish Congregations of America, United Israel Appeal, United Jewish Appeal, United Synagogue of Conservative Judaism, WIZO USA, Women's American ORT, Women's League for Conservative Judaism, Women's League for Israel, Women of Reform Judaism, Workmen's Circle, World Zionist Executive–US, and Zionist Organization of America.

19. Daniel J. Elazar, *People and Polity: The Organizational Dynamics of World Jewry* (Detroit: Wayne State University Press, 1989), p. 78.

20. Urofsky, *We Are One*, p. 445.

21. For a detailed analysis of the complicated web of the organized Jewish community in the United States, see Elazar, *Community and Polity*.

22. *Joint Program Plan for Jewish Community Relations, 1994–95*, National Jewish Community Relations Advisory Council, New York, p. 6. In 1994 the constituent organizations of NJCRAC were: American Jewish Committee, American Jewish Congress, B'nai B'rith/Anti-Defamation League, Hadassah, Jewish Labor Committee, Jewish War Veterans, National Council of Jewish Women, Union of American Hebrew Congregations, Union of Orthodox Jewish Congregations of America, United Synagogue of Conservative Judaism/Women's League for Conservative Judaism, Women's American ORT, and local Jewish community relations councils and committees throughout the United States.

23. Charles E. Silberman, *A Certain People: American Jews and Their Lives Today* (New York: Summit, 1985), p. 109.

24. Urofsky, *We Are One*, pp. 333–36.

25. Silberman, *A Certain People*, p. 345.

26. Theodore H. White, *America in Search of Itself: The Making of the President, 1956–1980* (New York: Harper & Row, 1982), p. 414. In New York State in 1980, the official vote compiled by the Federal Election Commission was 2,893,831 for Reagan, 2,728,372 for Carter, and 467,801 for Anderson.

Chapter 2. Memory of the Holocaust as an Issue in the American Jewish Community

1. Elie Wiesel, interview by author, New York City, August 8, 1990.
2. David M. Szonyi, *An Annotated Bibliography and Resource Guide* (New York: National Jewish Resource Center, 1985), gives a comprehensive listing of books, audiovisual materials, exhibits, curricula, memorials, research centers, and speakers' bureaus. In 1990, Social Studies School Service published its 32-page catalogue, "Teaching the Holocaust: Resources and Materials," which offers for sale to schools books, audiovisual materials, curricula, and other material dealing only with the Holocaust.
3. John W. Kingdon, *Agendas, Alternatives and Public Policies* (Boston: Little, Brown, 1984).
4. Boaz Evron, "Holocaust: The Uses of Disaster," *New Outlook* Discussion Paper (Israel: *New Outlook* magazine, n.d.), pp. 8–9.
5. Conor Cruise O'Brien, *The Siege* (New York: Simon & Schuster, 1986), p. 318.
6. Jacob Neusner, "A 'Holocaust' Primer," *National Review*, August 3, 1979, pp. 976–77.
7. Rabbi Irving Greenberg, interview by author, New York City, April 19, 1990.
8. Saul Friedlander, lecture presented at the Society for the Advancement of Judaism, New York City, February 4, 1990.
9. Melvin I. Urofsky, *We Are One* (Garden City, N.Y.: Anchor, 1978), p. 350.
10. Charles E. Silberman, *A Certain People: American Jews and Their Lives Today* (New York: Summit, 1985), pp. 182–83.
11. See Hannah Arendt, "A Reporter at Large: Eichmann in Jerusalem," *The New Yorker*, February 16 and 23, 1963; and *Eichmann in Jerusalem: A Report on the Banality of Evil*, rev. ed. (New York: Penguin, 1980), chap. 7.
12. Leonard Fein, *Where Are We? The Inner Life of America's Jews* (New York: Harper & Row, 1988), p. 18.
13. Michael Berenbaum, interview by author, New York City, March 12, 1990.
14. Wiesel, interview.
15. The first publications of these books in English in the United States were: Elie Wiesel, *Night* (New York: Hill & Wang, 1960), translated by Stella Rodway; Anne Frank, *Anne Frank: The Diary of a Young Girl* (New York: Doubleday, 1952); Gerda Weissmann Klein, *All But My Life* (New York: Hill & Wang, 1957); Raul Hilberg, *The Destruction of the European Jews* (Chicago: Quadrangle, 1961). All of these books are still in print, and more recent editions include: Wiesel, *Night, Dawn, The Accident: Three Tales* (New York: Hill & Wang, 1982); Frank, *The Diary of a Young*

Girl: The Definitive Edition (New York: Doubleday, 1995); Klein, *All But My Life* (New York: Noonday, 1992); Hilberg, *The Destruction of the European Jews: Revised and Definitive Edition*, 3 vols. (New York: Holmes & Meier, 1985).

16. Rochelle G. Saidel, *The Outraged Conscience: Seekers of Justice for Nazi War Criminals in America* (Albany: State University of New York Press, 1984), p. 7.

17. *Joint Program Plan for Jewish Community Relations, 1972–1973* (New York: National Jewish Community Relations Advisory Council), p. 11.

18. *Joint Program Plan for Jewish Community Relations, 1961–1962,* "The Eichmann Trial," pp. 15–16.

19. Early recommendations related to memorializing the Holocaust can be found in: the 1973–74 *Joint Program Plan*, pp. 12–13; the 1974–75 *Plan*, p. 14; the 1975–76 *Plan*, pp. 20–21; the 1976–77 *Plan*, p. 16; the 1977–78 *Plan*, p. 23; and the 1978–79 *Plan*, p. 13.

20. Greenberg, interview.

21. Neusner, "A 'Holocaust' Primer," pp. 976–77. Neusner was referring to Nathan Glazer, *American Judaism* (Chicago: University of Chicago Press, 1957).

22. Silberman, *A Certain People*, pp. 182–83.

23. David Sidorsky, ed., *The Future of the Jewish Community in America* (New York/Philadelphia: American Jewish Committee and Jewish Publication Society of America, 1973), p. 20.

24. Seymour Fox, "Toward a General Theory of Jewish Education," in Sidorsky, ed., *Future of the Jewish Community*, p. 262.

25. Daniel Elazar, "Decision-Making in the American-Jewish Community," in Sidorsky, ed., *Future of the Jewish Community*, p. 279.

26. Within Israel, the linkage of Zionism, the State of Israel, and the Holocaust has been a major vehicle and aim of memorialization. See, for example: Charles Liebman and Eliezer Don-Yehiya, *Civil Religion in Israel: Traditional Judaism and Political Culture in the Jewish State* (Berkeley: University of California Press, 1983); Tom Segev, *The Seventh Million: The Israelis and the Holocaust* (New York: Hill & Wang, 1993); James Young, *The Texture of Memory: Holocaust Memorials and Meaning*, Part III (New Haven: Yale University Press, 1993).

27. Arthur Hertzberg, *The Jews in America* (New York: Simon & Schuster, 1989), p. 382.

28. Ibid., p. 384. I have not discussed the policies of Breira and other alternative movements with regard to memorialization of the Holocaust because they have not been part of the organized American Jewish community as defined in Chapter 1—that is, those organizations belonging to the Conference of Presidents of Major American Jewish Organizations. The organized Jewish community has attempted to discredit, rather than encourage, the activities of the alternative peace movement. The Presidents'

Conference did not accept Americans for Peace Now as a member until 1993, and the decision to do so created much controversy.

29. Fein, *Where Are We?*, p. 63.
30. Jeshajahu Weinberg, interview by author, Washington, D.C., March 14, 1990.
31. Arthur Hertzberg, lecture presented at the Society for the Advancement of Judaism, New York City, February 4, 1990.
32. Samuel Norich, "What Holocaust Centers Tell Us About Ourselves," *The Forward*, March 6, 1987, p. 5.
33. *Directory of Holocaust Institutions* (Washington, D.C.: U.S. Holocaust Memorial Council, 1988), p. vii.
34. William L. Shulman, ed., *1995 Directory: Association of Holocaust Organizations* (New York: Holocaust Resource Center and Archives, Queensborough Community College, 1995).
35. Fein, *Where Are We?*, p. 62.
36. James E. Young, "Holocaust Memorials in America: The Politics of Identity," *Survey of Jewish Affairs*, vol. 10, William Frankel, ed. (London: Basil Blackwell, 1991).
37. Friedlander, lecture.

Chapter 3. Early Attempts to Create a New York City Holocaust Memorial

1. See S. L. Shneiderman, "To Memorialize the Six Million: The Monument Controversy," *Congress Bi-Weekly*, February 1965; and James Young, *The Texture of Memory: Holocaust Memorials and Meaning* (New Haven: Yale University Press, 1993), pp. 288–89.
2. A. R. Lerner, "The Case of the Memorial," unpublished and undated manuscript, filed under "American Memorial to the Six Million Jews of Europe, Inc.," Archives of YIVO Institute for Jewish Research, New York, p. 1.
3. Ibid., p. 2.
4. Young, *Texture of Memory*, p. 288.
5. Lerner, "Case of the Memorial," p. 2.
6. Ibid., p. 3.
7. Ibid., pp. 3–4.
8. Wolf Von Eckhardt, *Eric Mendelsohn* (New York: George Braziller, 1960), p. 30.
9. Lerner, "Case of the Memorial," pp. 7–8.
10. Ibid., p. 11.
11. Moses's anti-Jewish attitude is documented in Robert A. Caro, *The Power Broker* (New York: Vintage, 1975), pp. 411–12.
12. Lerner, "Case of the Memorial," pp. 19–20.
13. "Drive Underway for Riverside Drive Memorial," *West Side News*, April 1, 1948.

14. Letter from Mayor O'Dwyer to A. R. Lerner July 26, 1948, and address by Lerner at City Hall, October 20, 1948, filed under "American Memorial to the Six Million Jews of Europe, Inc.," Archives of YIVO Institute, New York.
15. This is documented in press releases and news articles of that time as well as in Eckhardt, *Eric Mendelsohn;* Bruno Zevi, *Erich Mendelsohn* (New York: Rizzoli, 1985); and Young, *Texture of Memory*, p. 290.
16. *The New York Times*, November 23, 1948, (fragment of clipping), Archives of YIVO Institute, New York.
17. Eckhardt, *Eric Mendelsohn*, p. 30.
18. "Memorial Model Shown at Museum," *The New York Times*, January 18, 1950, p. 9.
19. Shneiderman, "To Memorialize the Six Million."
20. Ibid.
21. Lerner, "The Case of the Memorial," pp. 16–17.
22. Ibid., p. 19.
23. Rebecca Read Shanor, *The City That Never Was* (New York: Viking, 1988), p. 219.
24. Charles R. Allen, Jr., *Nazi War Criminals in America: Facts . . . Action* (New York: Highgate House, 1985), pp. 49–57, details "Project Paperclip."
25. Howard Zinn, *The Twentieth Century: A People's History* (New York: Harper & Row, 1980), p. 128.
26. Naomi W. Cohen, *Not Free to Desist: The American Jewish Committee, 1906–1966* (Philadelphia: Jewish Publication Society, 1972), p. 346. See chap. 13, pp. 345–82.
27. "Part I: Open Letter to the Jewish People of the United States" by the editors; "Part II: Memorandum of the ADL (July 3, 1953)"; "Part III: The Harap Testimony Before the Un-American Activities Committee," *Jewish Life*, September 1953. See also Charles R. Allen, Jr., "A Talk with Velde Collaborators: An Interview That Reflects a Policy of Appeasement by Three Jewish 'Defense' Organizations Toward the McCarthyite Danger to Democracy," *Jewish Life*, October, 1953; also Cohen, *Not Free to Desist*, p. 354.
28. A. R. Lerner to Emil Shneiderman, February 24, 1965; memo from Shneiderman to Richard Cohen, American Jewish Congress, April 21, 1977 (concerning April 18 meeting); memorandum from Victoria Free to Richard Cohen, "Notes from a Press Conference at the Jewish Community Relations Council—March 24, 1977," March 25, 1977, filed under "American Memorial to Six Million Jews of Europe, Inc.," Archives of YIVO Institute, New York, N.Y.
29. Elie Wiesel, interview by author, New York City, August 8, 1990.
30. D. De Sola Pool, letter to the editor, *The New York Times*, June 20, 1952.

Chapter 4. Memorial Plans Change with the Political Climate

1. See Howard Zinn, *The Twentieth Century: A People's History* (New York: Harper & Row, 1980), pp. 152–62.
2. See James Young, *The Texture of Memory: Holocaust Memorials and Meaning* (New Haven: Yale University Press, 1993), chap. 6, for more details about Rapoport.
3. The letterhead of the coalition's stationery used the name "Committee to Commemorate the Six Million Jewish Martyrs." In addition to WAGRO, memorial sponsors were the American Jewish Committee, American Jewish Congress, Jewish Labor Committee, Jewish War Veterans, B'nai B'rith, Workmen's Circle, Farband–Labor Zionist Order, New York Board of Rabbis, National Council of Jewish Women, Bergen-Belsen Association, Club of Polish Jews, Jewish Nazi Victims of America, Federation of Polish Jews, Association of Yugoslav Jews, United Galician Jews of America, United Rumanian Jews of America, World Sephardi Federation, World Federation of Russian Jews, World Federation of Hungarian Jews, Danish-American Jewish Committee, Bulgarian Claims Committee, and World Federation of Ukrainian Jews (files of WAGRO, New York, N.Y.).
4. Nathan Rapoport, October 13, 1964, files of WAGRO, New York.
5. WAGRO-translated reprint of articles in the Yiddish *Daily Forward*, November 14, 1964, and *The Day–Jewish Journal*, November 15, 1964, files of WAGRO, New York.
6. "Conference of Jewish Organizations for the Memorial to the Six Million Martyrs and Heroes: Summary Report" of January 19, 1965, meeting, files of WAGRO, New York.
7. S. L. Shneiderman, "To Memorialize the Six Million: The Monument Controversy," *Congress Bi-Weekly*, February 1965.
8. The art commission consisted of seven members appointed by the mayor and four ex officio members. Of the appointees, it was required that one be a painter, one a sculptor, one an architect, and one a landscape architect. The other three appointees were to have no connection with the fine arts. The mayor was an ex officio member.
9. Minutes, Special Meeting of the New York City Art Commission, January 28, 1965, filed under "American Memorial to Six Million Jews of Europe, Inc.," Archives of YIVO Institute, New York, N.Y. A copy of the original disapproval of the Zygelboim Memorial Certificate 10804 is in the Zygelboim biographical files, archives of the Bund, New York, N.Y.
10. William E. Farrell, "City Rejects Park Memorials to Slain Jews," *The New York Times*, February 11, 1965, p. 1.
11. "Memorials in the Parks," editorial, *The New York Times*, February 13, 1965.

12. Farrell, "City Rejects Park Memorials."
13. William E. Farrell, "Two Jewish Leaders Protest Art Ban," *The New York Times*, February 12, 1965, p. 31.
14. Press release, Office of the Mayor, City of New York, for release: P.M. papers, March 6, 1965, and A.M. papers, March 7, 1965, files of WAGRO, New York.
15. William E. Farrell, "Mayor Promises a Monument Site," *The New York Times*, March 7, 1965.
16. Adolph R. Lerner to Emil (S. L.) Shneiderman, Rome, Italy, February 24, 1965, filed under "American Memorial to the Six Million Jews of Europe, Inc.," Archives of YIVO Institute, New York.
17. Ibid.
18. Martin Tolchin, "Times Square Memorial Urged," *The New York Times*, September 2, 1965.
19. Raymond Sokolov, "Rm to Let. Landmark Bldg. 77,000 Sq. Ft.," *The Wall Street Journal*, October 3, 1984, p. 28.
20. Tolchin, "Times Square Memorial Urged."
21. "Monument to Jews Scored at Meeting," *The New York Times*, December 31, 1965.
22. "Statement Made by Dr. Joachim Prinz, Chairman of Committee for Six Million," December 30, 1965, files of WAGRO, New York.
23. Helen Sutton, "Memorial to Jews: Where and When?" *New York Journal American*, March 16, 1966, p. 46.
24. Benjamin A. Gebiner and Vladka Meed to the New York City Art Commission, March 26, 1966, files of WAGRO, New York.

Chapter 5. The Holocaust Memorial Endeavor Continues

1. Benjamin Gebiner, "Chairman pro tem.," and Vladka Meed, "Sec'y pro tem.," to "Dear Friend," stationery of Committee to Commemorate the Six Million Jewish Martyrs, August 1966, files of WAGRO, New York, N.Y.
2. Ibid.
3. Arthur Rosenblatt to Benjamin A. Gebiner, October 13, 1966, files of WAGRO, New York.
4. Rosenblatt to Gebiner, November 21, 1966, files of WAGRO, New York.
5. Members of the art committee were: Harry N. Abrams, publisher of art books; H. Harvard Arnason, vice president of the Guggenheim Museum; Thomas S. Buechner, director of the Brooklyn Museum; David Finn, president of the Jewish Museum; Rene d'Harnoncourt, director of the Museum of Modern Art; Emily Genauer, art critic for the *New York World Journal Tribune;*

Bruce Glaser, director of Gallery of Israeli Art; Percival Goodman, architect; Robert Hale, retired from the Metropolitan Museum of Art; Dan Hunter, director of the Jewish Museum; Philip Johnson, architect; Louis I. Kahn, architect; Sherman E. Lee, director of the Cleveland Museum of Art; Abram Lerner, curator of the Hirshhorn Collection; Thomas M. Messer, director of the Guggenheim Museum; Charles Parkhurst, director of the Baltimore Museum of Art; and Meyer Schapiro, professor of art at Columbia University (then at the Fogg Art Museum, Harvard University).

6. Press release, February 18, 1967, files of WAGRO, New York.
7. Vladka Meed, interview by author, New York City, May 7, 1990.
8. August Heckscher to Benjamin A. Gebiner, March 22, 1968, files of WAGRO, New York.
9. "Dear Friends" letter from Gebiner and Meed, March 22, 1968, and "Dear Member" letter, undated and unsigned, files of WAGRO, New York.
10. Vladka Meed, interview.
11. Museum of Modern Art press release no. 102, for release October 17, 1968. Ada Louise Huxtable, "Plan for Jewish Martyrs' Monument Here Unveiled," *The New York Times*, October 17, 1968.
12. Howard Zinn, *The Twentieth Century: A People's History* (New York: Harper & Row, 1980), p. 237.
13. Benjamin A. Gebiner, interview by author, Bayside, N.Y., April 26, 1990.
14. Rebecca Read Shanor, *The City That Never Was* (New York: Viking, 1988), p. 219.
15. Gebiner, interview.
16. Memorandum by Jerry Goodman to Bertram Gold, October 23, 1968, Records Room, American Jewish Committee, New York, N.Y.
17. Bill from Louis I. Kahn to the Committee to Commemorate the Six Million Jewish Martyrs, November 6, 1968, Records Room, American Jewish Committee, New York.
18. David Lloyd Kreeger to Benjamin Gebiner, December 3, 1968, Records Room, American Jewish Committee, New York.
19. Jerry Goodman to David Lloyd Kreeger, July 18, 1969, Records Room, American Jewish Committee, New York.
20. Memorandum by David Geller to Bertram Gold, December 17, 1971, Records Room, American Jewish Committee, New York.
21. Vladka Meed, interview.
22. Benjamin A. Gebiner and Vladka Meed to Mayor John V. Lindsay, May 18, 1971, files of WAGRO, New York.
23. Marvin Schick to Benjamin A. Gebiner and Vladka Meed, May 28, 1971, files of WAGRO, New York. Schick, telephone conversation with the author, New York City, March 19, 1990.
24. Julius Schatz, interview by author, New York City, March 19, 1990.

25. Undated draft of correspondence, files of Vladka Meed, WAGRO, New York.
26. Executive Committee of Memorial to the Six Million Jewish Martyrs, Inc., to representatives of participating organizations, May 1974, files of WAGRO, New York.
27. Schatz, interview.
28. Files of Vladka Meed, WAGRO, New York.

Chapter 6. The Players Change but Still No Progress

1. Robert Born and Hirsh Altusky of WAGRO to Vladka Meed of Memorial to the Six Million Jewish Martyrs, June 29, 1978, files of WAGRO, New York, N.Y.
2. Memorandum from WAGRO, undated (but reference to thirty years after the Holocaust places it ca. 1975), files of WAGRO, New York.
3. Elie Wiesel, interview by author, New York City, August 8, 1990. Also see his "A Plea for the Survivors," written in 1975, in *A Jew Today* (New York: Vintage, 1979), pp. 218–47.
4. Benjamin Meed, President, WAGRO, to Charles G. Bluhdorn, December 9, 1976, files of WAGRO, New York.
5. Benjamin Meed to Mayor Abraham D. Beame, December 10, 1977, files of WAGRO, New York.
6. Michael Mehlman to Benjamin Meed, December 29, 1976, files of WAGRO, New York.
7. Janet Langsam to Benjamin Meed, files of WAGRO, New York.
8. Information sheet, Jewish Community Relations Council of New York, 1990.
9. Jim Sleeper, "Boom and Bust with Ed Koch," *Dissent—A Special Issue: In Search of New York* (Fall 1987), p. 437. See also Jim Chapin, "Who Rules New York Today?" *Dissent* (Fall 1987), pp. 471–478; Jack Newfield and Wayne Barrett, *City for Sale* (New York: Harper & Row, 1988).
10. Sleeper, p. 448.
11. American Jewish Congress memorandum from Victoria Free to Richard Cohen, "Notes from a Press Conference at the Jewish Community Relations Council—March 24, 1977," March 25, 1977, files of American Memorial to Six Million Jews of Europe, Inc., Archives of YIVO Institute, New York, N.Y.
12. Richard Ravitch, JCRC, April 7, 1977, to Benjamin Meed, files of WAGRO, New York; and to S. L. Shneiderman, Archives of YIVO Institute, New York.
13. Manny Behar, telephone conversation with author, December 20, 1990.
14. The "Martyrs' and Heroes' Remembrance Law, 5713–1953," which passed its final reading in the Knesset on August 19, 1953, is

reprinted in *Yad Vashem: The Holocaust Martyrs' and Heroes' Remembrance Authority, Jerusalem* (Jerusalem: Yad Vashem Publications, 1986). See Charles S. Leibman and Eliezer Don-Yehiya, *Civil Religion in Israel: Traditional Judaism and Political Culture in the Jewish State* (Berkeley: University of California, 1983) regarding the Holocaust as part of Israel's civil religion.

15. Richard Ravitch, interview by author, New York City, May 4, 1990.
16. See Elizabeth Rubin, "The Harrowing Tale of 'Holocaust Heights,'" *The Forward*, November 19, 1993, p. 1.
17. Memorandum from S. L. Shneiderman to Richard Cohen, American Jewish Congress, "Living Memorial for Six Million Jews," April 21, 1977, filed under "American Memorial to Six Million Jews of Europe, Inc.," Archives of Yivo Institute, New York.
18. Edward C. Banfield, *Political Influence* (New York: Free Press, 1961), p. 263.
19. Memorandum from S. L. Shneiderman to Richard Cohen.
20. Ernest Michel, interview by author, New York City, May 8, 1990.
21. Memorandum from S. L. Shneiderman to Richard Cohen.
22. Richard Ravitch to Benjamin Meed, September 26, 1977, files of WAGRO, New York. The date of the meeting was inadvertently omitted from the letter.
23. John E. Zuccotti to Richard Ravitch, December 12, 1977, Rickman files, Municipal Archive of the City of New York.
24. Ravitch, interview.
25. Mayor Edward I. Koch to President Jimmy Carter, September 29, 1978, Rickman files, Municipal Archive, New York.

Chapter 7. Holocaust Memorialization on the U.S. Government's Agenda

1. "Report for the Year Ending March 31, 1978: Conference of Presidents of Major American Jewish Organizations," New York, N.Y., p. 3.
2. Mark Siegel, interview by author, Washington, D.C., March 16, 1990.
3. Mark Siegel, Stuart Eizenstat, and Ellen Goldstein all said in interviews on March 16, 1990, that a national Holocaust memorial was originally Siegel's idea. Siegel's first memorandum on the topic has not been found by any of them or by the Jimmy Carter Library in Atlanta. However, the Carter Library does have a copy of Ellen Goldstein's June 21, 1977, reply to Siegel's request for a briefing on Holocaust memorials. His original memo to Jordan and Carter must have been written between March and June 1977.
4. "Report for the Year Ending March 31, 1978, pp. 7–8.

5. The key clause is: "Termination of all claims or states of belligerency and respect for and acknowledgement of the sovereignty, territorial integrity and political independence of every State in the area and their right to live in peace within secure and recognized boundaries free from threats or acts of force." See Alan M. Tigay, ed., *Myths and Facts 1980* (Washington: *Near East Report*, 1980), pp. 35–36.

6. Ibid., pp. 9–11.

7. Ibid., p. 12.

8. David Friedman, "Senators say if Carter wants all or nothing on his plane package deal he may wind up with nothing," Jewish Telegraphic Agency *Daily News Bulletin*, April 26, 1978, p. 1.

9. Siegel, interview.

10. Memorandum from Ellen Goldstein to Stuart Eizenstat, "Subject: Holocaust Memorial," March 28, 1978, DPS–Eizenstat Collection, Archives of the Jimmy Carter Library, Atlanta, Ga.

11. John W. Kingdon, *Agendas, Alternatives and Public Policies* (Boston: Little, Brown, 1984).

12. See Rochelle G. Saidel, *The Outraged Conscience: Seekers of Justice for Nazi War Criminals in America* (Albany: State University of New York Press, 1984), pp. 3–8, 103–38; and Charles R. Allen, Jr., *Nazi War Criminals in America: Facts . . . Action: A Basic Handbook* (New York: Highgate Press, 1986).

13. Kingdon, *Agendas, Alternatives and Public Policies*, pp. 92–94.

14. Note from Eizenstat to "B," April 4, 1978, DPS–Eizenstat Collection, Carter Library, Atlanta.

15. Memorandum from Stu Eizenstat and Bob Lipshutz to the president, "Subject: Holocaust Memorial," April 25, 1978, DPS–Eizenstat Collection, Carter Library, Atlanta.

16. Stuart Eizenstat, interview by author, Washington, D.C., March 16, 1990.

17. Elie Wiesel, interview by author, New York City, August 8, 1990. For more details about Wiesel's concerns about the commission and the later council, see Edward T. Linenthal, *Preserving Memory: The Struggle to Create America's Holocaust Museum*, (New York: Viking, 1995), pp. 22–51.

18. Eizenstat, interview.

19. Siegel, interview.

20. Helen Silver, "Carter Moves to Create a Memorial to the Victims of the Holocaust," Jewish Telegraphic Agency *Daily News Bulletin*, May 3, 1978, p. 3.

21. Memorandum from Stu Eizenstat and Bob Lipshutz to Tim Kraft, "Subject: President's Holocaust Memorial Commission," July 20, 1978, p. 5, DPS–Eizenstat Collection, Carter Library, Atlanta.

22. Memorandum from Ellen Goldstein to Stu Eizenstat, "Subject: Presidential Commission on the Holocaust Memorial," May 2, 1978, DPS–Eizenstat Collection, Carter Library, Atlanta.

23. Memorandum from Stu Eizenstat to the President, May 1, 1978, DPS–Eizenstat Collection, Carter Library, Atlanta.
24. Memorandum from Ellen Goldstein to Stu Eizenstat, "Subject: Briefing Memorandum Re: Memorial Commission Meeting," May 10, 1978, DPS–Eizenstat Collection, Carter Library, Atlanta.
25. Eizenstat, interview.
26. Memorandum from Ellen Goldstein to Stu Eizenstat, May 10, 1978.
27. Memorandum from Stu Eizenstat and Bob Lipshutz to Tim Kraft, July 20, 1978.
28. Memorandum from Stuart Eizenstat and Ellen Goldstein to the President, "Subject: Enrolled Resolution H.R. Res. 1014–Days of Remembrance of Victims of the Holocaust," September 9, 1978, Carter Library, Atlanta.
29. Memorandum from Bob Lipshutz and Stu Eizenstat to the President, "Subject: President's Holocaust Commission," September 18, 1978; memorandum from Ellen Goldstein to Stu Eizenstat, Bob Lipshutz and Ed Sanders, "Subject: Holocaust Commission", November 1, 1978, Special Advisor–Moses Collection, Carter Library, Atlanta. Members of the President's Commission on the Holocaust were Elie Wiesel, chairman; Congressman James J. Blanchard; Hyman Bookbinder (the American Jewish Committee's Washington representative); Senator Rudy Boschwitz; Professor Robert McAfee Brown; Dr. Gerson Cohen (chancellor of the Jewish Theological Seminary of America); Senator John C. Danforth; Professor Lucy Dawidowicz (Holocaust historian); Kitty Dukakis; Benjamin Epstein (of the Anti-Defamation League of B'nai B'rith); Rabbi Juda Glasner; Justice Arthur J. Goldberg; Professor Alfred Gottschalk (of Hebrew Union College); Congressman S. William Green; Father Theodore Hesburgh (University of Notre Dame president); Professor Raul Hilberg (Holocaust historian); Senator Henry M. Jackson; Professor Norman Lamm (head of Yeshiva University); Frank R. Lautenberg; Congressman William Lehman; Senator Claiborne Pell; Arnold Picker; Rabbi Bernard Raskas; Hadassah Rosensaft (survivor); Bayard Rustin; Marilyn Shubin; Isaac Bashevis Singer; Congressman Stephen J. Solarz; Senator Richard B. Stone; Sigmund Strochlitz (survivor); Mark Talisman (UJA-Federation Washington representative); Telford Taylor; Glenn E. Watts; and Congressman Sidney Yates. There was also an advisory board of twenty-seven people.
30. Wiesel, interview.
31. *Report to the President: President's Commission on the Holocaust* (Washington, D.C.: U.S. Government Printing Office, September 1979), p. 1.
32. Harold Seidman, *Politics, Position and Power* (New York: Oxford University Press, 1980), p. 43.
33. Congressman Stephen J. Solarz, "Remembering the Holocaust,"

Community Report, undated (February or March 1979), Washington, D.C., and Brooklyn, N.Y.

34. Herbert Rickman, interview by author, New York City, March 30, 1990.

35. "Remarks by Mayor Edward I. Koch (Delivered by Herbert P. Rickman, Special Assistant to the Mayor)," March 25, 1979, Brooklyn, N.Y., Archives of U.S. Holocaust Memorial Commission, Washington, D.C. At the commission's first meeting, held on February 15, 1979, historian Lucy Dawidowicz recommended New York City; and at a March 22, 1979 meeting of the commission's subcommittee on museum and monument, survivors Ben Mead and Yaffa Eliach also favored New York City. See Linenthal, *Preserving Memory*, pp. 57–58.

36. Untitled and unsigned handwritten notes from April 6, 1979, hearing held by S. William Green, archives of U.S. Holocaust Memorial Commission, Washington.

37. Congressman Marvin Greisman to Congressman S. William Green, April 5, 1979, files of U.S. Holocaust Memorial Commission, Washington.

38. Edward I. Koch, interview by author, New York City, May 18, 1990.

39. Rabbi Irving Greenberg, interview by author, New York City, April 19, 1990.

40. Hyman Bookbinder, telephone interview by author, Washington, D.C., March 16, 1990.

41. Eizenstat, interview.

42. *Report to the President*, September 27, 1979, p. 11.

43. Public Law 96-388, October 7, 1980, Washington, D.C. For more details on the creation of the U.S. Holocaust Memorial Museum in Washington, D.C., see Linenthal, *Preserving Memory*.

Chapter 8. Mayor Koch's Holocaust Memorial Task Force

1. Herbert Rickman, interview by author, New York City, March 30, 1990.

2. Manny Behar, telephone interview by author, December 21, 1990.

3. Remarks by Mayor Edward I. Koch at commemoration of the thirty-sixth anniversary of the Warsaw Ghetto uprising, Temple Emanu-El, Fifth Avenue, New York, April 22, 1979, Mayor Koch Accession Record Group, Special Assistant Herbert Rickman Subgroup, Municipal Archive of the City of New York, New York, N.Y.

4. Benjamin Meed, interview by author, New York City, May 7, 1990.

5. Harrison J. Goldin to Benjamin Meed, June 14, 1979, files of WAGRO, New York, N.Y.

6. Memorandum from Executive Committee of WAGRO to Mayor Koch and Governor Carey, "Subject: Holocaust Memorial in New York City," June 28, 1979, files of WAGRO, New York.

7. Ibid.

8. Benjamin Meed to Mayor Koch, June 26, 1979, files of WAGRO, New York.

9. Samuel J. Silberman to Mayor Koch, September 21, 1979, files of WAGRO, New York.

10. Benjamin Meed to Herbert Rickman, July 17, 1979, files of WAGRO, New York.

11. Elie Wiesel, interview by author, New York City, August 8, 1990; see also Wiesel, "A Plea for the Survivors" in *A Jew Today* (New York: Vintage, 1979), pp. 218–47.

12. Edward C. Banfield, *Political Influence* (New York: Free Press, 1961), p. 276.

13. Jack Newfield and Wayne Barrett, *City for Sale: Ed Koch and the Betrayal of New York* (New York: Harper & Row, 1988), p. 182.

14. Rickman, interview; Edward I. Koch, interview by author, New York City, May 18, 1990.

15. Meed, interview.

16. Koch, interview.

17. Rickman, interview.

18. Unsigned memorandum, "Meeting with George Kline [sic] Re: Holocaust Memorial Task Force," April 22, 1981, stationery of the Office of the Mayor, Mayor Koch Accession Record Group, Special Assistant Herbert Rickman Subgroup, Municipal Archive, New York.

19. Rickman, interview.

20. Koch, interview.

21. "First New Office Building in New York City in 5 Years," *The New York Times*, August 4, 1977, sec. 2, p. 1.

22. Robert A. Dahl, *Who Governs?* (New Haven: Yale University Press, 1961), chap. 10: "Leaders in Urban Redevelopment," pp. 115–40.

23. Koch, interview.

24. In 1977, Mayor Koch won 65 percent of the Jewish vote. Figures were provided by Jerry Skurnik, director of operations for both campaigns.

25. Edward I. Koch, *Mayor* (New York: Warner, 1984), pp. 297–98.

26. Press Release, Office of the Mayor, July 23, 1981, no. 203–81, Mayor Koch Accession Record Group, Special Assistant Herbert Rickman Subgroup, Municipal Archive, New York.

27. Dahl, *Who Governs?* p. 295.

28. Koch, interview.

29. George Klein to task force members, October 2, 1981, Mayor Koch Accession Record Group (82–27), Special Assistant Herbert Rickman Subgroup, Municipal Archive, New York.

30. George Klein to Benjamin Meed, January 20, 1982, files of WAGRO, New York, N.Y.
31. "Mayor's Task Force on the Holocaust: Ideas for a NYC Holocaust Memorial Center," no author cited, December 1981, Mayor Koch Accession Record Group (82-87), Special Assistant Herbert Rickman Subgroup, Municipal Archive, New York.
32. "Remarks by Hon. Herbert P. Rickman, Special Assistant to the Mayor, Introducing Public Hearings of Mayor's Holocaust Memorial Task Force," February 1, 1982, Mayor Koch Accession Record Group (82-87), Special Assistant Herbert Rickman Subgroup, Municipal Archive, New York.

Chapter 9. The New York City Holocaust Memorial Commission

1. For a discussion of Mayor Koch's relationship with developers, see Jim Sleeper, "Boom and Bust with Ed Koch," *Dissent—A Special Issue: In Search of New York* (Fall 1987), pp. 437–50; Jim Chapin, "Who Rules New York Today?" *Dissent* (Fall 1987), pp. 471–78; and Jack Newfield and Wayne Barrett, *City for Sale* (New York: Harper & Row, 1988). The letter of invitation to the commission is in the Mayor Koch Accession Record Group (82-27), Special Assistant Herbert Rickman Subgroup, Municipal Archive, New York, New York, N.Y.
2. Herbert Rickman, interview by author, New York City, March 30, 1990.
3. Mayor Edward I. Koch, interview by author, New York City, May 18, 1990.
4. Manhattan District Attorney Robert M. Morgenthau, telephone conversation with author, December 21, 1991.
5. First meeting of New York City Holocaust Memorial Commission, City Hall, September 14, 1982; remarks by George Klein from author's notes.
6. Press Release, Office of the Mayor, September 14, 1982, no. 244-82, Mayor Koch Accession Record Group (82-27), Special Assistant Herbert Rickman Subgroup, Municipal Archive, New York.
7. Associate chairpersons were Attorney General Robert Abrams, Congressman Joseph Addabbo, State Senate Majority Leader Warren Anderson, former mayor Abraham Beame, City Council President Carol Bellamy, former governor Hugh Carey, City Council Majority Leader Thomas Cuite, Senator Alfonse D'Amato, State Assembly Minority Leader James Emery, State Assembly Speaker Stanley Fink, Staten Island Borough President Anthony Gaeta, Brooklyn Borough President Howard Golden, City Comptroller Harrison J. Goldin, Congressman S. William Green, former governor Averell Harriman, former mayor Vincent

Impellitteri, former mayor John V. Lindsay, Queens Borough
President Donald Manes, Senator Daniel Patrick Moynihan, State
Senate Minority Leader Manfred Ohrenstein, State Comptroller
Edward V. Regan, Bronx Borough President Stanley Simon,
Manhattan Borough President Andrew Stein, former mayor
Robert F. Wagner, Sr., and former governor Malcolm Wilson.

8. Rickman, interview.
9. George Klein to Gerald Carmen, May 3, 1983, Mayor Koch
Accession Record Group (87-45), Special Assistant Herbert
Rickman Subgroup, Municipal Archive, New York.
10. "New York City Holocaust Memorial Commission, General
Meeting-Official Minutes, June 8, 1983," with cover letter dated
June 24, 1983; author's notes.
11. Certificate of Incorporation of New York City Holocaust Memorial
Commission, Inc., files of the commission, New York, N.Y.
12. Memorandum to GSA, Region 2, from New York City Holocaust
Memorial Commission, December 6, 1983, "Re: Informal Proposal
to Lease Space in the Old U.S. Custom House at Bowling Green,"
files of the commission, New York.
13. *The New York Times*, February 11, 1984.
14. Rickman, interview. Regarding the Indian museum, see Mayor
Koch to Dr. Roland W. Force, June 1, 1978, Mayor Koch Accession
Record Group, Special Assistant Herbert Rickman Subgroup-1978,
Municipal Archive, New York.
15. Eric Greenberg, "Custom House in N.Y. may become Holocaust
memorial," *The Jewish Week*, New York, March 9, 1984.
16. New York City Holocaust Memorial Commission, General
Meeting—Official Minutes, May 8, 1984.
17. Robert Dahl, *Who Governs?* (New Haven: Yale University Press,
1961), p. 90.
18. Official minutes of general meeting of commission, May 8, 1984.
19. Copies of letters listed are in files of author. Blumenfeld statement
is in "Hope Rises for N.Y. Holocaust Memorial" by Julius Liebb,
Jewish Press, October 5, 1984, p. 2.
20. David W. Dunlap, "Plans for Custom House Are Presented to
Board," *The New York Times*, August 2, 1984.
21. Owen Moritz, "A Split on Bowling Green," *New York Daily News*,
June 30, 1984.
22. "What to Do With the Customs House," editorial, *The New York
Times*, August 11, 1984.
23. Raymond Sokolov, "Rm to Let. Landmark Bldg. 77,000 Sq. Ft.,"
The Wall Street Journal, October 3, 1984, p. 28.
24. Joseph Berger, "Custom House Will Be Museum on Holocaust,"
The New York Times, October 18, 1984, p. B3.
25. Rickman, interview. Brendan Gill was the chairman of the New
York Landmarks Conservancy and a leader in efforts to revive the
Custom House. See David W. Dunlap, "Plans for Custom House
Are Presented to Board," *The New York Times*, August 2, 1984.

26. Report by Eisner and Lubin, Certified Public Accountants, March 21, 1985, New York, N.Y.

Chapter 10. Governor Cuomo Intervenes

1. Meyer S. Frucher, interview by author, New York City, February 4, 1991.
2. Ibid.
3. Mary Anne Ostrom, "Intelligencer: Mrs. Astor Argues Against Holocaust-Shrine Site," *New York* magazine, January 14, 1985, p. 10.
4. Adriel Bettelheim, "City's Holocaust Museum Seeks Exhibits, Funds," *The Jewish Week*, New York, February 22, 1985, p. 13.
5. David L. Blumenfeld to John M. Marcic, GSA, March 1, 1985, commission files, New York, N.Y.
6. John Webb, "To Keep the Memories Alive," *Daily News*, New York, March 3, 1985, p. 12.
7. For a detailed analysis of site selection, see Edward C. Banfield, *Political Influence* (New York: Free Press, 1961).
8. Stewart Ain, "Council Approves Concept of City Holocaust Memorial," *Long Island Jewish World*, February 28, 1985.
9. "New York City Council Adopts Resolution Urging City to Establish a Holocaust Memorial Center," Jewish Telegraphic Agency *Daily News Bulletin*, March 1, 1985, p. 4.
10. Mayor Edward I. Koch, interview by author, New York City, May 18, 1990.
11. Frucher, interview.
12. Koch, interview.
13. Frucher, interview.
14. Herbert Rickman, interview by author, New York City, March 30, 1990.
15. Ibid.
16. Michael Oreskes, "Battery Park City Offers Holocaust Museum a Site," *The New York Times*, April 5, 1985. See also Kevin Freeman, "New Location Approved in Principle for NYC Holocaust Museum and Memorial," Jewish Telegraphic Agency *Daily News Bulletin*, April 12, 1985, p. 3; and B. George Allen, "Proposed Holocaust Hall at Battery," *New York City Tribune*, April 10, 1985.
17. Governor Cuomo to GSA Administrator William Diamond, July 27, 1984.
18. Oreskes, "Battery Park City Offers a Site."
19. Banfield, *Political Influence*.
20. D. D. Guttenplan, "Klein's Square," *Village Voice*, December 15, 1987, p. 20.
21. Oreskes, "Battery Park City Offers a Site."

22. Freeman, "New Location Approved in Principle."
23. "New York City Holocaust Memorial Commission, General Meeting, Official Minutes, May 2, 1985"; and author's notes, May 3, 1985 meeting of New York City Holocaust Memorial Commission.
24. "New York City Holocaust Memorial Commission, Inc., Report as at December 31, 1985, Eisner & Lubin, Certified Public Accountants," New York City.
25. Frucher, interview.
26. Koch, interview.
27. Author's notes, commission meeting, Regency Hotel, New York City, June 16, 1986.
28. Ibid.
29. New York Holocaust Memorial Commission, Year End Fundraising Status Report, December 31, 1986.

Chapter 11. The Holocaust Museum as a Real Estate Deal

1. Brendan Gill, "The Sky Line: Battery Park City," *The New Yorker,* August 20, 1990.
2. Information on BPCA from "Battery Park City Fact Sheet," office of Ellen Rosen, BPCA, New York City, 1986; and *Manual for the Use of the Legislature of the State of New York, 1986–1987,* Albany, Gail S. Shaffer, Secretary of State, pp. 713–14.
3. Discussions between the commission and Olympia & York, which ultimately proved unsuccessful, were about making a significant contribution to the project. Olympia & York's Canadian parent company went into bankruptcy in 1993, but David Emil, president and CEO of BPCA, said in August 1994 that he was confident that the New York subsidiary would be able to continue to pay its rent. See David W. Dunlap, "Opening New Fronts at Battery Park City," *The New York Times,* September 4, 1994, sec. 9, p. 1.
4. "Memorandum to George Klein, Robert Morgenthau, Manfred Ohrenstein et al. from David Blumenfeld, August 20, 1986, re: Lease Signing Ceremony."
5. Press release, "Lease Signed for Site of Holocaust Memorial Museum at Battery Park City," BPCA, September 4, 1986.
6. J. Philip Rosen to Executive Committee, August 29, 1986, New York City, p. 1.
7. Ibid., p. 3.
8. Lease between BPCA and New York Holocaust Memorial Commission, signed September 4, 1986, p. 4.
9. Ibid., p. 16.
10. Lease between BPCA and Museum of Jewish Heritage, September 4, 1986, New York City, p. 9.

11. Ibid., p. 51.
12. Ibid., p. 1.
13. Author's notes, September 4, 1986 meeting at BPCA construction office, following lease signing.
14. "Memorandum from George Klein, Robert M. Morgenthau, and Manfred Ohrenstein to Executive Committee, Professional Staff, and Commission Invitees," September 12, 1986, New York, N.Y.
15. James Stewart Polshek to George Klein, December 1, 1986.
16. Jeffrey L. Pressman and Aaron Wildavsky, *Implementation* (Berkeley: University of California Press, 1979), p. xix.
17. Ibid., p. 109.
18. Author's notes from executive meeting of Holocaust commission, December 4, 1986, New York, N.Y.
19. Jeshajahu Weinberg, interview by author, Washington, D.C., March 14, 1990.
20. Author's notes from executive meeting of New York Holocaust Commission, September 15, 1987, New York.
21. Author's notes from executive meeting of New York Holocaust Commission, November 12, 1987, New York.
22. New York Holocaust Memorial Commission, End of Month Statement, December 31, 1987.
23. Pressman and Wildavsky, *Implementation*, p. 112.
24. The Museum of Jewish Heritage, memorandum from David Altshuler to Staff Planning Group, "Preparations for Decision to Break Ground and Begin Construction," January 18, 1988, New York, N.Y.
25. New York Holocaust Memorial Commission, minutes, meeting held March 15, 1988, Regency Hotel, New York, N.Y.

Chapter 12. New York State as a Fickle Landlord

1. Author's notes, committee meeting of New York Holocaust Memorial Commission, New York, N.Y., June 28, 1988.
2. Thomas J. Lueck, "City and State at Odds on Battery Park Hotel Plan," *The New York Times*, September 25, 1988, p. 38; and Neil Barsky, "Holocaust Museum and Hotel Linked," *New York Daily News*, September 25, 1988, p. 16.
3. Ibid.
4. Edward C. Banfield, *Political Influence* (New York: Free Press, 1961), p. 310.
5. Meyer S. (Sandy) Frucher, interview by author, New York City, February 4, 1991.
6. Dr. David Altshuler, interview by author, New York City, December 20, 1990.
7. George Klein and Robert Morgenthau to "Dear Friends," undated (fax dated November 2, 1988), New York.

8. Jeffrey L. Pressman and Aaron Wildavsky, *Implementation* (Berkeley: University of California Press, 1979), p. 94.
9. Ibid., p. 122.
10. Elizabeth Kolbert, "Albany Notes: Naming of Battery Park City Head Expected," *The New York Times*, September 18, 1988.
11. Joanna Molloy, "Holocaust Museum Deal Expected," *Battery News*, November 21, 1988, p. 14.
12. David Emil, interview by author, New York City, August 5, 1991.
13. Edward A. Adams, "Museum Jinxed Again: Holocaust Memorial Faces New Delays at Battery Park City," *New York Post*, December 8, 1988, p. 73.
14. Emil, interview.
15. Ibid.
16. Notes from Holocaust Commission meeting, Executive and Development Committees, December 14, 1988, New York, N.Y.
17. Pressman and Wildavsky, *Implementation*, p. 112.

Chapter 13. More Steps Backward and Forward

1. Author's notes, Holocaust Commission Executive Committee meeting, February 15, 1989, New York, N.Y.
2. Battery Park City Authority, News Release, February 23, 1989, New York, N.Y.
3. Statement by Mayor Edward I. Koch, Office of the Mayor, February 23, 1989, New York, N.Y.
4. "Statement by George Klein and Robert Morgenthau," New York Holocaust Memorial Commission, February 24, 1989, New York, N.Y.
5. Thomas J. Lueck, "Agency Revises a Museum Plan at Battery Park: To Require Donation by Condominium Builder," *The New York Times*, February 24, 1989, p. B3.
6. Statement of Cash Receipts and Disbursements, June 15, 1983 to May 31, 1989, A Living Memorial to the Holocaust–Museum of Jewish Heritage, New York, N.Y.
7. Author's notes, Holocaust Commission meeting, June 8, 1989, New York, N.Y.
8. Rochelle Saidel, "Yeshiva U. Says It Cancelled Dinner Honoring U.S. Businessman Who Aided Convicted War Criminal," Jewish Telegraphic Agency *Daily News Bulletin*, June 2, 1981, p. 3.
9. The commission's "popularization" of the grim history of the Holocaust through its association with Westheimer is reminiscent of the film industry's often gratuitous addition of sexual imagery to make movies about the Holocaust more appealing at the box office. This was true even of the lauded and Academy Award–winning *Schindler's List*.

10. Charles Dworkis, telephone interview by author, New York City, March 23, 1990.
11. Charles Dworkis, interview by author, New York City, April 19, 1990.
12. David Altshuler, interview by author, New York City, August 9, 1990.
13. David Altshuler, interview by author, New York City, December 20, 1990.
14. David Altshuler, interview by author, New York City, February 22, 1991.
15. David Altshuler, interview by author, New York City, August 5, 1991.
16. Kevin Sack, "Cuomo Seeking the Presidency? Yes, He Isn't, Maybe He Is," *The New York Times*, July 25, 1991, p. B5.
17. Jeffrey L. Pressman and Aaron Wildavsky, *Implementation* (Berkeley: University of California Press, 1979), p. 130.
18. Memorandum of Understanding between BPCA and the New York Holocaust Memorial Commission, Inc. and A Living Memorial to the Holocaust: Museum of Jewish Heritage, February 17, 1993, New York, N.Y., p. 12.

Chapter 14. Internal Power Struggles and Conflicts

1. Harold Seidman, *Politics, Position, and Power* (New York: Oxford University Press, 1980), p. 299.
2. Edward I. Koch, *Mayor* (New York: Warner Books, 1985), p. 297.
3. Jack Newfield and Wayne Barrett, *City for Sale: Ed Koch and the Betrayal of New York* (New York: Harper & Row, 1988), pp. 211–28.
4. Michael Harrington, "When Ed Koch Was Still a Liberal," *Dissent— A Special Issue: In Search of New York* (Fall 1987), pp. 595–602.
5. See Ricki Fulman, "Park to Recall Holocaust," *New York Daily News*, May 15, 1986, p. 2. The politics behind the event were discussed in the author's presence, in meetings with both Dinkins and Rickman in May 1986. In 1994–95, Manhattan Borough President Ruth Messinger and others were backing the construction of a monument to the Warsaw Ghetto uprising at the original Holocaust memorial site in Riverside Park. This projected monument was being planned at the same time that the Holocaust commission was focusing attention on its BPCA project. See Jon Kalish, "Monument Assignment," *The Jewish Week*, July 29–August 4, 1994, pp. 12–13.
6. Edward I. Koch, interview by author, New York City, May 18, 1990.
7. Meyer S. Frucher, interview by author, New York City, February 4, 1991.
8. "Morgy Thanks the Post for Baring Scam," *The New York Post*, September 17, 1987.

9. "The Morgy & Manny Show; DA and Senator May Meet as Panel Members," *The Daily News*, New York, September 24, 1987, p. 11.
10. Ronald Sullivan, "Senator's Trial Is Postponed Indefinitely: Delay May Hurt Case Against Ohrenstein," *The New York Times*, February 23, 1991, p. 27.
11. Chancery Office, Archdiocese of New York, to David Emil, February 24, 1989.
12. Linda M. Kirk to David Emil, New York City, April 21, 1989.
13. Terry Golway, "Battery Park City's Emil Is Assailed as a Meddler," *New York Observer*, August 5–12, 1991, p. 1.
14. Diana Jean Schemo, "New York Is Still Waiting for Its Own Holocaust Museum," *The New York Times*, December 12, 1993, p. 45.
15. Menachem Rosensaft, telephone interview by author, New York City, August 8, 1991.
16. Schemo, "New York Is Still Waiting."
17. Yehuda Bauer to David Altshuler, July 29, 1987.
18. David Altshuler to Yehuda Bauer, August 5, 1987.

Chapter 15. Why Is This Holocaust Museum Different from All Others?

1. Peter L. Berger and Thomas Luckmann, *The Social Construction of Reality* (Garden City, N.Y.: Doubleday Anchor, 1966), p. 123–24.
2. "A Living Memorial to the Holocaust–Museum of Jewish Heritage," brochure of the New York Holocaust Memorial Commission, 1990, New York, N.Y.
3. "Mayor's Task Force on the Holocaust: Ideas for a NYC Holocaust Memorial Center," no author cited, December 1981, Mayor Koch Accession Record Group (82-87), Special Assistant Herbert Rickman Subgroup, Municipal Archive, New York, N.Y.
4. See, for example, Berger and Luckmann, *Social Construction of Reality;* Karl W. Deutsch, *The Nerves of Government* (London and New York: Free Press, 1963); Clifford Geertz, *Local Knowledge* (New York: Basic Books, 1983); Erving Goffman, *The Presentation of Self in Everyday Life* (Garden City, N.Y.: Doubleday Anchor, 1959); Maurice Halbwachs, *Les cadres sociaux de la mémoire* (Paris: Presses Universitaires de France, 1952) and *The Collective Memory* (New York: Harper & Row, 1980); Karl Mannheim, *Ideology and Utopia* (London: Routledge & Kegan Paul, 1936); Barry Schwartz, "The Recovery of Masada: A Study in Collective Memory," *Sociological Quarterly* 27:2 (1986), 147–64; Barry Schwartz, Yael Zerubavel, and B.N. Barnett, "The Social Context of Commemoration: A Study in Collective Memory," *Social Forces* 61 (1982), 374–402.
5. Berger and Luckmann, *Social Construction*, p. 1.

6. Deutsch, *Nerves of Government.*

7. Ibid., p. 107.

8. An in-depth comparison and analysis of pre- and post-unification museum texts in such concentration camp memorials as Buchenwald, Sachsenhausen, and Ravensbrück would be an important contribution to the question of the politics of Holocaust memorialization. For more information on changes at Buchenwald, see Claudia Koonz, "Germany's Buchenwald: Whose Shrine? Whose Memory?" in *The Art of Memory: Holocaust Memorials in History*, edited by James Young (Munich and New York: Prestel-Verlag and The Jewish Museum, 1994), pp. 111–19.

9. Michael Berenbaum, *After Tragedy and Triumph: Modern Jewish Thought and the American Experience* (New York: Cambridge University Press, 1990), p. 163.

10. Michael Berenbaum, *The World Must Know: The History of the Holocaust as Told in the United States Holocaust Memorial Museum* (Boston: Little, Brown, 1993), p. 235.

11. By contrast, the exhibit that the German Democratic Republic created at Buchenwald was designed to connect the "fascism" of the Nazis to the capitalism of the United States and the other NATO countries.

12. Letter of invitation to become a charter supporter, United States Holocaust Memorial Museum, Washington, D.C., Spring 1991 (undated).

13. Ben Gallob, "ADL Joins Opposition to State Funds for Museum Planned by Wiesenthal Center," Jewish Telegraphic Agency *Daily News Bulletin*, June 25, 1985, p. 3. For background on controversies related to the museum, see Sheldon Teitelbaum and Tom Waldman, "The Unorthodox Rabbi," *Los Angeles Times Magazine*, July 15, 1990, pp. 6–11; and Gary Rosenblatt, "The Simon Wiesenthal Center: State-of-the-Art Activism or Hollywood Hype?" *Baltimore Jewish Times*, September 14, 1984.

14. Alisa Solomon, "An American Tragedy?" *The Village Voice*, New York, May 11, 1993, p. 35.

15. Allison Kaplan, "Jewish Population in U.S. Steady, but Traditional Areas See Decline," Jewish Telegraphic Agency *Daily News Bulletin*, August 30, 1990, p. 4.

16. Edward I. Koch, interview by author, New York City, May 18, 1990.

17. Berenbaum, *After Tragedy and Triumph*, p. 22.

18. Lease between BPCA and Museum of Jewish Heritage, September 4, 1986, New York City.

19. Memorandum of Understanding, Battery Park City Authority, New York Holocaust Memorial Commission, Inc., and A Living Memorial to the Holocaust: Museum of Jewish Heritage, July 26, 1991, New York City, p. 2.

20. Ibid., p. 7.

21. Ibid., p. 8.

22. Ibid., p. 8.
23. James E. Young, *The Texture of Memory: Holocaust Memorials and Meaning* (New Haven: Yale University Press, 1993), p. 288.

Chapter 16. A Holocaust Memorial for New York City—Fifty Years and Counting

1. David W. Dunlap, "Opening New Fronts at Battery Park City," *The New York Times*, September 4, 1994, sec. 9, p. 1.
2. Elizabeth Rubin, "The Harrowing Tale of 'Holocaust Heights,'" *The Forward*, New York, November 19, 1993, pp. 1, 5.
3. David Altshuler, "Building a Living Memorial," *The Forward*, New York, December 2, 1993.
4. Ernest W. Michel to the editor of *The Forward*, unpublished, New York, November 22, 1993, author's files.
5. Richard D. Hylton, "Developer Sued For $60 Million By Three Banks," *The New York Times*, March 25, 1991, p. A1.
6. Diana Jean Schemo, "New York Is Still Waiting for Its Own Holocaust Museum," *The New York Times*, December 12, 1993, p. 12.
7. According to *The Jewish Week*, three-fourths of the Jews who voted in the 1994 gubernatorial race gave their vote to Mario Cuomo. See Stewart Ain, "Out of Sync," *The Jewish Week*, November 11–17, 1994, pp. 24–25. For background on Senator D'Amato's role in the election, see Francis X. Clines, "Just Don't Call Me King, D'Amato Says of Pataki Victory," *The New York Times*, November 10, 1994. p. B1.
8. New Release, "Governor Cuomo and Mayor Giuliani Announce That Construction of A Living Memorial to the Holocaust–Museum of Jewish Heritage Will Begin This Fall," Battery Park City Authority and A Living Memorial to the Holocaust–Museum of Jewish Heritage, August 18, 1994, New York, N.Y.
9. According to a New York Times/WCBS-TV news poll taken on September 29 and October 2, 1994, Governor Cuomo was in a "virtual dead heat" with the Republican candidate, New York State senator George Pataki. The statewide telephone poll showed Pataki with 44 percent, Cuomo with 41 percent, and 12 percent undecided. See "Deep Discontent With Cuomo Strengthens Pataki, Poll Shows" by Kevin Sack, *The New York Times*, October 5, 1994, p. 1. Further evidence of the political implications of the timing of the lease signing and ground breaking was the complaint by the Democratic candidate for New York State comptroller, H. Carl McCall, that Governor Cuomo forgot to invite him to the August lease signing. See "Ideology Contrast Adds Some Flavor to Comptroller Race" by Sam Roberts, *The New York Times*, September 19, 1994, p. B4.

10. According to Claudia Koonz, all of the major concentration camp memorials in the German Democratic Republic followed the mandate of a 1955 government commission that their prime goal was to connect fascism with the capitalism of the members of NATO. See her "Germany's Buchenwald: Whose Shrine? Whose Memory?" in *The Art of Memory: Holocaust Memorials in History*, edited by James Young (Munich and New York: Prestel-Verlag and The Jewish Museum, 1994), pp. 111–19.

11. The Ravensbrück memorial site uses these figures for the total of women and the total of survivors, estimating that 10 percent of the inmates were Jewish. At present, only 55,000 names have been verified with official documents, although newly opened Russian archives are expected to provide more documentation. Many women, especially Jewish women, passed through the camp on their way to or from Auschwitz or other camps. No one is certain how many of these Jewish women were actually in the official Nazi records. Because the last months of the camp's existence were chaotic and the Nazis burned some records in the crematorium before fleeing at the end of April, 1945, it may be impossible to ever know exact statistics. Hundreds of Jewish women were among the 1,300 survivors who gathered at the camp to commemorate the fiftieth anniversary of liberation, April 22–24, 1995.

12. I was unable to see this exhibit because it was closed for renovation. It was actually initiated under the German Democratic Republic, after journalist Charles R. Allen, Jr., and I, and perhaps others, pressured the Ravensbrück survivors organization, which was largely Communist. However, it did not open until 1992, according to Christa Schulz, assistant to the museum director. Before then, the Ravensbrück women were memorialized by nationality, in keeping with Communist ideology. Every country that had a Ravensbrück survivors committee was allowed to create its own small exhibit. Thus, for example, although there were Polish Jewish women at Ravensbrück, the religious content of the Polish exhibit was entirely Catholic in nature. The Jewish exhibit was created by the museum staff, rather than by a memorial committee.

13. For an account of the changes that were made at Buchenwald between reunification and 1994, see Koonz, "Germany's Buchenwald." Information on the movement to memorialize the murder of Nazi prisoners is based on a conversation with Werner Händler, International Secretary of Survivors of Sachsenhausen Concentration Camp, Berlin, April 26, 1995. See also Claus Dumde, "8. Mai, Herr Kinkel und die ‚roten Winkel'," *Neues Deutschland*, Berlin, April 25, 1995, p. 2.

14. According to Sidney Verba, political culture "consists of the system of empirical beliefs, expressive symbols, and values which defines the situation in which political action takes place." See his

"Comparative Political Culture" in *Political Culture and Political Development*, edited by Sidney Verba and Lucian Pye (Princeton, N.J.: Princeton University Press, 1965), p. 513. The description of Yad Vashem is from Charles S. Leibman and Eliezer Don-Yehiya, *Civil Religion in Israel: Traditional Judaism and Political Culture in the Jewish State* (Berkeley: University of California Press, 1983), p. 151. Beginning in January 1995, the Israeli government decided to "merely suggest" that official foreign guests visit Yad Vashem. However, presidents, prime ministers, and foreign ministers would still be taken there routinely. See Clyde Haberman, "Israelis Ask If Holocaust Is Right Image, Memorial No Longer On Official Itinerary," *The New York Times*, January 14, 1995, p. A5.

15. Aviva Cantor, "Special Interview: 'Americanizing the Holocaust' Worries Israelis Doing Holocaust Research," Jewish Telegraphic Agency *Daily News Bulletin*, April 24, 1987, p. 4.

16. Yossi Klein Halevi, "Who Owns the Memory?" *The Jerusalem Report*, February 25, 1993, pp. 28–33.

Select Bibliography

Alexander, Edward. "Stealing the Holocaust." *Midstream* (November 1980): 46–50.

Banfield, Edward C. *Political Influence*. New York: Free Press, 1961.

Bauer, Yehuda. *American Jewry and the Holocaust: The American Jewish Joint Distribution Committee, 1939–1945*. Detroit: Wayne State University Press, 1981.

——. "Whose Holocaust?" *Midstream* (November 1980): 42–46.

Berenbaum, Michael. *After Tragedy and Triumph: Modern Jewish Thought and the American Experience*. New York: Cambridge University Press, 1990.

——. "The Nativization of the Holocaust." *Judaism* 35, no. 4 (Fall 1986): 447–57.

——. "On the Politics of Public Commemoration of the Holocaust." *Shoah* (Fall/Winter 1981–1982): 6–9, 37.

——. *The World Must Know: The History of the Holocaust as Told in the United States Holocaust Memorial Museum*. Boston: Little, Brown, 1993.

Berger, Peter L., and Thomas Luckmann. *The Social Construction of Reality*. Garden City, N.Y.: Doubleday Anchor, 1966.

Bodnar, John. *Remaking America: Public Memory, Commemoration, and Patriotism in the Twentieth Century*. Princeton: Princeton University Press, 1992.

Boyarin, Jonathan. *A Storm from Paradise: The Politics of Jewish Memory*. Minneapolis: University of Minnesota Press, 1992.

Brenna, Susan. "Housing Memories of Genocide." *New York Newsday*, September 2, 1988.

Cantor, Aviva. "Holocaust Consciousness." *Jewish Women/Jewish Men: The Legacy of Patriarchy in Jewish Life*. San Francisco: HarperSanFrancisco, 1995.

————. "Special Interview: 'Americanizing the Holocaust' Worries Israelis Doing Holocaust Research." Jewish Telegraphic Agency *Daily News Bulletin*, April 24, 1987.

Chapin, Jim. "Who Rules New York Today?" *Dissent—A Special Issue: In Search of New York* (Fall 1987): 471–78.

Connerton, Paul. *How Societies Remember.* New York: Cambridge University Press, 1989.

Dahl, Robert A. *Who Governs?* New Haven: Yale University Press, 1961.

Deutsch, Karl W. *The Nerves of Government.* London and New York: Free Press, 1963.

Dunlop, David. "Holocaust Memorial Museum to Rise in Battery Park City." *The New York Times*, August 19, 1994.

Edelman, Murray. *Constructing the Political Spectacle.* Chicago: University of Chicago Press, 1988.

————. *The Symbolic Uses of Politics.* Urbana: University of Illinois Press, 1967, 1985.

Elazar, Daniel J. *Community and Polity: The Organizational Dynamics of American Jewry.* Philadelphia: Jewish Publication Society, 1976.

————. *People and Polity: The Organizational Dynamics of World Jewry.* Detroit: Wayne State University Press, 1989.

Eliade, Mircea. *The Sacred and the Profane.* New York: Harcourt, Brace, 1956.

Elon, Amos. *The Israelis: Founders and Sons.* New York: Holt, Rinehart & Winston, 1971.

Evron, Boaz. "Holocaust: The Uses of Disaster." *New Outlook* Discussion Paper. Israel: *New Outlook* magazine, n.d.

Fein, Leonard. *Where Are We? The Inner Life of America's Jews.* New York: Harper & Row, 1988.

Feingold, Henry L. *The Politics of Rescue.* New York: Holocaust Library, 1970.

————. *Bearing Witness: How America and Its Jews Responded to the Holocaust.* Syracuse: Syracuse University Press, 1995.

Friedlander, Saul. *Memory, History, and the Extermination of the Jews of Europe.* Bloomington: University of Indiana Press, 1993.

————. *Reflections of Nazism: An Essay on Kitsch and Death.* New York: Harper & Row, 1984.

————. "The Shoah Between Memory and History." *Jerusalem Quarterly* 53 (Winter 1990).

————, ed. *Probing the Limits of Representation: Nazism and the "Final Solution."* Cambridge, Mass.: Harvard University Press, 1992.

Geertz, Clifford. *Local Knowledge.* New York: Basic Books, 1983.

Gill, Brendan. "The SkyLine: Battery Park City." *The New Yorker,* August 20, 1990.

Goldberg, J. J. and Naomi Godfrey. "Two Holocaust Museums Finally Bypass Hurdles." *The Jewish Week,* New York, April 28, 1989.

Goldberger, Paul. "A Memorial Evokes Unspeakable Events with Dignity." *The New York Times,* April 30, 1989.

Goldmann, Nahum. *The Jewish Paradox.* New York: Grosset & Dunlap, 1978.

Greenberger, Robert. "The Genesis of the Holocaust Museum." *Jewish Journal,* New York, May 12, 1989.

————. "Painful Witness." *Regardie's* (November 1988): 61–69.

Grose, Peter. *Israel in the Mind of America.* New York: Schocken, 1984.

Halbwachs, Maurice. *Les cadres sociaux de la mémoire.* Paris: Presses Universitaires de France, 1952.

————. *The Collective Memory.* New York: Harper & Row, 1980.

Handleman, Don. *Models and Mirrors: Towards an Anthropology of Public Events.* New York: Cambridge University Press, 1990.

Hartman, Geoffrey, ed. *Bitburg in Moral and Political Perspective.* Bloomington: Indiana University Press, 1986.

————. *Holocaust Remembrance: The Shapes of Memory.* Cambridge, Mass. and Oxford: Blackwell, 1993.

Hertzberg, Arthur. *Being Jewish In America: The Modern Experience.* New York: Schocken, 1979.

————. *The Jews in America.* New York: Simon & Schuster, 1989.

Hirsch, Herbert. *Genocide and the Politics of Memory.* Chapel Hill: University of North Carolina Press, 1995.

Hirt-Manheimer, Aron, ed. "Holocaust Memorials: How Much Is Enough?" *Reform Judaism* (Fall 1987): 8–9.

Hochhauser, Herbert. "Jews for Sale: Could They Have Been Saved? Evian Conference, July 1938." In *In Answer. . . . Is the Story True? Why Did the World Community Not Respond? What are the Lessons?* edited by Franklin H. Littell, Irene Shur, and Claude R. Foster, Jr. West Chester, Pa.: Sylvan, 1988.

Husock, Howard. "Red, White and Jew: Holocaust Museum on the Mall." *Tikkun* 5, no. 4 (July/August 1990): 32.

Jick, Leon A. "The Holocaust: Its Use and Abuse Within the American

Public." *Yad Vashem Studies 14*. Jerusalem: Yad Vashem Martyrs' and Heroes' Remembrance Authority, 1981.

Kammen, Michael. *Mystic Chords of Memory: The Transformation of Tradition in American Culture*. New York: Alfred A. Knopf, 1991.

Katz, Stephen T. *The Holocaust in Historical Context*, vol. 1. New York: Oxford University Press, 1994.

Kingdon, John W. *Agendas, Alternatives and Public Policies*. Boston: Little, Brown, 1984.

Klein, Dennis B., ed. *Dimensions: A Journal of Holocaust Studies* 3, no. 4, "Are Memorials Reflecting History?" New York: Anti-Defamation League of B'nai B'rith, 1987.

Klein Halevi, Yossi. "Who Owns the Memory?" *The Jerusalem Report* (February 25, 1993): 28–33.

Koonz, Claudia. "Germany's Buchenwald: Whose Shrine? Whose Memory?" In *The Art of Memory: Holocaust Memorials in History*, edited by James Young. Munich/New York: Prestel-Verlag and The Jewish Museum, 1994.

Kushner, Tony. *The Holocaust and the Liberal Imagination*. Oxford: Blackwell, 1994.

Lang, Berel. *Act and Idea in the Nazi Genocide*. Chicago: University of Chicago Press, 1990.

Langer, Lawrence. *Admitting the Holocaust*. New York: Oxford University Press, 1995.

Lazin, Frederick A. "The Reaction of the American Jewish Committee to the Crisis of German Jewry, 1933–1939." In *In Answer. . . . Is the Story True? Why Did the World Community Not Respond? What Are the Lessons?* edited by Franklin H. Littell, Irene Shur, and Claude R. Foster, Jr. West Chester, Pa.: Sylvan, 1988.

Liebman, Charles S., and Eliezer Don-Yehiya. *Civil Religion in Israel: Traditional Judaism and Political Culture in the Jewish State*. Berkeley: University of California Press, 1983.

Linenthal, Edward T. "Contested Memories, Contested Space: The Holocaust Museum Gets Pushed Back." *Moment* (June 1993): 46–53.

———. *Preserving Memory: The Struggle to Create America's Holocaust Museum*. New York: Viking, 1995.

Lipstadt, Deborah. *Denying the Holocaust: The Growing Assault on Truth and Memory*. New York: Free Press, 1993.

Littell, Franklin H. "Inventing the Holocaust: Christian's Retrospect." Unpublished paper presented June 17, 1993, at the Ninth International Historical Conference of Yad Vashem, Jerusalem.

Lopate, Phillip. "Resistance to the Holocaust" (and responses to article). *Tikkun* 4, no. 3 (May/June 1989): 55–70.

Magida, Arthur. "Planning a Holocaust Museum." *Jewish Journal*, New York, April 15, 1983. Reprinted from *Baltimore Jewish Times*.

Maier, Charles S. *The Unmasterable Past: History, Holocaust, and German National Identity*. Cambridge, Mass.: Harvard University Press, 1988.

Mais, Yitzchak. "Institutionalizing the Holocaust: Issues Related to the Establishment of Holocaust Memorial Centers." *Remembering for the Future*, Theme II. Presented at an international scholars' conference, Oxford, July 10–13, 1988, pp. 1778–89.

Marrus, Michael R. *The Holocaust in History*. Hanover/London: University Press of New England, 1987.

Mayo, James. *War Memorials as Political Landscape*. New York: Praeger, 1988.

Miller, Judith. *One, By One, By One*. New York: Simon & Schuster, 1990.

Milton, Sybil. "The Memorialization of the Holocaust: Museums, Memorials, and Centers." *Genocide: A Critical Bibliography* 2, edited by Israel Charney, 299–320. New York: Facts on File and Mansell, 1991.

———, and Ira Nowinski. *In Fitting Memory: The Art and Politics of Holocaust Memorials*. Detroit: Wayne State University Press, 1991.

Muschamp, Herbert. "Shaping a Monument to Memory." *The New York Times*, April 11, 1993.

Neusner, Jacob. "Can Judaism Survive the Twentieth Century?" *Tikkun* 4 (1989): 39.

———. "A 'Holocaust' Primer." *National Review*, August 3, 1979, 975–79.

———. "New York's Museum of Jewish Heritage." *The National Jewish Post and Opinion* 54, no. 27 (March 30, 1988).

Newfield, Jack, and Wayne Barrett. *City for Sale*. New York: Harper & Row, 1988.

Nora, Pierre. "Between Memory and History: *Les lieux de mémoire*." *Representations* 26 (Spring 1989): 12.

Norich, Samuel. "What Holocaust Centers Tell Us About Ourselves." *The Forward*, March 6, 1987.

Novick, Peter. "Holocaust Memory in America." In *The Art of Memory:*

Holocaust Memorials in History, edited by James Young. Munich/ New York: Prestel-Verlag and The Jewish Museum, 1994.

Porat, Dina. *The Blue and the Yellow Stars of David: The Zionist Leadership in Palestine and the Holocaust.* Cambridge, Mass.: Harvard University Press, 1990.

Pressman, Jeffrey L., and Aaron Wildavsky. *Implementation.* 2d ed. Berkeley: University of California Press, 1979.

Rosenblatt, Gary. "The Simon Wiesenthal Center: State-of-the-Art Activism or Hollywood Hype?" *Baltimore Jewish Times,* September 14, 1984.

Rosenfeld, Alvin H. "The Holocaust in Jewish Memory and Public Memory." *Dimensions: A Journal of Holocaust Studies* 2, no. 3 (Fall 1986). New York: Anti-Defamation League of B'nai B'rith.

Roskies, David G. *Against the Apocalypse: Responses to Catastrophe in Modern Jewish Culture.* Cambridge, Mass.: Harvard University Press, 1984.

Ross, Robert W. "An Early Intervention That Failed." In *In Answer. . . . Is the Story True? Why Did the World Community Not Respond? What Are the Lessons?* edited by Franklin H. Littell, Irene Shur, and Claude, R. Foster, Jr. West Chester, Pa.: Sylvan, 1988.

Rubenstein, Richard L. *The Cunning of History: Mass Death and the American Future.* New York: Scribner's, 1975.

Rubin, Elizabeth. "The Harrowing Tale of 'Holocaust Heights.'" *The Forward,* November 19, 1993.

Ryback, Timothy. "Bringing Auschwitz Back to Life." *The New Yorker,* November 15, 1993.

Saidel, Rochelle G. "Forty-six years and Counting: Creating a Holocaust Memorial Museum in New York City." Unpublished paper presented at the New York State Political Science Association annual meeting, Hunter College, New York, April 1993.

———. "The Holocaust in the Political Culture of Israel." *Midstream* 35, no. 7 (October 1989): 17–21.

———. *The Outraged Conscience: Seekers of Justice for Nazi War Criminals in America.* Albany: State University of New York Press, 1984.

———. "The Political Genesis of the U.S. Holocaust Memorial Museum." Unpublished paper presented at the 23d Scholars Conference on the Holocaust and the German Church Struggle, University of Tulsa, Oklahoma, March 1993.

———. "The Politics of Memorializing the Holocaust: Creating a

Holocaust Memorial Museum in New York City." Ph.D. dissertation, City University Graduate Center, New York, 1992.

————. "The Politics of Memorialization: Creating a Holocaust Memorial Museum in New York City." *Proceedings of the Eleventh World Congress of Jewish Studies* 3: 147–54. Jerusalem: World Union of Jewish Studies, 1994.

Scheindlin, Raymond P. "Museum of Life, Museum of Death." *Tikkun* 8, no. 6 (November/December 1993): 85.

Schemo, Diana Jean. "New York Is Still Waiting for Its Own Holocaust Museum." *The New York Times,* December 12, 1993.

Schwartz, Barry. "The Recovery of Masada: A Study in Collective Memory." *Sociological Quarterly* 27, no. 2 (1986): 147–64.

————, Yael Zerubavel, and B. N. Barnett. "The Social Context of Commemoration: A Study in Collective Memory." *Social Forces* 61 (1982): 374–402.

Scruggs, Jan C., and Joel Swerdlow. *To Heal a Nation: The Vietnam Veterans Memorial.* New York, 1985.

Segev, Tom. *The Seventh Million: The Israelis and the Holocaust.* New York: Hill & Wang, 1993.

Seidman, Harold. *Politics, Position, and Power.* New York: Oxford University Press, 1980.

Seldin, Ruth R. "American Jewish Museums: Trends and Issues." *American Jewish Year Book 1991: A Record of Events and Trends in American and World Jewish Life.* New York: American Jewish Committee/Jewish Publication Society, 1992.

Shanor, Rebecca Read. *The City That Never Was.* New York: Viking, 1988.

Shneiderman, S.L. "To Memorialize the Six Million: The Monument Controversy." *Congress Bi-Weekly,* February 1965.

Silberman, Charles E. *A Certain People: American Jews and Their Lives Today.* New York: Summit, 1985.

Sleeper, Jim. "Boom and Bust with Ed Koch." *Dissent—A Special Issue: In Search of New York* (Fall 1987): 437–50.

Solomon, Alisa. "An American Tragedy?" *The Village Voice,* New York, May 11, 1993.

Sorkin, Michael. "Reconstructing the Holocaust." *The Village Voice,* New York, June 23, 1987.

Teitelbaum, Sheldon, and Tom Waldman. "The Unorthodox Rabbi." *Los Angeles Times Magazine,* July 15, 1990, 6–11.

Urofsky, Melvin I. *We Are One.* Garden City, N.Y.: Anchor, 1978.

Vidal-Naquet, Pierre. *Assassins of Memory*. New York: Columbia University Press, 1992.

Weintraub, Judith. "Passing on the Memory of the Holocaust." *The Washington Post*, February 2, 1990.

Weyl, Martin. "How Do Museums Speak the Unspeakable?" *The New York Times*, June 11, 1989.

Wiesel, Elie. *A Jew Today*. New York: Vintage, 1979.

Wohlgelernter, Eli. "Interactive Remembrance." *The Jerusalem Post Magazine*, April 16, 1993.

Woocher, Jonathan. "Sacred Survival: American Jewry's Civil Religion." *Judaism* 34 (Spring 1985): 151–62.

Wyman, David. *The Abandonment of the Jews: America and the Holocaust, 1941–1945*. New York: Pantheon, 1984.

Yankelovich, Skelly and White/Clancy, Shulman. "American Public Awareness of and Attitudes Toward the Holocaust 1: A Case for Further Education. 2: The United States Holocaust Memorial Museum." Prepared for the United States Holocaust Memorial Council and the Anti-Defamation League of B'nai B'rith, 1991.

Yerushalmi, Yosef Hayim. *Zakhor: Jewish History and Jewish Memory*. Seattle: University of Washington Press, 1982.

Young, James E. "'After the Holocaust: National Attitudes to Jews': The Texture and Meaning of Memory: Holocaust Memorials and Meaning." *Holocaust and Genocide Studies* 4, no. 1 (1989): 63–76. Oxford: Maxwell Pergamon Macmillan.

———. "The Biography of a Memorial Icon: Nathan Rapoport's Warsaw Ghetto Monument." University of California Press, *Representations* 26 (Spring 1989).

———. "Holocaust Memorials in America: The Politics of Identity." *Survey of Jewish Affairs*, William Frankel, ed., vol. 10. London: Basil Blackwell, 1991.

———. "Israel's Memorial Landscape: Sho'ah, Heroism, and National Redemption." In *Lessons and Legacies: The Meaning of the Holocaust in a Changing World*, edited by Peter Hayes, 279–304. Evanston: Northwestern University Press, 1991.

———. "Memory and Monument." In *Bitburg in Moral and Political Perspective*, edited by Geoffrey Hartman. Bloomington: Indiana University Press, 1986.

———. *The Texture of Memory: Holocaust Memorials and Meaning*. New Haven: Yale University Press, 1993.

———, ed. *The Art of Memory: Holocaust Memorials in History*. Munich/New York: Prestel-Verlag and The Jewish Museum, 1994.

Zinn, Howard. *The Twentieth Century: A People's History*. New York: Harper & Row, 1980.

Index

Rochelle G. Saidel holds a Ph.D. degree in political science from The Graduate School and University Center of the City University of New York. She was awarded the National Foundation for Jewish Culture's 1994 Musher Publication Prize for the manuscript of this book. Her research focuses on the memorialization of the Shoah, and on the experiences of Jewish women during the time of the Third Reich. She is also the author of *The Outraged Conscience: Seekers of Justice for Nazi War Criminals in America* (State University of New York Press, 1984) and of many articles and academic papers. Dr. Saidel is currently a visiting scholar at NEMGE—The Center for the Study of Women and Gender, and a scientific consultant for NAPENA—The Center for North American Studies, both at the University of São Paulo, Brazil. In 1995 she represented the university at the NGO Forum on Women, held in conjunction with the United Nations Fourth World Conference on Women in Beijing; and in the summer of 1996 she was an NEH Visiting Scholar at Brandeis University.